Heathen, Hindoo, Hindu

AMERICAN REPRESENTATIONS OF INDIA, 1721–1893

Michael J. Altman

OXFORD
UNIVERSITY PRESS

Oxford University Press is a department of the University of Oxford. It furthers
the University's objective of excellence in research, scholarship, and education
by publishing worldwide. Oxford is a registered trade mark of Oxford University
Press in the UK and certain other countries.

Published in the United States of America by Oxford University Press
198 Madison Avenue, New York, NY 10016, United States of America.

CIP data is on file at the Library of Congress
ISBN 978–0–19–065492–4

9 8 7 6 5 4 3 2 1

Printed by Sheridan Books, Inc., United States of America

For Emily, my partner in everything.

Contents

Acknowledgments

THIS BOOK EXISTS because of a number of people besides me. I may have written the book, but they made it possible.

One reason this book exists is the influence of my parents. There is an image in my mind of my father eating lunch. He has a bowl of soup, a radio playing some sort of either sports or political talk, and a book propped up in front of him. He leans forward over the bowl, into the pages of the book, as steam floats up. I think he was reading Agatha Christie. Dad left books everywhere in our house. Piles of them. He and my mother told me that I could write a book. Without them I would not have known that writing a book was a thing one could do in the world.

Another reason this book exists is the support of the Department of Religious Studies at the College of Charleston. I am thankful to Zeff Bjerken, Elijah Siegler, Lee Irwin, and John Huddlestun for being excellent teachers and mentors. It was in Zeff's seminar on religion after 9/11 where I first read *Orientalism*. Without that department I would not have known that religious studies was a thing one could study in the world.

Another reason this book exists is that Leela Prasad took the time to be patient with me while I was at Duke University and helped me figure out how I could bridge my interest in colonial India and religion in America. Her generosity of spirit and encouragement as I began to dig into the sources that are now in this book made this whole thing possible. The two years I spent at Duke were amazing because of the scholarly community between the various universities in the area. I am thankful to Jason Bivins, Grant Wacker, and Tom Tweed for all of the guidance they gave me as a young master's student with no idea what he was doing. I am especially thankful to Tom who first mentioned that I should go look and see what nineteenth-century magazines might say about India. I am also thankful to the Ph.D. students I met at Duke and the University of North Carolina, who have now become colleagues and friends. I'm especially grateful to Angela Tarango, Seth Dowland, Kate Bowler, Mandy McMichael, and Elesha Coffman, who took the time to humor my ridiculous arguments over lunch in the graduate lounge.

Another reason this book exists is that Bobbi Patterson is the most joyful person in the world. The moment I stepped foot onto the campus at Emory University, she made me feel like it was home. The Graduate Division of Religion at Emory was an amazing place to grow into a scholar, and every student and faculty member of the American Religious Cultures track made it feel like a family. I'm especially grateful to Ben Brazil, Dennis LoRusso, Kenny Smith, and Samira Mehta for humoring my ridiculous arguments in seminars and in the graduate lounge. At Emory, Brooks Holifield and Russ Richey taught me to think like a historian. Paul Courtright led me through the history of colonial India. Through it all, Gary Laderman was the Dude. Gary always gave me enough rope to do whatever I wanted, but he always cut me down before I tied myself up in a tree. He is my teacher, my mentor, and my friend. Thanks, Dude.

Another reason this book exists is that Steven Ramey was chairing a search committee and recommended that the Department of Religious Studies at the University of Alabama hire me as a full-time instructor. A year later they hired me as an assistant professor. I am so proud to be a part of this department. I am thankful to have a department chair as forward thinking and supportive as Russell McCutcheon. His commitment to developing the other junior faculty in our department is a model for senior scholars everywhere. I am grateful to have amazing colleagues in the department who genuinely appreciate each other and work for a common goal. I am humbled by our outstanding students, who challenge me in the classroom and humor my ridiculous arguments in the student lounge.

This book also exists because of my family. My three boys have grown up with this book. Steinichen, my oldest, was born within days of me finishing the master's thesis that became this book. While I was at Emory, Ollister was born. Then a few days before my dissertation defense, Gideon was born. In a very real way, this book is theirs. But don't worry, boys, you don't have to read it.

I discovered religious studies at the College of Charleston. I also fell in love. Emily Steinichen Altman has been my partner through all of this. She never doubted me, even when I doubted myself. She is the love of my life and my best friend. This book would not be here without her. A true acknowledgment of my gratitude to her would require a sky-writer, fireworks, and an Elton John song.

There are Hindus, but there is no Hinduism.

Preface

IN ITS FIRST incarnation, this book was a project about Hinduism in nineteenth-century America. As I started out, I knew what Hinduism was—it was a religious tradition, it was something people taught courses like "Introduction to Hinduism" about (I was even a teaching assistant for such a course). So, I went to three nineteenth-century magazines and began to hunt for Hinduism. The thing was, I never really found "Hinduism." Instead I found descriptions of "heathens," translations of Sanskrit texts, "Hindoos," "Gentoos," "Brahmins," "the Vedam," "Vishnoo," "Kreeshna," "widow burning," "caste," and all sorts of other representations, images, texts, descriptions, and narratives. Nonetheless, in its initial form, I wrote about all of these things as "Hinduism in nineteenth-century America." I had found Hinduism in a period long before most American religious historians thought there was such a thing in American culture. Original contribution to the field made.

After that initial foray into the sources from the period, I realized that there was a bigger story to tell than merely the discovery of some interesting representations of "Hinduism" in three magazines. So, I decided to expand my archive and cover as much as I could from the earliest references all the way up to the World's Parliament of Religions. As I expanded my archive, it became clear that I was not finding "Hinduism" in these sources. I was finding that whole list of terms noted earlier and more. But surely all these terms were just a variety of ways to describe and reference the same thing, right? If it was not "Hinduism," then what was it? So, I coined a new term: Hindu religion. In this new and expanded version of the project, I used "Hindu religion" to name the single object that I thought all of these texts, terms, authors, and representations described.

And then I had a wonderfully terrible realization. My "Hindu religion" was no different from the nineteenth-century author's "religion of the Hindoos" or "Brahmanism" or "heathenism." Indeed, "Hindu religion" did not name a single object to which all of these other terms referred. Instead, it was simply another term in the long list of terms that Americans like me had used to describe something about the people of India and their practices and beliefs. I had written myself into the very history I was trying to analyze.

A second realization followed. The way to approach these sources was to take their own language seriously and not to assume that I knew what they were *really* talking about. That is, I should not assume that "Brahmanism," "religion of the Hindoos," "heathenism," and, eventually, "Hinduism" all referred to the same object. These were not various (mis)representations of Hinduism, the religious tradition we all know. Nor were these steps in a developmental knowledge of this one thing we now know better, called Hinduism. Each of them was its own representation. Yes, they referred to one another and inflected one another, but they also served their own social, cultural, and political purposes. "Brahmanism" was not "Hindoo religion," which was not "heathenism," which was not "Hinduism." Neither was one of them the "right" representation and the others "wrong." My task, then, was not to find "Hinduism" in nineteenth-century America, nor was it to trace the development of American representations of "Hindu religions" from "heathenism" to "Hinduism." My task was to analyze the variety of ways in which Americans represented religion in India and pay particular attention to how subjects constructed each of these representations and to what ends they put them. That is what I have done in this book.[1]

To accomplish that task, I have stuck close to the language of the texts and authors in my analysis. Where authors have discussed "Hindoo religion," I have analyzed Hindoo religion. Where they have described "Brahmanism," I have analyzed Brahmanism. The double-O "Hindoo" in my prose may be striking to some readers. That moment of shock is important because it reminds readers that when a nineteenth-century author writes about the Hindoo, he or she is not necessarily writing about what might today be identified as "Hinduism." Noah Webster's dictionary entries for "Hindoo" and "Hindooism" during the period revealed the ambiguous nature of these terms. In 1828 the only entry is for "HIN'DOO, n. An aboriginal of Hindoostan, or Hindostan." By 1849 the entry is extended to "HIN'DOO-ISM, HIN'DU-ISM, n. The doctrines and rites of the Hindoos; the system of religious principles among the Hindoos." That same definition is repeated in the 1864 edition.[2] Just what those "doctrines and rites" were and what that system was remained wide open. Dictionaries reflect the common usage of a word. In common usage throughout the nineteenth century, "Hindoo" and "Hindooism" were empty terms referring to "those people in India" and "whatever it is those people in

India are doing." The variety of ways Americans filled these empty terms is the sub-ject of this book. So, though these terms do not get so-called scare quotes through-out this book, the reader is asked to read with scare quotes at hand.

It is important to note from the outset that I am not arguing that Hinduism is *merely* a construction. Nor am I arguing that there is no such thing as Hinduism *really*. The temples Indian-Americans have built across the United States testify to the fact that Hinduism is very real and very much a part of the American religious landscape. Rather, my argument in this book is about the construction of a series of categories that Americans used to understand religion in India, to understand themselves, and to argue about the definition of religion in their nation and cul-ture. Hindu Americans who read this book will most likely not recognize them-selves in the representations of Indian religion they find in these nineteenth-century American sources. Nor should they. But I hope Hindu Americans will find a valuable history of how the categories of heathen, Hindoo, and Hindu emerged in American culture and shaped American understandings of South Asia.

We can trace the path of Hindu religious movements more precisely than that of the words; the movements entered through Chicago.

WENDY DONIGER, *The Hindus*

Prologue

ON SEPTEMBER 11, 1893, a Bengali monk stood before a crowd of Americans inside the Hall of Columbus in Chicago at the World's Parliament of Religions. He wore a saffron robe and turban. Observers described him as "a large, well-built man, with superb carriage of the Hindustanis." He was "the popular Hindoo monk who looks so much like McCullough's Othello," Swami Vivekananda. Vivekananda addressed his "sisters and brothers of America" to a rousing applause that lasted several minutes.[3] When he spoke, the audience heard a "perfect English masterpiece." As one audience member wrote:

> His personality dominant, magnetic; his voice, rich as a bronze bell; the controlled fervor of his feeling; the beauty of his message to the Western world he was facing for the first time—these combined to give us a rare and perfect moment of supreme emotion. It was human eloquence at its highest pitch.[4]

His opening address attracted fans. "Scores of women" walked over their benches to get near the young swami afterward. A few days later, Vivekananda delivered a lecture titled "Hinduism as a Religion." As one of his Western disciples described it, "in this stunning talk Swamiji gave coherence and unity to the bewildering number of sects and beliefs that through untold ages have gathered and flowered under the name Hinduism."[5] As religious studies scholar Vasudha Narayanan notes, "most people trace the history of Hinduism in America to this famous address."[6] Following the Parliament, Vivekananda toured the country, speaking about Vedanta philosophy and yoga. He founded the Vedanta Society, which built the first Hindu temple in America. He has been remembered as "a model of success from an earlier generation, representing the Indian religious teacher who aspires to come to the United States to proclaim Hinduism."[7]

Most stories of Hinduism in the United States begin with Vivekananda. In some cases, religious historians will begin with a brief Transcendentalist and Theosophist prologue. Such narratives begin by noting that Ralph Waldo Emerson, Helena Blavatsky, and other American religious liberals read and were influenced by Indian texts such as the Bhagavad Gita. Nonetheless, in most narratives the arrival of Vivekananda signaled the real beginning of Hinduism in America. As the story goes, other gurus, such as Yogananda, followed Vivekananda and spread yoga and meditation throughout America before World War II. Then, in 1965, changes in immigration laws opened up the United States to South Asian immigrants who came to America, built temples, societies, and institutions, and took their place in the religiously plural American society. Following this narrative, studies of Hinduism in the United States have focused on the twentieth century, immigrant Hinduism, new religious movements, and gurus.[8] These studies render Hinduism as an object carried to the United States by South Asian teachers, gurus, and immigrants. They are stories of ever expanding progress, increase in numbers and knowledge, and greater and greater pluralism.[9]

There are serious problems with these accounts of "Hinduism in America." First, such narratives treat Hinduism as if it were a stable object that moves from one place to another, rather than an ever-shifting discourse. Scholars use the arrival of immigrants after 1965 as a metaphor to explain the American encounter with Indian religion before 1965. For example, sociologist Prema A. Kurien has described how "Hinduism arrived in the United States long before Hindu immigrants did."[10] She cited travelogues, missionary accounts, and translations of "Hindu scriptures" as leading to the arrival of Hinduism in America. Religious studies scholar Vasudha Narayanan has split "Hinduism in the United States" between "the history of ideas and practices that are derived from Hindu traditions" and "the history of Hindus in this country." She further divides the history between the era before large-scale South Asian immigration began in 1965 and the era afterward. During the nineteenth century, "ideas and practices originating in Hinduism came at a time when Hindus were not allowed into the country."[11] Narayanan and Kurien read the immigrant pattern back onto the movement of ideas. Just as people who identified as "Hindu" came to America after 1965, they argue, so too did ideas identified as "Hinduism" or "Hindu traditions" migrate in the earlier period.

In these narratives, "Hinduism" moves like a giant wooden box carried across the oceans from India to America. But, as this book argues, there was no solid, singular, unified Hinduism to ship. There was no box. Rather, pieces of driftwood—a translation of the Bhagavd Gita here, a missionary report there, an image of Krishna taken from Calcutta—floated along a triangular network between Britain, North America, and India. Americans fashioned a variety of representations, images, and ideas out of these fragments, and they labeled them by a variety of terms: Hindoo, Hindoo religion, Brahmanism, heathenism, and on and on.

These studies also fail to account for the full history of American encounters with religion in India. Though they do describe the arrival of Hinduism before 1965, the Transcedentalist-Theosophist-Vivekananda-1965 history misses American discourses about the people and religions of India that begin in the late eighteenth century. These accounts ignore a larger history of American interest in India by assuming that Hinduism is made of certain "ideas or practices," "Hindu traditions," or scriptures. Thus, Cotton Mather's comparison between the "heathens" of Malabar and the "heathen" natives of Martha's Vineyard, or missionary reports about "the Juggernaut," have not been included in the history of "Hinduism in America." These representations do not match the model of Hinduism that scholars have been looking for. Scholars have defined Hinduism and then have gone back to look for it in the archive.

Religious historian Stephen Prothero has attempted to account for the full variety of American encounters with India in some of his work. Prothero has repeatedly gathered these disparate representations of and encounters with Indian religion under the term "Hinduism." Yet, this is not the term found in the historical archive. Prothero has argued that "of all the religions of Asia, Hinduism has the longest history in the United States" and wrote about the "Hindu tradition." He took every reference to, representation of, or encounter with "Hindoos," "Gentoos," "heathens," or "pagans" in India that he found and folded them into "Hinduism."[12] Across a handful of articles, Prothero's work on Hinduism in America reflects his belief that Hinduism is a stable world religion. Whether they knew it or not, according to Prothero, Americans who read or wrote about the religion of the Hindoos were *really* writing about Hinduism.

These various problematic and incomplete narratives of Hinduism in the United States share an assumption about the nature of Hinduism itself. These studies treat Hinduism as a stable religion with some sort of essential characteristic or list of traits that define it. Yet, "Hinduism" is a fraught term in religious studies. Scholars continue to struggle with a definition for Hinduism.[13] Is it a unified religion? A civilization containing multiple religious traditions? A nineteenth-century construct? If it was constructed, then by whom? For some scholars, Hinduism did not exist prior to the British colonization of India. As historian of religions Richard King has argued, "Hinduism," as a unified and systematic religion, emerged during the nineteenth century as Western Orientalists and South Asians encountered one another in colonial India. As he so bluntly puts it, "the notion of 'Hinduism' is itself a Western-inspired abstraction, which until the nineteenth century bore little or no resemblance to the diversity of Indian religious belief and practice."[14] British colonial power in India constructed "Hinduism" by locating the core of Indian religion in Sanskrit texts and defining Indian religion according to Judeo-Christian assumptions. King concluded that "it remains an anachronism to project the notion of 'Hinduism' as it is commonly understood into pre-colonial Indian history" and that before the colonial period there is no "religion called 'Hinduism' that might be taken to represent the belief system of the Hindu people."[15]

The so-called constructivist argument has been rejected by scholars who see a unified religion of the Hindus in the pre-colonial archive. David N. Lorenzen has distinguished "the English word itself" from "a single religious community." Lorenzen has argued that "the evidence suggests that a Hindu religion theologically and devotionally grounded in texts such as the *Bhagavad-Gita*, the Puranas, and philosophical commentaries on the six *darśanas* gradually acquired a much sharper self-conscious identity through the rivalry between Muslims and Hindus in the period between 1200 and 1500 and was firmly established long before 1800."[16] Andrew J. Nicholson has most recently rehashed and extended this argument.[17] In the introduction to the Hinduism volume of the recent *Norton Anthology of World Religions*, Wendy Dongier offered a "cluster" definition for Hinduism:

> The religion commonly known as Hinduism has existed from at least 1500 B.C.E. (if one begins with the earliest text, the *Rig Veda*) or even perhaps 2500 B.C.E. (if one includes the Indus Valley Civilization, from which we have rich archeological evidence but not deciphered texts) to the present. And it has thrived over a wide geographical area, enriched by many different language groups and types of cultures. So wide is this span of time and space, and so diverse the ideas and myths and rituals and images that it encompasses, that some scholars resist calling it a single religion. But the widespread scholarly convention of gathering together the many forms of these ideas and myths and rituals and calling them "Hinduism" is supported by the intertextual tradition of the Hindus themselves, who tie the earliest texts to the latest in an unbroken chain (what they call a *param-para*, "from one to the other") and distinguish themselves from other religions (Buddhism, Islam, Christianity) by various terms, including, for the past four hundred years, "Hinduism." In that spirit, the present anthology brings together texts from the widest reaches of time and space under the umbrella term "Hinduism."[18]

For these scholars, generally textualists of South Asia, something—be it philosophy, identity contra Muslims, or a set of texts—unified Hindus in India prior to the arrival of the East India Company.

Taken at face value, these appeared to be contradictory and opposite sides of the argument about the history of Hinduism. Religious historian Brian Pennington outlined the debate in a clear "on the one hand, on the other hand" style:

> On one side of the debate over the appropriateness or utility of the term "Hinduism" are the constructionists, those who claim that in the scholarly practice the category Hinduism vacuums up a miscellany of Indic traditions, ideas, and communities that, at their core, have so little in common that their collective identification under this umbrella is at best misleading and at worst an exercise in ideological subterfuge. . . . On the other side of the issues echo a varity of voices that insist that, however, diffuse, variegated, multivalent, and internally contested, "Hinduism," as an analytic category and descriptive label is both meaningful and reasonably true to observed social and historical realities.[19]

It is a matter of constructivist versus correspondence definitions: Richard King's nineteenth-century construction versus Wendy Doniger's ancient pan-Indian Hinduism. But, these two definitions actually have a lot in common. They are both origin narratives.

At first blush, King and the other constructivists appeared to offer a radical departure from their colleagues who argued for a unified and ancient religion called Hinduism. They were *deconstructing* Hinduism, after all—except that they did not deconstruct Hinduism, they simply moved the origin story to a later date. A religion called Hinduism still existed; it was just not as old as some would argue. Rather than originating in 2500 B.C.E., as Doniger argued, it began in the colonial period. Furthermore, even though critics labeled him a "constructivist," a latent essentialism snuck into King's definition of Hinduism. Even though Hinduism was constructed in the colonial period, he still delinated between "accurate" and "inaccurate" readings of Indian texts. For example, he made a point to highlight how American writer Theos Bernard's description of the *darśanas*, or Indian schools of philosophy, was "historically inaccurate, as even a cursory examination of the philosophical texts of each school will demonstrate."[20] Hinduism was a construction, but be sure you get it right. So, while they disagree about the date of origin, both the constructivists and the unifiers agreed that there was a "correct" or "accurate" Hinduism.

These scholars have argued over how and when Hinduism came into being. Whence this object called Hinduism? But I want to pursue a different question, one that does not approach Hinduism as a given object—as that box that sailed to America. As Will Sweetman has argued, " 'Hinduism' has no ontological status, it is not an entity. It is rather a tool of analysis."[21] So how did this tool of analysis end up in America? What made this sort of analysis thinkable? In his study of "the Other" in Western anthropology, Bernard McGrane described how he was "not interested in the fact and nature of their existence, but I'm very much interested in the fact and nature of their conceivability."[22] Rather than asking how Hinduism arrived in America, I want to know how Hinduism became conceivable in America. That is, how is it possible for anyone to speak of "Hinduism" at any point in time? What makes it thinkable? Instead of finding its origin, I want to trace its *emergence*. "Emergence is always produced through a particular stage of forces," and an analysis of emergence "must delineate this interaction, the struggle these forces wage against each other or against adverse circumstances."[23] So, what forces and interactions produced Hinduism in specific times and places? The question of emergence or conceivability demands that the scholar account for the forces and circumstances that made the idea of "Hinduism" thinkable.

Asking how Hinduism became conceivable requires grounding the question in a specific time and place, because the answer will change accordingly. What made Hinduism conceivable in colonial Bengal? What made Hinduism conceivable in London? And what made Hinduism conceivable in the United States? The question of conceivability is richer, deeper, and more interesting than a simple claim that "Hinduism is a construction." "Hinduism is a construction" is an argument about origins. The question of conceivability, of emergence, is genealogical. "Genealogy" as a method has a variety of definitions and brands: Nietzsche's genealogy, Foucault's genealogy, Deluze's genealogy, Asad's genealogy, and so on. For my purposes, genealogy means an attention to the powers, identities, forces, constraints, agents, and discourses that form a particular category. It means paying attention to the connection between categories, the ways they overlap, include, and exclude one another. It traces how the formation of one category draws on the others and produces yet more.[24]

This study is genealogical insofar as it analyzes a series of sites that produced representations of religion in India and led to the formation of "Hinduism, the world religion from India" in American culture and thought. Genealogy "opposes itself to the search for origins."[25] This genealogy of Hinduism in America does not search for the origin—when it arrived or when it was constructed—but, rather, it isolates various and disparate sites of emergence and the "numberless beginnings." A number of diverse representations, encounters, and images of religion in India emerged in American culture before 1893. They did not form a discrete evolution or chain of thought from one to the other. Heathens did not lead to Hindoos and then to Hindus and then to Hinduism. When Vivekananda walked on stage in 1893, "Hinduism" was not the culmination of these earlier representations. Rather, Hinduism as a world religion emerged in the midst of various representations of religion. They made Hinduism conceivable, but they were not its direct antecedents.

As a genealogy of Hinduism in American culture, this book does not trace a direct history from "heathenism" to "Hinduism." Rather, I analyze different examples of how Americans represented religion in India. I call these representations of "religion in India" not because I think they are necessarily representations of "religion" but because the sources themselves categorize them as such. That is, they are "religion" insofar as the sources and writers claim they are. I then trace connections between the representations and examine the forces, arguments, conflicts, and identities at play in each representation. Americans wrote a lot about India in the nineteenth century, and a complete account of all the representations of religion in India would be impossible. I have chosen to focus on representations that share connections with each other or with movements and events that historians regard as the major streams of American religious history. I also chose representations that were widely circulated or enduring. Nearly all of the sources for this book came from published works and periodicals. At one level, the decision of what to include was my own arbitrary one. At another level, the narratives of American religious history currently dominating the field dictated it. Thus, I include evangelical Christians, liberal religionists, metaphysicals, and the World's Parliament of Religions. The result of these decisions is a study of white people who lived mostly in the northeastern United States. I hope further work will open up how non-white Americans imagined India and represented Indian religion.

All of the representations discussed in this book emerged in American culture through debates about the category "religion." As the following chapters will show, Americans deployed representations of religion in India in their arguments about religion in America. In some cases "the religion of the Hindoos" was the "heathenism" or "superstition" that marked the boundary of "true religion." In other cases, "Brahmanism" provided the contemplative side of religion necessary to form a Universal Religion. For some Americans, India was the land of esoteric religious power. For others, India provided an example of brown heathen despotism, in contrast to white Christian democracy in America. Throughout the nineteenth century, India provided a useful foil for Americans as they debated the contours of religion.

When Americans talked about religion in India, they were not really talking about religion in India. They were talking about themselves. So, I have focused my analysis on the ways these representations of religion in India functioned as arguments about what it meant to be "American." As these representations show, white

Protestant Americans used India as a "sort of surrogate and even underground self," as Edward Said called it, to make sense of their own conflicts and differences.[26] Each of these representations, then, revealed more about the Americans involved then it did anything about people in India. One way to argue about being American was to argue about heathens, Hindoos, and Hindus.

1 Heathens and Hindoos in Early America

COTTON MATHER BELIEVED in a connection between America and Asia. He believed that the Native Americans had arrived on the continent from Asia sometime after the biblical flood. He also believed in a world with Christian Europe at its center and the heathen lands of the East Indies and West Indies on the outskirts. Mather's 1721 *India Christiana* reflected the connections he saw between the East and West Indies on the boundary of Christendom. It contained a sermon Mather gave to the Commissioners for the Propagation of the Gospel Among the American Indians at Samuel Sewell's house, followed by two letters, one from Mather to the Dutch Lutheran mission in South India and a response from the Dutch missionary John Ernest Grundler.[1] *India Christiana* highlighted the ways Mather saw the work among the Indian "heathens" as the same whether it was in America or India. He called his fellow Euro-Americans to "the Promise made unto our SAVIOUR, *I will give the Heathen for thine Inheritance, and the Uttermost of the Earth for thy Possession.*"[2] The New England Puritans and the Dutch missionaries found themselves on the borderlands of European influence, and both had been charged with spreading the "joyful sound" of the Gospel in a heathen wilderness. Mather never mentioned Hindus, "Hindoos," or "Gentoos" in his writings about India's religions. Whether in Martha's Vineyard or on the west coast of India, Indians were Indians, heathens were heathens, and they all needed the Gospel.

By the end of the century, Americans would write about Hindus, Hindoos, Gentoos, yogis, and "sanyasins." Relying on accounts from British Orientalists, East

India Company officials, and missionaries, American authors began writing about "the religion of the Hindoos" for an American audience. The category of heathenism took on a taxonomical status as the genus for various species of false religion. The "religion of the Hindoos" was one such species. This transition occurred as American writers engaged in a transatlantic debate about the nature of religion and the relationship of Christianity to the rest of the world. As Enlightenment thinkers replaced Christianity with reason as the grid for understanding human difference, heathenism took on a new importance within debates about the truth and boundaries of Christianity. By the end of the century, these European debates would spur a few writers in the newly formed United States to describe "the religion of the Hindoos."

Heathenism and Religion in the Enlightenment

The descriptions of the heathen, in both the West and East Indies, in Mather's *India Christiana* reflected Enlightenment understandings of non-Christian Others and the questions surrounding reason and religion in European thought during the period. The Reformation, the European wars of religion, and new European knowledge about the New World, Africa, and Asia led to a number of questions surrounding the nature of "religion," the means for authorizing "true religion," and the relationship between Christianity and the various other "religions" around the world.[3] As Bernard McGrane put it, "In the Enlightenment 'religion' was first constituted as a general category, i.e. 'religion' became a concept detached from Christianity, from Christianism, and, in an oedipal-like operation, usurped its place. . . . Christianity became a species of the new genus 'religion.'"[4] Religion thus became a category that could hold differences within Europe, as in the wars of religion, and differences between Europe and its outside, as in the various religions of the New World, Asia, and Africa.

For example, in *The Reasons of the Christian Religion* (1667), Puritan divine Richard Baxter surveyed the state of religion in the world and came to a number of conclusions. He found religion to be nearly universal. "All the world, except those called Heathens, are conscious of the necessity of supernatural Revelation; yea, the Heathens themselves have some common apprehension of it."[5] He then discerned "four sorts of Religion. . . . The meer [*sic*] Naturalists, called commonly Heathens and Idolaters: the Jews: the Mahometans: and the Christians."[6] Baxter found some heathens better than others. He recognized the wisdom of heathen philosophers such as Aristotle and Plato, but "except these Philosophers, and very few more, the generality of the Heathens were and are foolish Idolaters, and ignorant, sensual brutish men."[7] Baxter's fourfold taxonomy of Christians, Mahometans, Jews, and heathens would be the organizing system of thought about religious difference well into the nineteenth century. Within this system, the heathen was identified by his ignorance—the "ignorant, sensual brutish men," as Baxter called them. As McGrane summarized it, "the self-identity of the Enlightenment is aligned with the knowledge *as opposed to* the identity of the unenlightened, alien Other that is aligned with ignorance."[8] It was ignorance that marked the difference between the European and the non-European Other.

Within this context, it is not surprising that Mather never used the words "Hindu," "Hindoo," or "Gentoo." Instead, he always referred to the "Malabarians" or the "heathen." Similarly, in his letter printed in *India Christiana*, Grundler called the Malabarians "deluded Heathen People."[9] "Heathen" served as a category that encompassed every non-European, non-Jewish, non-Muslim Other. Mather described the natives of North America, the heathens he had observed himself, in terms that emphasized their ignorance. He called them "the most forlorn *Ruins of Mankind*, and very doleful Objects. Their way of living was lamentably Barbarous. Beyond all Expression Dark were their Notions of a God; and *Chepian*, or the *Evil God*, had as great a share as *Kautantowit*, or the *Good God*, in their Adorations, The *Manicheans* (as great a Tribe of *Hereticks* as ever were in the World) may boast of *these*, as being really *Theirs*."[10] A lack of knowledge (dark notions) led to a lack of civilization (barbarous way of living) and a misunderstanding of religious truth (heresy).

Mather always approached the heathen through the frame of missionary work. If the heathen was heathen because of his ignorance, the solution was to bring him into knowledge. As he wrote, the goal of Christian missions was "to *Humanize* these Miserable *Animals*, and in any measure to *Cicurate* them & *Civilize* them" but even more "to Raise these Miserables up, unto an Acquaintance with, and an Experience of, the **Christian Religion**, and bring them not only to *Know* something of their SAVIOUR, but also to *Live unto GOD by Him*."[11] Knowledge would lead to civilization and the humanization of the heathen. By giving Indians religion qua Christianity, they could be humanized and saved.

Cotton Mather's earliest representation of people in India lacked any sense that the heathen in Asia differed very greatly from the heathen in North America. It would take two major changes to usher in a new American understanding of East Indians as fundamentally different from West Indians. First, Americans would have more firsthand experiences with India through maritime trade and, second, an explosion of European knowledge about India and its people would come through the work of the first generation of British Orientalists.

The Orient in Bits and Pieces: The East India Marine Society of Salem

Cotton Mather saw India as a mission field on the margins of Christian Europe, but after the American Revolution, another group of New Englanders imagined India as a land of trade and wealth. They hoped to see free trade, not Christian mission, spread around the world. "The Fair of America and the wealth of India—in the pursuit of each a *Good Hope* is half the voyage." So toasted the men of the East India Marine Society of Salem (EIMS) and their guests in 1825. It was a big day for the society. They celebrated their twenty-sixth anniversary, they opened the new East India Marine Hall, and they welcomed President John Quincy Adams as their guest. The toast, one of many, reflected the mariners' view of the past quarter-century of trade with Asia.

Indian wealth proved important to the maritime trade on which the early republic depended. According to cultural historian Susan Bean, "in 1791, 92 percent of U.S. revenues were generated from impost and tonnage duties." These revenues "derived from far-flung voyages and exotic cargoes provided a measure of financial stability to the federal government."[12] Furthermore, all of this trade gave the mariners and merchants of New England a cosmopolitan outlook that valued independence and the right to freely trade around the world.

Writing to Secretary of State James Madison in 1806, Salem mariner and congressman, Jacob Crowninshield argued for the advantages of the trade at Calcutta:

Calcutta is on the Ganges. It is a place of great trade. It exports vast quantities of rice for the supply of all India, of late years Sugar and Indigo, and its cotton and silk goods have always been much admired. We send from 30 to 50 ships annually to Calcutta. The outward cargo is chiefly Dollars, iron, lead, Brandy, Madeira and other wines, a variety of European articles, tar, large and small spars. It is estimated that we have imported in some years at least three millions of dollars worth of goods from Calcutta.[13]

Trade with India became important to the budding American economy. In 1807 imports from India tallied over $4 million.[14] The lucrative trade connecting New England to India economically also led to moments of cultural exchange.

The East India Marine Society sat at the crux of cultural and economic exchange between Asia and America. Founded in 1799 by mariners who had ventured around the Cape of Good Hope, the society formed to support the families and widows of mariners killed at sea and to gather and maintain information about the best routes to the East Indies. Beyond these two goals, though, the society also maintained a "cabinet of curiosities" filled with items brought back from Asia and the Pacific. It was, as one member toasted in 1804, a cabinet so "that every mariner may possess the history of the world."[15] The cabinet was a hodgepodge. It included items from natural history to minerals to cultural objects. A catalog from 1821 listed items ranging from "a portion of human intestine (Duodenum) with the capillary vessels filled with an injection of red wax, showing the folds (Valvulae conniventes) in which the lacteals open to take up the chyle" to pieces of minerals to a shark's backbone to "a print of the Temple of Elephanta, near Bombay."[16] The cabinet was a place at once scientific and exotic.

What started as a cabinet of curiosities became a museum for the society's members and folks in town. But it was a museum filled with items out of context. Only the whimsy of the patrons and mariners held the collection together. As one historian of the museum has written, "to the mariner [the artifact] was a curious souvenir; to the museum-goer it became a model, a synecdoche. Individual patrons had donated discrete items, often for reasons unique to them, but the museum synergized those artifacts, and from that synergism emerged an image that could have been quite different from the intent of the patron-mariner or the reality of the far-away land."[17] The image that emerged was not an image of India, China, or Java. It was an image of "the Orient," an internally undifferentiated "other-place" that was exotic, rich, and open to scientific inquiry.

For the first few years of its existence, the EIMS celebrated its anniversary with a procession through town featuring Oriental artifacts from the museum and a palanquin from Calcutta upon which the society members would ride. Salem clergyman William Bentley described one such procession in 1804. "Each of the brethren bore some Indian curiosity & the palanquin was borne by the negroes dressed nearly in the Indian manner. A person dressed in Chinese habits & mask passed in front. The crowd of spectators was great."[18] Bentley had apparently gotten used to the Salem gentleman costumed in the Chinese habit. Three years earlier he had disapproved of the Mandarin dress in the parade: "The dressing of one of their company in a Mandarin's dress, was no compliment paid to themselves on the occasion. Might they not rather have given the dress to one of their Servants or have exhibited a figure to the wondering multitude."[19] Reverend Bentley missed the meaning of the procession in his critique. The goal was not just to exhibit the Oriental objects; the goal was to display mastery and ownership over them. The men of the EIMS desired to publicly display that they inhabited the East as comfortably as they did the streets of Salem. They did so with a parade of African Americans carrying a palanquin full of mariners, the "Indian curiosity," and the Chinese habit. As their bodies moved down the streets of Salem, Massachusetts, decked in pieces of the Orient, the EIMS members declared in public that the East was not that far from home. They, and their traveling mariner bodies, bridged the gap between the familiar world of New England and the exotic world of the Orient.

India and the Orient often appeared in America as things, cloth mostly. Remembering her childhood in Salem during the early nineteenth century, Caroline Howard King wrote, "the wonders of India [were] so near our front doors, when my mother wanted a new set of china or a fresh camel's hair shawl or scarf, it was as easy a thing for her to speak to the Captain of the next ship starting to India as it would be now for us to order them at Brigg's or Hovey's."[20] But even earlier than King's lifetime, Indian cotton goods made their way to the American colonies by way of London up until the decade of the revolution.[21] The museum provided an exotic shadow to the familiar domestic goods of the East India trade in New England homes. The scarf and the idol came from the same place, but one went into the New England home and the other into the museum. One was worn on the body of a woman as a fashion, while the other was part of the mariner's exotic collection.

Out of context and with but a phrase or two of description, a number of artifacts from India ended up in the East India Marine Society Museum with Indian or "Hindoo" labels. The 1821 catalog lists "a group of idols worshipped in Bengal" gifted by Ephraim Emerton. These "idols" were images of Rama, Sita, and Jagaddhatri, molded in clay and painted beautifully. Reverend William Bentley himself donated a "model of a fakir molded in clay." The museum also held a copper image of Ganesa from Java, noted as "the god of Prudence and Sagacity among the Hindoos," a "Burso, or Monument erected to the memory of the dead, in India, by the Hindoos," "beads worn by the Pundahs and Fakirs in India," and two items dealing with the infamous Temple of Elephanta. The first was a print of the temple, and the second, "a Hand, broken from a Statue of Granite, in the Temple on the Island of Elephanta, near Bombay," given by Benjamin Lander. The collection also included pieces of native clothing, Christian scriptures translated into Indian languages, and tools from India. Most of the items did not carry the date that they were donated to the museum, so all that can be said is that they were there before 1821, though it is likely that most of them arrived in the first decade of the century.[22]

The label of "Hindoo" given to these items reflected the mariners' interest in Indian culture during the period. The society's members took little interest in Indian texts or doctrines of religion. Unlike the British Orientalists, EIMS mariners dealt in material objects, not texts, and they dealt with merchants in Indian ports, not brahmin pandits in colonial bureaucracies. Thus the "Hindoo" items they brought back centered on holy ascetics, images of deities, and the fabulous Temple of Elephanta. What held the items together in the collection, what made them Hindoo, was their association with ascetics, idols, and temples.

However, the overall impression of Oriental mystique overshadowed and overwhelmed any representation of a Hindoo religious system. While some items did offer museumgoers a glimpse of the exotic Hindoos, the collection of foreign cultural objects and natural specimens more strongly represented an undifferentiated Orient, rather than any single culture or religion. Visiting the museum as a young girl, Caroline Howard King remembered it as having had a "mysterious attraction." She described her attraction to the museum and a set of life-sized models of Indians near its entrance:

> Indeed it was an experience for an imaginative child, to step from the prosaic streets of a New England town, into that atmosphere redolent with perfumes from the East, warm and fragrant and silent, with a touch of the dear old Arabian Nights about it. From the moment I set my foot in that beautiful old hall, and was greeted by the solemn group of Orientals, who, draped in Eastern stuffs and camel's hair shawls stood opposite the entrance, until the hour of closing came, and Captain Saul went through this never-failing ceremony of presenting me with a strip of sandal wood cut from a huge log that stood near the door, or a sweet-smelling Tonquin Bean, the hours were full of enchantment, and I think I came as near fairy-land as one ever can in this work-a-day world.[23]

The museum was not a passage to India per se, but instead a passage to a "fairy-land" full of Oriental enchantment. King's words imply that it was a land of her imagination—a land that was not real. Yet she could smell the "perfumes of the East," feel the museum's warmth, and hold on to the strip of sandalwood. The materiality and sensuality of the museum were real. It launched her childhood imagination into an Orient populated by the clay models in the entrance and touched by the Arabian nights. Indian artifacts melded with models of "Orientals," foreign tools, and natural specimens within the walls of the museum to make it a place of fantasy, imagination, and an undifferentiated exotic Orient.[24]

While King experienced the museum as a passage to the Orient, others in town believed that the museum played an important role in the progress of science and human knowledge. In an open letter to the society published in the *Salem Gazette*, an anonymous admirer lauded the society for its collection and distinguished the society from "many men of sordid and contracted minds [who] consider a Museum as they do fire works, that give pleasure only while seen."[25] On the contrary, the society was "enlightened by science and refined by taste" and was "filled with admiration at every thing which throws light on the history of nations, or exhibits the beauties, or displays the wonders of nature."[26] The author saw potential in the society's work for exploring the history of humanity.

> The country from which you bring us information has been emphatically called the "cradle of the world"; there we are to look for the earliest beginnings and slow progress of Art, and the still slower march of Science. Your researches united to the researches of others, will assist the philosopher in discussing that hitherto but partially explored subject, the powers and faculties of the human mind; by showing him the influence of climate, laws, superstition and habit on society.[27]

Rather than the imaginative world of King, this museumgoer found a very real world of rational science within the hall of the society. Every item shed light on the progress of human development. The museum represented an Orient that held the secrets of human history and that was open for scientific investigation. The image of Rama and Sita and the broken granite hand from Elephanta pointed to the development of art and the influence of "superstition and habit." Again, the items from India did not represent any sort of "Hinduism," or even "Hindoo religion." Rather, they represented an Orient that was "the cradle of the world" and that held the answers to questions about the development of the human mind. The author imagined this Orient as primitive and promised to reveal the development and advancement of Anglo-American culture in comparison.

The East-India trade in New England brought Indian objects and materials into American hands. While most often these things were clothes, at times they were also pieces that fit into the construction of Hindoos as idolaters. The EIMS processions and museum used pieces of Indian material culture to represent the Orient as both "the cradle of the world" that could be scientifically examined and an imaginative fairyland of the exotic Other. In the hands of the East India Marine Society, Hindoo items became part of a larger representation of the foreign, Oriental Other. The Orient was either the land of luxury goods and fantastical mystery or the land that held the ancient secrets of human development. In either case it stood in stark contrast to the modernizing, industrializing, and rational New England. The East may have been just outside the door, but everything changed when one crossed the threshold.

India through British Eyes

When American trade with India began in the 1790s, the British had already been trading in India for over a century, but it was not until the second half of the eighteenth century that widespread discussion of India in Britain or even Europe took hold. Early missionaries such as Roberto Nobili and Bartholomäus Ziegenbalg wrote of their encounters with the people of India in the seventeenth and early eighteenth centuries, respectively, yet the impact of these accounts paled in comparison to later British works.[28] Indeed, superiors refused to allow Ziegenbalg's works on religion in Malabar to be published during his lifetime. One work did appear in Berlin in 1791 without Ziegenbalg's name on the title page, but his two German-language texts were not officially published until 1867 and 1926.[29] In the second half of the eighteenth century, as the British extended their power on the subcontinent, their knowledge of Indian society and culture grew steadily. As historian P. J. Marshall noted, "once the British began their conquests in the second half of the century, Europe came more and more to see India through British eyes."[30] Likewise, Americans who wanted to know something of the heathen of India would turn to British sources.

Two early works, John Zephaniah Holwell's *Interesting Historical Events Relative to the Provinces of Bengal and the Empire of Indostan* (1767) and Alexander Dow's *History of Hindostan* (1768) found an audience in Britain and North America. Dow and Holwell included very little new information in their books. But the timing of their publication led to greater public interest than previous accounts.[31] Both Holwell and Dow went to India as part of the British East India Company. Holwell rose to a brief stint as governor of Bengal, and Dow died a colonel in the Company's Bengal Army. Neither of them knew Sanskrit. Yet, as Marshall noted, their importance "lies less in the novelty of what they said than in the audience that they reached. Both authors were widely reviewed and discussed in Britain."[32] Both of them had their works translated into French (and Holwell's book was also translated into German) within a couple years of their initial publication.

Despite Holwell's and Dow's popularity, the biggest breakthrough in European knowledge about India came two decades later with the formation of the Asiatic Society of Bengal. Founded by William Jones in 1874, the society consisted of various East India Company officials and British civil servants. Jones himself came to India to fill an appointment to the Indian Supreme Court. At meetings of the society, various amateur Orientalists read papers about the art, religion, culture, and language of India. The society published papers from their meetings in a journal, *Asiatick Researches*, beginning in 1789. Much of the society's success was due to the support it enjoyed from the governor of Bengal, Warren Hastings. Hastings had a vision for a British civil service force of "Orientalized service elite competent in Indian languages and responsive to Indian traditions."[33] Thus, British knowledge about India served British colonial interests in India.[34]

The compilation and translation of Nathaniel B. Halhead's *Code of Gentoo Laws* exemplified this connection between Orientalist knowledge and colonial governance. The British government in Bengal had charge over the civil courts, and Hastings aimed to ensure that Indians would be governed by Indian laws. As Bernard Cohn described Hastings's approach, "in his discussion of his plans, Hastings was translating for a British audience theories and practices from one culture to another. India had an ancient constitution which was expressed in what came to be thought of as two codes, one Hindu and the other Muslim."[35] Muslim legal and textual traditions made that code easier to identify, but the British did not know where to find the Hindu code. Hastings had a plan. He assembled eleven Bengali pandits and charged them with compiling all of the relevant Indian literature. He appointed Halhead to supervise them. The pandits made their compilation, translated it into Persian, and then Halhead, who did not know Sanskrit, translated the Persian into English. The result was *Code of Gentoo Laws*, published in 1776. But, as Marshall noted, the *Code* was a practical failure. "It did not inspire complete confidence and was never accepted as a final authority; it merely provided the pandits with another source to interpret."[36] Failure though it was in India, it was well received in Europe and was translated into French and German in 1778.

Hastings's patronage led to two other important works by the first generation of British Orientalists. First, Hastings gave a leave of absence to a young writer, Charles Wilkins, so he could learn Sanskrit. Wilkins decided to attempt a translation of the Mahabharata. In 1785 Wilkins published his translation of the Bhagavad Gita, one portion of the larger Mahabharata. Second, dissatisfied with Halhead's *Code*, William Jones sought out the earliest possible compendium of Indian law. He found it in the Sanskrit Manusmrti, which he translated and published as *The Institutes of Hindu Law: Or, the Ordinances of Menu* in 1794. *Asiatick Researches, Code of Gentoo Laws, The Institutes of Hindu Law*, and Wilkins's *The Bhagavat-Geeta* all reached American readers in the early nineteenth century. In India, "the knowledge which this small group of British officials sought to control was to be the instrumentality through which they were to issue commands, and collect ever-increasing amounts of information. This information was needed to create or locate cheap and effective means to assess and collect taxes, and maintain law and order."[37] But this colonial knowledge did not remain in India. These texts traveled along networks connecting India, Britain, and America. As they circulated beyond their colonial context, they were drawn up into larger debates about the nature of religion, the historicity of the Bible, and the superiority of Christianity ongoing in Europe and the United States.

Hannah Adams, the Religious Encyclopedist

One book sparked Hannah Adams's interest in religion: Thomas Broughton's *An Historical Dictionary of All Religion s from the Creation of the World to This Present Time* (1756). A gentleman boarding with the Adams family taught her Latin and Greek and brought along a portion of Broughton's work dealing with Arminians, Calvinists, and some other denominations. Broughton's treatment of the Christian sects triggered an interest in religious controversy that left Adams "disgusted with the want of candor in the authors" for their "most unfavorable descriptions of the denominations they disliked, and applying to them the names of heretics, fanatics, enthusiasts, &c."[38] So, Adams decided to compile her own account of the various denominations in the world and she planned to do so according to some rules:

1. To avoid giving the least preference of one denomination above another: omitting those passages in the authors cited, where they pass their judgment on the sentiments of which they give an account: consequently the making use of any such appellations as *Hereticks, Schismaticks, Enthusiasts, Fanaticks,* &c. is carefully avoided.
2. To give a few arguments of the principal sects, from their own authors, where they could be obtained.
3. To endeavor to give the sentiments of every sect in the general collective sense of that denomination.
4. To give the whole as much as possible in the words of the authors from which the compilation is made, and where that could not be done without to greet prolixity, to take utmost care not to misrepresent the ideas.[39]

Adams aimed at an impartial and fair account of the world's variety of theological positions throughout history, compiled from the best authors she could acquire. The result was published in 1784 as *An Alphabetical Compendium of the Various Sects Which Have Appeared in the World from the Beginning of the Christian Era to the Present Day* and went through four editions with various titles. Her description of the "Gentoos" in the first edition is the earliest description of religion in India published by an American.

As the inspiration from Broughton's work signals, Hannah Adams's four editions took part in a larger European project of cataloging religions during the seventeenth century. Travel and colonial expansion in the sixteenth and seventeenth centuries led to an explosion of European knowledge of non-European Others. European writers then set to organizing this knowledge, especially the knowledge of the world's religious diversity. In English, this began as early as Samuel Purchas's *Purchas his Pilgrimage: Or Relations of the World and the Religions Observed in all Ages and Places discovered, from Creation unto this Present* in 1613.[40] The most popular and duplicated book in this tradition was Bernard Picart and Jean Frederic Bernard's *Cérémonies et coustumes religieuses de tous les peuples du monde* (1723–1737). Picart and Bernard's work "channeled various streams of knowledge and criticism in one direction, summing up what was known about the world's religions and giving that knowledge a new significance."[41] The book went through numerous translations, piracies, and editions well into the nineteenth century in Europe and the United States.[42] Adams's work must be understood as an American entry into this field of religious encyclopedism.

The four editions of Adams's text reflect the larger Enlightenment understanding of religion that undergirded European encyclopedias of religions. David Pailin identified two principles that guided Enlightenment thinking about religion: "The first of these principles is that religious faith is fundamentally a matter of assent to certain truths. The second is that these truths can be determined to be such by the proper use of human reason."[43] As Peter Harrison recounted, the category "religion" emerged as a radically cognitive term during the Enlightenment:

> It would be expected that "religion" and the strategies for its elucidation would develop in tandem. For this reason "religion" was constructed along essentially rationalist lines, for it was created in the image of the prevailing rationalist methods of investigation: "religion" was cut to fit the new and much-vaunted scientific method. . . . As we shall see, inquiry into religion of a people become a matter of asking what was believed, and if it was true. The emergence of the idea of religion thus entailed tests of religious truth, theories of religion, comparisons of "religions," in short, a whole set of rules which governed the manner in which the nascent concept was to be deployed.[44]

While Adams resisted assessing the truth of the various religions she cataloged in her books, she nonetheless approached religion as a rational phenomenon. Religion was a matter of what various groups of people believed. In her four editions she took account of the various Christian sects that have engaged in theological controversies over the centuries. In the back of the book she added an appendix that took account of the world's non-Christian religions, including the religion of the "Gentoos" of India.

Adams's descriptions of Gentoo religion relied on Europe in two ways. First, she took a rationalist Enlightenment approach to religion through her focus on the categories of texts, beliefs, and sects. In Adams's rendering, Gentoo religion shared the same post-Reformation model of sectarianism as European and American

Christianity. Thus, she took little interest in reports of temples or rituals because her larger project was an account of religious beliefs and theological disputes. Over the four editions the material she cited changed, but the focus remained on what the "Gentoos" or "Hindoos" believed, the texts that supported these beliefs, and the doctrinal differences between Indian sects. Second, as she functioned as an author-compiler, her accounts across all four editions relied upon the European, mostly British, sources she had at her disposal. While Adams may not be the representative reader, nonetheless, the texts in the footnotes of her four editions accounted for the changing knowledge of Asia available to American readers through British sources.

The emphasis on what people in India believed appeared in the first edition of *An Alphabetical Compendium* from 1784. Adams compiled a section (spanning a page and a half) on the Mogul Empire that was almost exclusively focused on the beliefs of the "Gentoos, or as others call them, Hindoos." She began by sketching an outline of Gentoo beliefs. "They pretend that *Brumma* [Brahma], who was their legislator both in politics and religion, was inferior only to God; and that he existed many thousands of years before our account of the creation. The *Bramins*—for so the Gentoo Priests are called—pretend, that he bequeathed to them a book, called the *Vidam* [Veda], containing his doctrines and instructions."[45] She also mentioned that the Veda was lost but the brahmins have the "Shastah" [Shastra], which contains commentary in Sanskrit. Brahma served as a "Moses" figure of sorts who dispensed religious and political law. His doctrines included belief in a supreme being who creates a world with "a regular gradation of beings, some superior, and some inferior to man," the immortality of the soul, and a future state of rewards and punishments in the form of "Pathegorian Metampsychosis," or reincarnation.[46]

These beliefs fell into the wrong hands, however. Adams recounted how the brahmin priests, in hopes of inculcating these doctrines in the lower classes, took "recourse to sensible representation of the *Deity* and his attributes; so that the original doctrines of Brumma were changed into idolatry."[47] Adams then described three idolatrous sects found in India: "the *Banians*, the *Persees* and the *Faquirs*." Her focus remained on the beliefs of these sects. The Banians believed in "the transmigration of souls" and so they would not harm animals. The Persees, or Parsees, worshipped fire, and the Faquirs, or fakirs, "are a kind of *Monks*, and live very austere, performing many severe acts of mortification."[48] The section closed by noting that all Indians shared a belief in the sacrality of the Ganges and washed in it often.

Adams's account of Gentoo beliefs narrated a story of declension from a primitive monotheism, a common theme in Enlightenment thinking about non-Christian religions. Adams took her account of Brahma and the Veda directly from William Guthrie's popular *A New System of Modern Geography*, first published in 1770 as *Geographical, Historical, and Commercial Grammar*. Adams, via Guthrie, narrated the declension of Gentoo belief from the monotheism of the Veda to heathen idolatry. This decline occurred because of the superstitions of priestcraft. The brahmins led the people astray. In Adams's telling, the brahmins failed to bring the "lower classes" up to their level by educating them with the proper beliefs, as a good New England minister did with his flock. Rather, the brahmins used idols to appeal to irrational senses instead of reason. Irrational idolatry displaced rational religion. Adams thus represented India as an upside-down place where religion declined away from truth instead of progressing toward it. This explanation of heathen religion through priestcraft and decline from a primitive monotheism was common throughout English thought, most notably in the theories of the English Deists.[49] People were naturally drawn to a rational belief in a monotheistic god, the theory went, but priests interjected themselves as selfish intermediaries that instituted heathen rituals, deities, and institutions that deceived the people. Despite the declension narrative, Adams tried to present a neutral portrayal of Gentoo belief, organized around Enlightenment categories of what counted as religion.

In the 1791 edition of her work, renamed *A View of Religions*, Adams continued to represent Gentoos through Enlightenment categories. She shifted to a new source, however: Holwell's 1767 *Interesting Historical Events Relative to the Provinces of Bengal, and the Empire of Indostan*. Holwell based his text on an unidentified "Shastah" that he believed was at least 4,866 years old and contained the most ancient statement on religion in the world. Marshall described Holwell as a deist and "undoubtedly a Christian, if of a very eccentric kind."[50] As such, Holwell read his Shastah as an example of an ancient monotheistic religion and compared it unfavorably with the contemporary religious worship in India. Holwell detested the "degenerate, crafty, superstitious, litigious and wicked" Indians of his own time, but he viewed their ancient teachings as "rational and sublime" and the brahmins that lived by the ancient "Shastah" as "the purest models of genuine piety that now exist, or can be found on the face of the earth."[51] This "twofold philosophy," as Harrison described it, had a long history in European thought but took on new importance among Enlightenment deists.[52] Twofold philosophy posited "a division between popular 'superstition' and esoteric 'religion.' The human race is divided into two groups . . . the credulous, superstitious mob and the intellectual elite."[53] Enlightenment deists suggested that the twofold philosophy was a universal feature of all religion, and so Holwell was quick to identify and focus on the esoteric and monotheistic core that he believed was the "true" and "sublime" religion of the Gentoos.

So, when Adams turned to Holwell as a source, she tried to keep her promise of neutrality, but still reproduced a meandering summary of Gentoo theology and the "fundamental doctrines of the Bramins, as they are taught in Shastah." According to Adams, as taken from Holwell, brahmins believed in one omnipotent God who created three lesser divinities (Brahma, Shiva, and Vishnu) and a host of angelic beings. These angelic beings, at the instigation of "Moisasoor," rebelled. God threw the rebellious beings out of heaven to "languish forever in sorrow and darkness." The three lesser divinities interceded on behalf of the rebels and convinced God to create a new world where the rebels may live out their punishment in mortal bodies and work for redemption and entrance back into heaven and God's presence. "Consequently, the sprits which animate every mortal form, are delinquent angels in a state of punishment, for a lapse from innocence, in a pre-existent state."[54] Again, Adams focused on beliefs and doctrines in her extract from Holwell. She presented Gentoos as believers in a story of a fall from innocence, a monotheistic supreme God, rebellion by God's creatures, and a search for redemption and future reward. These "fundamental doctrines of the Bramins" shared affinities with Adams's and Holwell's own liberal Christianity.

The attempt at a neutral tone continued when Adams extracted Holwell's account of sati in India. Via Holwell, Adams recounted "a *voluntary sacrifice*, of too singular a nature to pass unnoticed; which is that *of the Gentoos wives burning themselves with the bodies of their deceased husbands.*"[55] The extract emphasized the voluntary nature of sati and attempted to explain the doctrine behind it. Women are "nurtured and instructed in the firm faith that this *voluntary sacrifice* is the most glorious period of their lives" and afterward their "celestial spirit . . . flies to join the spirit of their deceased husbands, in a state of purification" while their children are "raised in dignity and honor."[56] In Holwell's full text, he prefaced the section Adams extracted by noting, "if we view these women in a just light, we shall think more candidly of them and confess they act upon heroic, as well as rational and pious principles."[57] While Adams muted Holwell's admiration for the women in the name of neutrality, she retained the generally tolerant tone of his account. In later depictions by other American writers, sati exemplified the irrational violence of Indian religions, but Adams allowed it to remain voluntary and rational in her text.

Adams added one more extract to her 1791 edition, this time taken from Halhead's preface to his 1776 *A Code of Gentoo Laws*. Adams extracted a section of Halhead's preface in which he remarked on the need to recognize the goodness in every religion. It was Halhead's plea for religious tolerance. He wrote, "the diversities of belief among mankind, are a manifest demonstration of the power of the Supreme Being. . . . Having introduced a numerous variety of crafts, and a multiplicity of different customs, he views in each particular place, the mode of worship which he has appointed."[58] God took pleasure in "attendants at the mosque," and "the adoration of idols" because he is "the intimate of the Mussulmen, the friend of the Hindoos, the companion of the Christians, and the confident [*sic*] of the

Jews."[59] What Halhead wrote as an argument for finding value in the Indian law he translated, Adams shifted to a statement about sectarian tolerance within Indian religion. She prefaced Halhead with her own words: "There are among the Gentoos, upward of thirty sects. Theirs is the most tolerant of all religions."[60] Halhead was not discussing the tolerance of Indians, but rather the tolerance required of the reader approaching their religious law. Adams shifted the subject of Halhead's text to the exemplary tolerance of the Hindus themselves. They are tolerant of one another's sectarian differences, unlike the various Christian disputes she recorded earlier in the book. This call for tolerance was driven home in the appendix of Adams's work, where she listed five beliefs shared by all Christians and argued that the diversity of religious opinions beyond these five are "under the direction of an all-perfect Being, who governs in infinite wisdom."[61] Thus, in Adams's hands, Halhead's statement supported Adams's belief about the limits of Christian sectarianism and the universality of God.

When she published the third edition of *A View of Religions* in 1801, Adams presented an even more unified message about the state of religion in the world. In the newly expanded introduction, Adams offered a series of historical narratives accounting for the state of religion in the world at the time of Jesus' birth. The introduction narrated how the pure religion of Jesus Christ had slowly accrued outside influences and had diversified into various sects. The central theme of her work, then, was an exploration of these sects and this diversity. As her biographer Gary Schmidt put it, "she painted a disarrayed world searching for the Deity—sometimes rationally and philosophically, sometimes desperately, sometimes enthusiastically."[62] The third edition was the most cohesive version of the text yet, using the introduction to set up the problem of religious diversity, exploring that diversity in parts I and II, and then concluding at the end of her appendix that there would be a time "when the knowledge of the truth shall be universally extended; when all superstition shall be abolished; the Jews and Gentiles unitedly become the subjects of Christ's universal empire; and the *knowledge of the Lord fill the earth, as the waters cover the sea.*"[63] Neutral description gave way to theological explanation. The world was full of human strivings for God, and those strivings would eventually culminate in a global moment of Christian unity.

This vision changed Adams's section on religion in India. She expanded it to twelve pages by adding a large chunk of information from two major new sources, Thomas Maurice's *Indian Antiquities* (1793–1800) and the reports of the British Baptist missionaries stationed at Serampore. By replacing Holwell's theological account with Maurice's, keeping the section from Halhead's *Gentoo Code*, and adding accounts from the Baptist mission, Adams's third edition gave readers a presentation of a "Hindoo system" built from the most recent British sources. This third edition signals a transition from a description of beliefs held by a people, the Gentoos, to a systematic form of doctrine. The change in spelling from "Gentoo" to "Hindoo" marked a greater systematization in the representation of Indian religions. In her description of the "Hindoo system," Adams argued for an original monotheism buried deep in the history of India, described the Hindoo search for salvation, and hoped for the spread of the Christian message among Indians.

Adams's cohesive description of "the Hindoo system" relied upon the work of Thomas Maurice. For his part, Maurice relied heavily on the work of William Jones. Thus, Jones's work systematizing Hindoo religion trickled down through Maurice to Adams. The question of how the various heathen people of the world fit into biblical history plagued European thinkers during the Enlightenment.[64] Jones was especially interested in placing the Sanskrit texts within the chronology of the Bible. In his 1790 "On the Chronology of the Hindus," which appeared in volume two of *Asiatick Researches*, he did just that, concluding that the earliest Sanskrit texts were written after the book of Genesis. Similarities between the Bible and the Sanskrit texts, he argued, reflected the shared origin of humanity as described in Genesis. Thus, Adams (by way of Maurice, by way of Jones) began by accounting for the origins of the "Hindoo nation" through the biblical narrative. The Hindoos descended from either Noah or his son Shem. After the biblical flood, these descendants traveled from the site of the ark at Ararat to the western edge of India, where they flourished and "practiced the purest rites of the patriarchal religion, without images and temples."[65] This pure, monotheistic, "primitive theology" consisted of two primary ideas: "That God vouchsafed a revelation to man in a state of innocence, concerning the divine nature, will, and mode of worship; that the Deity is not a solitary occult, inaccessible being, but perpetually present with all his creatures and works."[66] The pure ancient monotheism quickly eroded, however, when "the descendants of Ham invaded and conquered India and corrupted their ancient religion." [67] However, there were remnants of the original monotheism in the Vedas. The Vedas shared a common ancestry with Christianity in the primeval monotheism of Noetic natural theology.

Adams never explicitly compared Christianity with the Hindoo system beyond connecting the two through the Noetic history. However, the theological doctrines of the Hindoo system that she emphasized carry with them implications of a comparison with Christianity. Again, drawing from Jones and Maurice, Adams described Brahma, Vishnu, and Shiva as representatives of the creative, sustaining, and destroying powers of divinity, respectively. "This threefold divinity, armed with the terrors of almighty power, pursue, through the whole extent of creation, the rebellious Dentah, headed by Mahasoor, the great malignant spirit."[68] While she never used the term "trinity," the threefold divinity could likely have instigated comparisons with the Christian trinity in both her own mind and the mind of the reader. Similarly, she described the nine incarnations of Vishnu as "the Deity descending in an [*sic*] human shape to accomplish certain awful and important events, as in the three first; to confound blaspheming vice, to subvert gigantic tyranny, and to avenge oppressed innocence, as in the five following; or finally, as in the ninth, to abolish a gloomy and sanguinary superstition."[69] Again, the incarnation of the deity to accomplish great things could have reminded Christian readers in New England of the incarnation of Jesus. Adams never made explicit note of these similarities between her description of the Hindoo system and Christianity. Nonetheless, she selected material from Jones and Maurice that were most similar to Christian doctrines.

The "saniassi," or sanyasin, made his debut in the 1801 edition and took a prominent place in Adams's description of Indian religion. The sanyasin, a holy ascetic, became the figure that best represented the Hindoo struggle toward salvation. According to Adams, he believed that his spiritual discipline could "unbar the gates of eternity, and procure an immediate entrance into paradise."[70] Adams explained how the sanyasin vowed to conquer his body and his passions, left his family and friends, and headed to the desert where "famine and misery are the companions of his solitude."[71] There he was "absorbed in profound meditations on the Deity" that unite him with the Deity and give him special powers to "call down the stars from heaven," "bring up demons from the lowest bobun of Naraka," and "disembody the soul, which, for a while, leaves its earthly mansion in utter insensibility, and after taking a wide ethereal flight, returns to animate the breathless clay."[72] Eventually, the sanyasin's austerities would lead his soul to permanent liberation and he would achieve disembodied paradise.

Adams connected the figure of the sanyasin—a figure that seems at first glance the farthest from Adams's own Yankee Christian sensibilities—to the Christian God. In describing the final destination of the sanyasin's soul, she copied from Maurice the description of the soul that "finally mingles with, and is absorbed in the essence of the supreme Brahme, who, the veil of mythology laid aside, is no other than the *ineffable, infinite,* and *eternal God.*"[73] Adams allowed the broad and liberal Christianity of William Jones and Thomas Maurice to bleed through in her text. Maurice's narrative, taken from Jones, of an ancient monotheism, shared by Hindoos and Christians, that slowly degraded in India paralleled Adams's own narrative of the diversification of Christianity along sectarian lines after Christ. Putting these two narratives alongside one another, Vedic monotheism became a long-lost cousin of true Christianity, and the sanyasin became absorbed into a God that is bigger than the sectarian claims of either Indians or Americans.

Though Adams compared the Hindoo system with Christianity throughout her description of religion in India, she did not equate them. To be sure, Adams believed Christianity to be the most excellent religion, as reflected in her 1804 book, *The Truth and Excellence of the Christian Religion Exhibited*. Though it had various schisms and sects, Christianity still held universal truth found in the common doctrines Adams outlined in the appendix. However, this did not mean that truth was exclusive to Christianity. For Adams, as for Maurice, elements of universal truth were buried in the ancient religion of the Hindoos, in the text of the Vedas, and in the soteriological desires of the sanyasin. Furthermore, using Jones's chronology, Maurice argued that the Hindoo system proved the universal truth of Christianity. The places where the Hindoo system and biblical chronology aligned evidenced "the great truths of revelation; and thus the Indian Antiquities cannot fail of being considered of national benefit."[74] Where the Bible and the ancient Indian texts agreed, they proved the universal truths of Christianity. Where the two systems departed, they testified to the uniqueness of the Christian revelation.

Because she believed in the supremacy of Christianity over the partial truth within the Hindoo system, Adams hoped the Indians would accept Christianity. She closed her section on the Hindoo system by describing the work of the Baptist missionaries at Serampore, led by the indefatigable William Carey. Drawing on a series of reports from 1795–1800, Adams noted that the missionaries had assembled a congregation of 200 to 600 people, they had learned Bengali and Hindustani, the New Testament had been translated into Bengali, a press had been set up for printing scriptures and tracts, and soon the entire Bible would be translated and printed. Adams began her description of religion in India with the Vedas, and she ended it with the translation of the Bible. The ancient truth of Hindoo monotheism had degraded and been buried in the Vedas but could be restored through the work of Christian missionaries and the divine revelation of the Bible in an Indian tongue. With the arrival of the missionaries, Adams's declension narrative of religion in India could be reversed. No longer left with only the partial monotheism of the Vedas, the missionaries would bring India the unique revelation of the Bible necessary for true religion. The missionaries brought Christianity, and with it, the promise of Christian progress.

In 1815, Thomas Williams of London, who had published the first British edition of Adams's *A View of All Religions*, decided it was time for a second edition. Williams took the 1801 edition of Adams's text and repurposed it. While he added and subtracted some of the content, the most important change Williams made involved rearranging the contents into an alphabetical dictionary. Williams removed the division between Christian and non-Christian sects that had organized the previous editions and arranged everything into briefer, alphabetically organized entries. Williams titled the new edition *A Dictionary of All Religions and Religious Denominations*. While Adams did not like many of the substantive changes Williams made to the tone and content of the second edition, she did approve of the new organization. In 1817, she published her own edition, titled *A Dictionary of All Religions and Religious Denominations: Jewish, Heathen, Mahometan, Christian, Ancient and Modern*, which took Williams's edition, kept some of his additional content, edited it, and, most important, kept the dictionary style of organization.[75] The new edition, as Thomas A. Tweed noted in his updated introduction, "avoided a bivalent classification that undercut all subsequent distinctions and overvalued one tradition."[76] The resultant text "added to the reader's sense of vastness and variability of the [religious] terrain."[77] The fourth edition contained only a small amount of new material about religion in India, but the new dictionary style opened up a view of Hindoos as part of a religious world with many diverse sects across time and space.

The content of *Dictionary of All Religions and Religious Denominations*, like that of the previous edition, relied on British sources for its content. The text spoke in conflicting voices, however, because it blended Adams's and Williams's research. The article under "Hindoos" was similar to the section on religion in India in the third edition, but with a few extra details about the spread of missionary work. It maintained a tolerant and William Jones–influenced Orientalist tone. There was, however, a new entry for "Yogeys," taken from Williams's edition, that drew on the writing of evangelical missionary apologists Claudius Buchanan and William Ward. This entry focused on the physical disciplines of the yogi such as "casting themselves down on spikes" or hook-swinging.[78] In this way, the fourth edition spoke about Indian religion in two voices. The text contained a rupture between the sympathetic Orientalism of Maurice and Jones, which focused on texts and beliefs in the "Hindoos" article, and the zealous missionary evangelicalism of Buchanan and Ward, which only saw violent pagan blood rituals in the "Yogeys." This rupture in the text and this difference between the British sources prefigured a larger rupture in American discourse on religion in India between liberal and evangelical Protestants that began in the 1820s and 1830s. Liberals focused on the wisdom and truth in ancient Hindu texts and practices such as yoga and meditation, while evangelicals railed against the idolatry, violence, and barbarism of the benighted Hindoo heathens. Thus the twofold philosophy split, with different writers representing either the "superstitious" or "esoteric" side of religion in India. Beginning in Adams's *Dictionary*, Americans articulated multivocal and conflicting representations of religion in India.

By the time she published the fourth edition of her work, Hannah Adams had secured her place as an influential writer among the New England intelligentsia. She also had opened up the field of comparative religion in America. As the reviewer of her *Dictionary* wrote in the *North American Review*, Adams was "in such full possession of publick regard, from the benefit conferred by her writings, and the merits of her several productions are so generally known, that we do not deem it necessary to enter into an elaborate investigation of the manner in which she has executed this new edition of a very useful book."[79] Adams's books were useful resources for the New England reading public to investigate the variety of religious beliefs throughout history and across geography. Adams quilted various British sources together to construct a representation of a Hindoo system with sacred texts, doctrines, and sects analogous to Christianity. Adams's comparative approach reached its pinnacle in the organization of her fourth edition. The alphabetical structure allowed her to see Hindoos and yogeys (as well as other "heathens") where Cotton Mather could not. By viewing religion taxonomically, she opened up the possibility that there could be more to heathenism than mere false idolatry. Yet Adams never used the term "Hinduism" or even "Hindooism." At times she wrote of a "Hindoo system" or "religion of the Hindoos," but "Hindoo" was either a noun, as in "a Hindoo," or an adjective for something else—"Hindoo law" and "Hindoo religion." Her description of the Hindoo system imagined a religious system that stretched across the Indian continent, but it was not yet a religion in its own right. It was still another example of heathenism. So, while her four editions opened up the boundaries of "religion," Hindoos only appeared within the marginal and diverse category of heathenism.

It is important to note that Adams's project was motivated by Christian theological disputes that had their roots in the European Enlightenment. As James Turner has argued, "to class Adams as a 'prophet and pioneer' of the academic discipline of religious studies . . . is seriously to overestimate her competence and underestimate the extent to which the internal quarrels of Christianity motivated her."[80] But Turner's assessment misses that the Christianity of her project is part of her "prophet and pioneer" status. The study of comparative religion in the United States following Adams was a Christian project. It was also characterized by many of the same Enlightenment categories of belief, text, and sect that she used. Furthermore, in the nineteenth century the Americans who engaged with non-European religions, especially religions in India, often came from a broadly Christian religious background and encountered religions in India with religious, and often Christian, motivations. The Enlightenment project of comparing religions became the Christian thing to do.

Joseph Priestley's Defense of Moses

While Hannah Adams was in the midst of her various editions in Boston, out in Pennsylvania an English immigrant worked on his own comparative religion project. Joseph Priestley published *A Comparison of the Institutes of Moses with those of the Hindoos and Other Ancient Nations* in 1799. Adams concerned herself with accounting for the diversity of human religions. Priestley, however, concerned himself with questions of origin and truth. Adams was interested in breadth, Priestley in depth. The question "whence the law of Moses?" drove the arguments of Priestley's book and his representation of "Hindoo law." Priestley engaged in a largely European argument in his book, even if he wrote from the middle of the United States. He argued against the claim by French Orientalist Louis-Mathieu Langlès that the Pentateuch derived from the older text of the Vedas. His *Comparison* was more than the first in-depth study of Indian religions published in the United States. It was a work in Christian apologetics and Enlightenment thought on natural religion, reason, and revelation. In *Comparison*, Priestley defended the unique revelation found in the Old Testament. The institutes of Moses were superior to those of the Hindoos, Priestley argued, because they did not rely on human reason alone. Humans needed revelation to find truth.

Like Adams, Priestley narrated a story of declension in Indian religious history, depended upon British sources, and focused on brahminical and Vedic texts for his representation of "the religion of the Hindoos." Unlike Adams, he also spent a good deal of time describing Hindoo religions as superstitious, violent, and lascivious. Priestley deployed Hindoo religion to prove the superiority of the Christian biblical revelation over the vagaries of heathen imagination. For Priestley, the violence and superstition of the heathen Hindoos evidenced the limits of natural religion and the necessity of the unique revelation of the Christian scriptures. As one historian wrote, "he wrote not to praise but to diminish the Oriental religions, and he sought to reassert the claim of Christianity as the one true faith." [81] At first blush, Priestley appears to be "a rather narrow-minded bigot."[82] He was that, but he was also a theological controversialist, and the first intellectual in America to think that Hindoo religions merited a thorough understanding.

Priestley's description of Hindoo religions followed a declension narrative that begins with an ancient monotheism and ends with contemporary superstition. Even more than Adams, Priestley emphasized a twofold approach to religion in India that separated out the ancient monotheism from the contemporary superstition. The text consisted of twenty-four sections emphasizing four major themes: the antiquity of Hindoo religions and Hindoo texts, cosmology and theology, the role of religion in social organization, and religious customs and practices. These themes moved chronologically from monotheism in ancient times to "licentious superstition" in contemporary reports.

Priestley pinpointed the beginning of Hindoo culture in the wake of the biblical flood. Drawing on William Jones's chronology, he wrote, "the oldest accounts of the Hindoo nation do not in reality go any farther back than to the deluge mentioned in the books of Moses, and that their religious institutions were consequently posterior to that event."[83] In these early times, the Hindoos held to the belief of a singular supreme being. That belief quickly faded. "That there is one God, the original author of all things, was retained in the East, and especially by the Hindoos; but they thought there were many inferior deities presiding over different parts of the system."[84] For Priestley, the various deities found in Hindoo scriptures doomed the Hindoo system. "If this be not a system of polytheism, leading to every evil arising from polytheism elsewhere, I do not know how to define the word."[85] These "evils" included the caste system, oppression of women, sati, superstition, and "licentious rites." Lacking divine revelation, the Hindoos fell into a religious system of imagination that led into the darkness of superstitious heathenism.

Like Hannah Adams, Priestley built his representation of Hindoo religion from European sources. Priestley believed that the Vedas were the most important text for understanding the religious law and beliefs of the Hindoos. Since the Vedas had yet to be translated, however, Priestley believed he could rely on the words of the brahmins and the few sources that had been translated, such as Halhead's *Code of Gentoo Laws* and Jones's *Institutes of Hindu Law*. He showed no awareness of Charles Wilkins's translation of the Bhagavad Gita, which would be so important to Americans after the turn of the century. Priestley supported these translated sources with other British sources, such as Holwell's *Interesting Historical Events* and Alexander Dow's *History of Hindostan* (1768). Much like Adams, Priestley patched together these various British sources into an publication that carried a Vedic and brahminical bias. Through the Orientalist texts at his disposal, Priestley represented the Hindoo system as Vedic texts and brahmin practice.

While Priestley emphasized the role of the Vedas and Manu in his representation of Hindoo religion, he also spent a large amount of space, roughly five chapters of the text, examining various Hindoo practices and devotions. Aside from a handful of references to Jones's *Institutes of Hindu Law*, the vast majority of his examples came from the writings of British officials and European travelers. For Priestley, the theological errors of polytheism and idolatry led directly to superstition and dark practices. Similar to the rupture between the "Hindoo" and "Yogeye" articles in Adams's text, there was a tension in Priestley's text between the two Hindoo systems in Priestley's sources. On the one hand, his Orientalist sources presented the Sanskrit texts of the Vedas and Manu, and on the other, missionaries and travel sources described popular practices.

Priestley bridged the Orientalist and traveler representations of Hindoo religions by arguing that the theology of the Hindoos was not sublime, as the Orientalist might think, but was in fact flawed, and that these flaws manifested in contemporary practices decried by travelers and missionaries. For example, Priestley derided Hindoo prayer as "no proper address to the Supreme Being, expressive of the sentiments of humility, veneration, and sublimation, but the mere repetition of certain words, the pronunciation of which can only be supposed to operate like a charm."[86]

Priestley also described Hindoo veneration of the cow, water, and fire as super-stition. He linked veneration of fire and water to other ancient religions' similar veneration and credited it to the great power of the elements. The sacrality of the cow flummoxed him. "There are many other useful animals, at least nearly, as use-ful, the sheep for instance, for which the Hindoos profess no particular regard . . . the origin of this superstition is so remote, that we have no means of tracing it."[87] Priestley devoted an entire chapter to "the licentious rites of the Hindoo." He argued that there were "serious consequences of adopting erroneous principles, even such are commonly called metaphysical ones" and pointed to temple prostitutes as the greatest example of wrong belief leading to wrong practice.[88] Though he could not always explain how, Priestley believed the inferior theology found in the Vedas led to the benighted superstition of Hindoo practice. The relationship between super-stition and inferior theology proved the necessity of biblical revelation for morality and truth.

For Priestley, the difference between Hindoo religion and biblical religion hinged on the superiority of revelation over imagination. God revealed the biblical text to Moses, but the Vedas and Manu originated in the human imagination. Priestley denied reason's ability to aid in the human discovery of truth in some form of natural religion. Left to their own devices, humans used their imagination, not their reason, to invent religious systems. The Vedas may happen upon truth here or there, but they were cut from a wholly different cloth than the Hebrew texts. In his conclusion, he wrote,

> The absurdity of the Hindoo system is as apparent as the superior wisdom of Moses. . . . And yet while the Hebrews made no discoveries in science, they had a religion perfectly rational, and that of the Hindoos was absurd in the extreme. This surely, is an argument of internal kind in favour of the divine ori-gin of the Hebrew religion.[89]

Or, as he summed it up a bit later, true religion "must necessarily have derived from revelation."[90] In *Comparison,* Priestley engaged in a centuries-long Enlightenment debate about the relationship between reason, revelation, and true religion and defended Moses against unbelieving European intellectuals. Reason was not enough, he argued. Imagination could not compare with revelation.

Hindoo Religion and American Enlightenment

Priestley's text had little of the publishing success that Adams's four editions enjoyed, perhaps because he published in the backwoods of Pennsylvania and not among the intellectuals of Boston. At least one influential American took interest in his comparative investigation of Hindoo religion, however. John Adams had a rocky up-and-down relationship with Priestley in the 1790s. He almost had the Englishman deported. By the early nineteenth century, though, Adams had taken an interest in Asian religions that led him to Priestley's works.[91] In a December 1813 letter to Thomas Jefferson, Adams offered a critical reading of Priestley's later work, *The Doctrines of Heathen Philosophers Compared with that of Revelation* (1804). A few months later, he told Jefferson, "I have been looking into Oriental History and Hindoo religion" and had gathered together whatever sources he could find, including Priestley's *Comparison*.[92] Adams complained to Jefferson that Priestley's text did not fulfill his curiosity about Hindu religions. He was frustrated that "the original Shasta, and the original Vedams are not obtained, or if obtained not yet translated into any European Language."[93] He also thought Priestley tipped the scales in favor of the Hebrew text by not finding texts "more honourable to the original Hindo [*sic*] Religion than anything he has quoted."[94] The marginalia in Adams's copy of *Comparison* revealed his shock at the "Ridiculous Observances" of the Hindoos, as well as his interest in comparing Hindoo religions with Catholicism. Adams's notes were heaviest in the early sections where Priestley discusses texts and theology and then later in the section on Hindoo devotions. [95]

Adams came to Priestley as part of his lifelong interest in the questions that dominated the European Enlightenment:

> Throughout his life John Adams had read quantities of English Deists and their orothodox opponents. The nature of Christ and immortality, the significance of revelation, the meaning of spirit and matter, were problems about which he had an enduring curiosity, and if he often expressed vexation with the refinements of theological quibbling, he does not seem to have been able to turn his back on the vast flow of religious literature. Since in Deistic controversy the teachings of Christianity and pagan religion was a central issue, Adams had explored the rival English views on the character of heathenism from Cudworth through Priestley.[96]

It is within this context, as an American interested in problems that had plagued European thought since the seventeenth century, that all of the American works representing religion in India in the eighteenth and early nineteenth century must be understood.

By 1817 Adams had gotten hold of the works of William Jones from Europe. He wondered to Jefferson in May of that year, "is it necessary to Salvation to investigate all these Cosmogonies and Mythologies? Is Bryant, Gebelin, Dupuis, or Sir

William Jones, right?"[97] In July, Adams described his thirst for comparative religious knowledge.

> Let me go back to twenty. Give me a million of Revenue, a Library of a Million of Volumes, and as many more as I should want. I would devote my Life to such an Oeuvre as Condorcet tells us, that Turgot had in contemplation, all his Lifetime. I would digest Bryant, Gebelin, Dupuis, Sir William Jones and above all the Acta Sanctorum of the Bolandists.[98]

For John Adams, William Jones and Joseph Priestley were part of his larger Enlightenment questions. As in the work of Hannah Adams and Priestley, the Hindoos were interesting to Adams insofar as they were part of the answer to questions about Christian truth, divine revelation, and human reason. Manuel has claimed that "John Adams died a mythographer *manqué*." Perhaps, but at the same time, "Hindoo religion" emerged in American culture as would-be mythographers and religious encyclopedists like Hannah Adams and Joseph Priestley engaged the European debates about the gods through European sources. In the decades following Priestley and Adams, American writers would being to generate their own accounts of religion in India, and one "Hindoo" writer would find an audience in the United States.

2 Missionaries, Unitarians, and Raja Rammohun Roy

JEDIDIAH MORSE PULLED Hannah Adams into New England's conflicts over Unitarian clergy. In his aptly titled 1814 publication, *An Appeal to the Public on the Controversy Respecting the Revolution in Harvard College, and the Events Which Have Followed It; Occasioned by the Use Which Has Been Made of Certain Complaints and Accusations of Miss Hannah Adams, Against the Author,* Morse connected two debates from the past decade: his fight with Hannah Adams over a schoolbook on New England history and the rise of Unitarian theology at Harvard and beyond. In his mind, a liberal conspiracy was afoot, attacking him personally from all sides. He believed his theological opponents used the argument with Adams and her liberal friends over a New England history book to impugn his character and attack his orthodox theology.

It all began in 1804 when Morse and Elijah Parish published their *Compendious History of New England.* The book aimed "to reduce [New England history] to a form, order, and size, adapted to the use of the higher classes in schools and to families."[1] The Morse and Parish publication troubled Adams because she had published the larger *A Summary History of New-England* in 1799 and aimed to publish an abridgment for the same family and school market. She saw the publication of *Compendious History* as an infringement on her publication plans and a detriment to her income. In 1805 she published *Abridgement of the History of New England for the Use of Young Persons,* putting her work in direct competition with Morse. Morse claimed that both authors were acting as competitors in the free market, while Adams argued that it was immoral for Morse to impinge upon the income of a poor widow trying to make ends meet. Liberal clergy, opponents of Morse's strict Calvinism, came to Adams's aid.

The same year Adams published her history book, the selection of Henry Ware as the Hollis Chair of Divinity at Harvard ignited another dispute with Morse at its center. Ware was a Unitarian and Morse, a strict Calvinist orthodox and an Overseer on the college board, loudly disapproved of the appointment. He saw it as part of a larger liberal conspiracy to take control of the Massachusetts clergy. Morse published his opposition to the appointment in March 1805 as a pamphlet titled *The True Reasons on Which the Election of a Hollis Professor of Divinity in Harvard College, Was Opposed at the Board of Overseers*. He then went on to found *The Panoplist*, an evangelical magazine critical of the spreading liberalism, in June 1805. Morse also brokered a deal between Old Calvinists and New Divinity clergy to establish Andover Seminary in 1808 as a stronghold of evangelical theology and an alternative to liberal Harvard. Morse built the bulwarks for the theological battle between Calvinists and Unitarians in New England.[2]

The two disputes coalesced when Hannah Adams's liberal friends in the clergy came to her aid and impugned Morse's character for stealing from a widow. Morse fought off the liberals on both fronts through private letters and communications. Finally he brought everything out in the open in 1814 with *An Appeal*. He argued that the liberals advocated for Adams because of the dispute over Ware's appointment. In his view, it was all part of the encroachment of liberalism in the churches. "The *use* which has been made of the groundless complaints and accusations of Miss Hannah Adams, by my adversaries in this controversy, has undoubtedly led to this publication; and the *Revolution* in the religious character of Harvard College, is the prominent event, which has imparted so much importance to these complaints as to justify it."[3] Morse went on to accuse the liberals of an "ingenious policy of assailing the principles of the orthodox, by attempting to fix a stigma on their moral character."[4] Morse's publication inflamed the conflict in New England to a fever pitch. Morse and other evangelicals called for separation between the Trinitarian Calvinists and the Unitarians.

Jedidah Morse's crusade against liberalism brought representations of India into American print culture during the first third of the nineteenth century. Morse founded Andover Seminary, where the first wave of American missionaries to South Asia trained. He also helped found the American Board of Commissioners for Foreign Missions (ABCFM) that sent those missionaries. Then he founded *The Panoplist*. That magazine became the official publication of the ABCFM and a regular publisher of missionary reports from India. Beyond Morse's work, the debate between Unitarians and Trinitarians set the stage for America's encounter with Rammohun Roy. Roy was an Indian reformer in Bengal whose writings became part of the Unitarian argument against the trinity. Through evangelical expansion and Protestant theological controversy, Yankees encountered new representations of religion in India.

India in Evangelical Missionary Print: "Obscenity and Blood"

An angel named Serenus visited Eugenia, the narrator in the story "Fragment of a Vision," and whisked her away to "present a fairer prospect of the unbounded love of Christ." The angel carried her along sunbeams through "regions of ether" until they landed on the "fertile plains of India."

> I looked and with amazement beheld innumerable crowds of the swarthy inhabitants of Hindoostan celebrating an idolatrous festival. The barbarous rites, the horrible clangour [*sic*] and confusion, with the dread of superstition of the poor, blinded votaries, displayed to my imagination a scene that rent my heart and filled my breast with sorrow and tumult.[5]

Eugenia pitied the Indians in her heart, while her ears "were pained with the loud and noisy babblings of the multitude." The angelic travel guide directed Eugenia's attention to the banks of the Ganges River, where she saw devotees bathing themselves in the waters and heard "the feeble cries of the helpless infants, who in vain struggled against the swellings of the flood." The scenes deeply disturbed Eugenia. She said a silent prayer for God to save the people of India.[6]

Sensing Eugenia's distress at these sights and sounds, Serenus took her to the home of a dying Indian man. At first it appeared to be another scene of calamity, but, though he was dying, the man's soul "as if unwilling to quit the body, still lingered to breath the last testimony of Jesus' love."[7] The Indian man was a Christian and exclaimed with his dying breath,

> Tell them, I bowed to idols; but did I put my trust in idols now, I should sink lower than the grave. Tell them, I performed the rites of the Ganges; but there is no water that cleanseth from the sin, besides the water of the river that 'proceedeth out of the throne of God and of the Lamb!'[8]

And then he died. When the man died, the vision of India fled, leaving Eugenia with "the grateful recollection" of a soul won for Christ.[9]

Published in the *Massachusetts Missionary Magazine*, "Fragment of a Vision" contained many images and themes through which American evangelicals represented Hindoos in the first third of the nineteenth century.[10] Just as the angel

Serenus whisked Eugenia to a foreign land, the missionary print culture of the early nineteenth century brought evangelical readers to the mission field. In the pages of missionary print, evangelicals encountered religions in India as bloody, obscene, and idolatrous. These representations emphasized the Hindoos' need for the rational and divine light of the gospel to save them from deluded heathenism.

The Massachusetts Missionary Magazine was one of many evangelical periodicals that sprang up in New England during the first decades of the nineteenth century. Revivals in upstate New York and the Cumberland River Valley consisted of camp meetings full of Methodists and Baptists. But in New England, evangelicals channeled their fervor into various religious societies, including missionary societies. With each new missionary society came a new missionary journal with news of the heathen overseas. These journals brought New England evangelicals a global vision for Christian revival. As historian Oliver Wendell Elsbree described it, "With the rise of the missionary journal proper, as the official organ of the local missionary society, the public was educated on the subject of foreign missionary enterprises with ever increasing effectiveness. It was the period of world politics, and serious people were thinking in terms of humanity as never before."[11] Jedidah Morse and other evangelicals established the institutional structures for a global missionary movement while fighting theological controversies with Unitarian Christians. They also brought missionary reports from around the world into the hands of Yankees. Evangelical representations of religions in India appeared in missionary journals within the dual context of revivalist missionary zeal and theological controversy.

The earliest images of Hindoos popular in the New England evangelical press came from the works of East India Company chaplain and missionary advocate Claudius Buchanan.[12] Buchanan presented Hindoo religion as a bloody, violent, superstitious, and backward religious system that needed to be overcome by the bright light of the gospel. Buchanan presented this image of Hindoo religion to Americans through a piece of Indian religious culture that dominated their imaginations for the rest of the century: the Juggernaut.

"Juggernaut" was the Anglicization of the god Jagannath, seated at a temple in Puri, Orissa, on the east coast of India.[13] The image of Juggernaut in the United States began with a letter from Buchanan, written at Tanjore and originally published in the British *Christian Observer*, but then reprinted throughout New England evangelical publications.[14] In the letter, Buchanan offered his observations from ten days spent at the Jagannath temple. He described the worship of "hundreds of thousands" of pilgrims and the great festival of the "Rutt Iatra" (Ratha Yatra) when the god is pulled outside the temple on a giant cart. More important, he described "human victims" who showed their devotion to the god "by falling under the wheels of the moving tower in which the Idol is placed."[15] In his description of Juggernaut, Buchanan provided a specific example of what he and other missionaries described as the "sanguinary superstitions" of Hindoo religion.

Buchanan also described Juggernaut in biblical terms for his evangelical audience. Juggernaut was "the chief seat of Moloch in the whole earth," referencing the god whose worship was forbidden in Leviticus 18:21. Buchanan saw "the place of the skulls, called Golgatha," a reference to the place of Jesus' crucifixion in the New Testament, "where the dogs and vultures are ever expecting" the corpses of the devotees.[16] The multitude worshipping Moloch-Juggernaut was "like that in the Revelations" but, rather than Hosannas to Christ and his second coming, they yell in "applause at the view of the horrid shape and at the actions of the high-priest of infamy, who is mounted with it on the throne."[17] The whole scene was "the valley of Hinnon," where children were sacrificed to the false gods in the Old Testament.[18] This biblical description worked by inverting traditional Protestant tropes. Rather than the Golgatha where Jesus' death atoned for sin, Juggernaut was a place of meaningless bloodshed. The worship was not the beautiful eschaton of the second coming, but "horrid." It was the valley of idolatrous blood shed to false gods, not the temple of worship to the one true God. Buchanan drove this point home by noting the difference between the scene of Juggernaut and the Indian Christians he met at Tanjore. At Tanjore "the feeble-minded Hindoo exhibits Christian virtues, in a vigour which greatly surprises me! Here Christ is glorified."[19] Through his description, Buchanan constructed an image of Juggernaut as the diametric opposite of Christianity: full of meaningless worship, unredeeeming death, blood that failed to atone, and horror instead of beauty.

Buchanan most fully described the bloody Juggernaut in his most famous work in America, *Christian Researches in Asia* (1811). In *Christian Researches*, Buchanan built on the description of Juggernaut found in his earlier letter. Once again he emphasized the blood of the rituals at Puri. Recounting the Ratha Yatra, Buchanan described a man who offered himself up as a sacrifice to the god by throwing his body under the cart. "He laid himself down in the road before the tower as it was moving along, lying on his face, with his arms stretched forwards . . . and he was crushed to death by the wheels of the tower."[20] Buchanan declared that the god "is said to *smile* when the libation of the blood is made."[21] When he saw the image of the god for himself, Buchanan described "a frightful visage painted black, with his distended mouth of a bloody color."[22] For Buchanan, the bloody smile of Juggernaut epitomized Hindoo religion and its sanguinary rites.

While he had described the blood of Juggernaut in his earlier letter, in *Christian Researches* Buchanan added a new quality of licentiousness to it. He started with the exterior of the temple. "As other temples are usually adorned with figures emblematical of their religion; representations (numerous and various) of that vice, which constitutes the essence of *his* worship. The walls and gates are covered with indecent emblems, in massive and durable sculpture."[23] During the Ratha Yatra, a priest pronounced "obscene stanzas" and "a boy of about twelve years was then brought forth to attempt something yet more lascivious . . . the child perfected the praise of his idol with such ardent expression and gesture, that the god was pleased . . . and the multitude emitting a sensual yell of delight, urged the car along." Next, "an aged minister of the idol then stood up, and with a long rod in his hand, which he moved with indecent action, completed the variety of this disgusting exhibition." Buchanan admitted that he "felt a consciousness of doing wrong in witnessing it."[24] Buchanan struggled to fully describe the horror he found in Juggernaut. On the one hand, he struggled with the language of the devotees, which he did not know, and relied on interpreting gesticulations. On the other hand, his English prose struggled to express the scene and maintain propriety. The sexuality Buchanan tried to describe was always just a little outside of his words. For Buchanan, Juggernaut's obscenity and sexuality exceeded proper language for an evangelical readership.

Along with the blood and obscenity of Juggernaut, Buchanan paid special attention to the noise of Juggernaut's worshippers. In the preceding quote, he described "obscene songs" and "a sensual yell of delight." In *Christian Researches* he described "a kind of *hissing* applause" from the women "who emitted a sound like that of *whistling*, with their lips circular, and the tongue vibrating: as if a serpent would speak by their organs, uttering human sounds" that he compared with the hissing of Satan's assembly in Milton's *Paradise Lost*.[25] Shouts, songs, hissings, "the sound of a great thunder," and acclamations filled the worship of Juggernaut, as described by Buchanan. These were not sweet melodious sounds. Rather, "the voices I now heard, were not those of melody or of joyful acclamation; for there is no harmony in the praise of Moloch's worshippers."[26] It was a noisy and disorderly affair that shocked his senses. True religion was melodious, interior, ordered. Where he saw idolatry, Buchanan heard cacophony.

Buchanan also surveyed Indian Catholicism in *Christian Researches*. He found little difference between Catholics and Hindoos. Touring through South India, he wrote, "Of the Priests it may truly be said, that they are, in general better acquainted with the Veda of Brahma than with the Gospel of Christ. In some places the doctrines of both are blended . . . [I] witnessed (in October 1806) the Tower of Juggernaut employed to solemnize a Christian festival." The priest accompanying Buchanan "surveyed the idolatrous cart and its painted figures . . . seemingly unconscious himself of any impropriety in them."[27] The link between Hindoo practice and Catholicism engaged a larger Protestant critique of Catholics at home in Britain. As historian of religion Brian K. Pennington has argued, the strong connection between Indian idolatry and British anti-Catholicism "partook of a history of opposition to Roman Catholic ritual, belief, and polity" and suggests "a pervasive Protestant Christian rationalism that was suspicious of the ritual use of images and any other institutional religious forms not governed by individual reason."[28] Idolatry and superstition united Catholicism and Hindoo religions as forms of religion that required the enlightenment of rational Protestant Christianity.

Buchanan's writings in general, and *Christian Researches* in particular, gave American evangelicals their first images of religions in India during the early nineteenth century. In the United States, *Christian Researches* went through numerous editions and was promoted in burgeoning evangelical magazines like *The Panoplist*.[29] Various evangelical magazines in New England published reviews and extracts of *Christian Researches* that extracted the descriptions of Juggernaut and its "sanguinary superstitions."[30] Writing about Buchanan's influence in Britain, Pennington has argued that "idol worship" in general became the practice that held together a pan-Indian system of Hindoo religion in the minds of nineteenth-century evangelicals.[31] This observation about Buchanan's influence in Britain holds true for the United States as well. In the United States, Buchanan's accounts of Juggernaut represented Hindoo religion as a system of idolatry that stretched across India and set the pattern for later reports by American missionaries writing home. The Juggernaut that Buchanan constructed also became a symbol of blood and death beyond idolatry. For example, a temperance article in *The Panoplist* used Buchanan's account "of the sanguinary rites at Juggernaut" as a comparison to the "monstrous vice" of alcohol that "has shrines on the banks of almost every brook" and "four thousand self-devoted human victims, immolated every year upon its altars."[32] Here Juggernaut was shorthand for violent, mindless death. American drunkenness was a form of idolatry as ignorant and destructive as Hindoo heathenism, and both demanded the sacrifice of human lives. Buchanan's Juggernaut became the dominant image of religion in India in the imaginations of evangelicals for the next half-century.

When American evangelicals sent missionaries to India, they sent home new images of Hindoo idolatry. The founding of the ABCFM by New England Congregationalists in 1810 provided an opportunity for representations of religions in India penned by American missionaries to enter evangelical print culture. The ABCFM had its roots in the evangelical New England network that Jedidah Morse had worked so hard to cultivate. Its first missionaries came from Andover Seminary, and *The Panoplist*, later renamed *The Missionary Herald*, became its official periodical. In 1812 the ABCFM sent out their first batch of missionaries headed for India: Adoniram and Nancy Judson, Samuel and Harriet Newell, Roxanna and Samuel Nott, Luther Rice, and Gordon Hall.[33] Hall and the Notts settled in Bombay and Samuel Newell joined them there in 1815 after the death of his wife and

child in Ceylon. The ABCFM mission station at Bombay sent home numerous journals and letters describing Hindu religious culture, which evangelicals published in
The Panoplist and *The Missionary Herald*. In these missionary reports the themes
established by Buchanan appear over and over again. According to American missionaries, Hindoos practiced a bloody, licentious, noisy, superstitious, and Catholic
religion.[34]

Picking up where Buchanan left off, American missionary journals continued to
publish accounts of Juggernaut. In 1813, *The Panoplist* published a letter dated June
1812 from Harriet Newell, Samuel Newell's wife. Newell described the bathing and
worship of Juggernaut at Calcutta, where the Newells awaited permission to travel
south to Ceylon. She wrote, "The idol Juggernaut was taken from his pagoda, or
temple, and bathed in some water taken from the river Ganges, which they consider sacred."[35] After bathing the idol, devotees began bathing in the river as well,
"where they said their prayers, counted their fingers, poured muddy water down
their infants' throats, and performed many other superstitious ceremonies."[36]
Newell read these actions within the Protestant framework of sin and atonement.
For Newell, all of these actions reflected a desire on the part of devotees to find
atonement for their sins—atonement only available through "the blood of Jesus,
which does indeed cleanse from all sin."[37] In 1833 the ABCFM published an engraving of Juggernaut's cart. The text accompanying the image gave a history of the festival taken from British missionary William Ward and the now infamous account
of the Ratha Yatra from Buchanan. Having read about Juggernaut for two decades,
New Englanders now had a picture of the towering cart, the mass of people, and the
gesticulations of the devotees.[38]

Missionary reports of Hindoo religion's bloody character also included accounts
of blood sacrifices and hook-swinging. Hook-swinging, or *charak puja*, involved
devotees attaching hooks into the flesh of their backs and then being hung from
various forms of tall poles that would swing them around in a circle.[39] Writing from
Bombay, Samuel Newell and Gordon Hall described devotees offering the sacrifice of a rooster to the goddess of wealth, "Luxumee," or Lakshmi, and applying the
blood of the animal to their foreheads. Newell and Hall also noted that the sacrifice
of sheep was common among Hindoos and that "the *life* and *blood* of the animal, are
principally regarded by these idolaters, in making their offerings to their gods."[40] In
another account, Hall offered one image of the "scores of sheep" sacrificed and the
details of the ritual, including the opening up of the belly and removal of the liver.[41]
The specter of human sacrifices often haunted these accounts of animal sacrifice.
As one missionary report mentioned, "*there is good evidence that human sacrifices,
within a few years past, and within a few miles of Bombay, have been repeatedly made
on various occasions to local deities.*"[42]

Along with animal sacrifice, missionaries described "female sacrifice" in their reports. Sati, the practice of widow immolation on their husbands' funeral pyres, represented the utter violence of Hindoo religion to missionaries and their audiences back home. Narratives containing eyewitness accounts of sati can be found throughout nineteenth-century American missionary literature. But most of these accounts are reprinted from British or Indian sources. Indeed, while ABCFM missionaries decried sati, it does not appear that they ever witnessed the act firsthand.

An extract from the journal of the ABCFM mission at Bombay published in the *Panoplist* included a narrative taken from the *Bombay Courier*. The ABCFM missionaries claimed the narrative was enough "to excite in every Christian mind the deepest commiseration for the deluded idolators, and the most ardent and active zeal for their conversion."[43] The narrative that followed told the story of a "Rajah" who died of smallpox in "Kathmandoo" (Katmandu). Upon his death, one of his "Ranees (queens,) one of the concubines of the Rajah, with five of their female attendants were to burn with the remains of the master."[44] The author then gave a detailed account of the ritual that included the lighting of the pyre with "the shouts and groanings of the multitude." For American missionaries, sati provided a violent example of how heathen Hindoo religion led to death and suffering. They used this image to generate support for their work among evangelical audiences. Indeed, when the British colonial government began work to ban sati in the 1830s, the ABCFM's magazine took notice and followed the process closely.

The Bombay missionaries may never have witnessed sati, but they did have firsthand experiences with hook-swinging. One account from the Bombay missionaries described a man and woman who each took a turn being hoisted twenty-five feet in the air by two hooks in their back. The woman "seemed to manifest greater fortitude and contempt of pain than the man did . . . she voluntarily flung herself about by a variety of action, which must have greatly augmented her pains."[45] Missionaries generally interpreted animal sacrifice and hook-swinging as "the degraded, deplorable, perishing condition of the heathen."[46] But the missionaries also tended to interpret these blood sacrifices as a sign that the Hindus were not wholly unredeemable. Applying their own evangelical views of Christ's atoning sacrifice, the Bombay missionaries asked the reader "what should put it into the minds of these unenlightened heathens, that the shedding of blood could have any efficacy in appeasing of God against sin? Let the unbeliever solve this question, if he can."[47] As historian Carl Jackson has noted, bloody practices such as hook-swinging defined religion in India for American missionaries and "represented the very essence of Hindu teaching" to them.[48] Bloody rituals pointed to the darkness of Hindoo heathenism and the hope that real atonement for sin could be found when the blood of Jesus replaced the blood of sheep, roosters, goats, and hook-swingers.

Along with blood, missionaries described sex and obscenity as central to religion in India. In their published accounts, the Bombay missionaries condemned what they called obscene and sexual dancing that accompanied Hindoo festivals. Missionaries railed against "those parts of the Hindoo system, which recommend and enforce impurity, licentiousness, and indecency, by annual exhibitions."[49] For example, one account described how during a festival "in the afternoon and evening there was, particularly among the lower sorts of people, abundance of music and dancing; males and females engaging in an indecent manner."[50] Another account described "*naches* (dances)" wherein "some places women were in men's clothes, and in others men were in women's clothes. . . . The females are common prostitutes but by the natives are not considered less religious on that account. . . . Their dress, and all their movements, were designed and well calculated, to excite all the passions which are for the interest of their abandoned profession."[51] Spectators of these dances seemed "gratified and delighted in the same proportions as the exhibitions are removed from decency."[52] Missionaries struggled, like Buchanan, with the proper language to describe Indian eroticism. The editors of *The Panoplist* prefaced the preceding description with a note that the scenes in the missionary report "are so scandalously obscene, as not to admit of description in a Christian country." In another case, a missionary described the phallic shape of the lingam (an image of the god Shiva) as "a significant emblem of what decency forbids to be named; and *such was the deity*."[53] From festival worship to the forms of the gods, everywhere the missionaries looked they found obscene sexuality in Hindoo religion and struggled to put it into words.

Much like Buchanan's description of Juggernaut, the ABCFM missionaries consistently described chaotic noise accompanying the licentiousness of Hindoo religion. Accounts of rituals included descriptions of musicians with "ragged-sounding instruments" that played a "hideous clang" and music "struck up with redoubled violence."[54] Another report noted, "the Hindoo holidays of the *Sheemgah* are just closed. For ten days past we have heard nothing but the noisy music of these people."[55] It was not just festivals in the streets either. Even a temple "resounded with the inharmonious notes of a band of native musicians, celebrating the praises of the cocoa-nut god."[56] For some missionaries, the cacophony of Hindoo worship reflected larger spiritual disease. Bombay missionary William Ramsey described how the sounds he heard on a Sunday afternoon had a profound effect on him. "The sound of the *tom-toms* and the accompanying screeching noise of the jackals on the banks of the river chilled my very soul, and threw a damp over my spirits that I cannot well describe." Ramsey wondered when the "dismal sound of idolatrous revels" would become "hymns of praise to God and to the Lamb."[57] The dissonant noise of Hindoo worship contrasted with the harmony of the Christian hymn, just as the violent and bloody rituals differed from the single redemptive sacrifice of Jesus. Missionaries represented Hindoo religions as the cacophonous antithesis to harmonious Christian piety.

The ABCFM missionaries in Bombay also paid attention to Indian Catholicism and found little to separate it from Hindoo religion. Hall and Newell offered American readers a view of a Catholic Good Friday procession in Bombay. "Today we have witnessed among the Catholic Christians a scene not much inferior in grossness to the idolatry of the heathen: viz. a representation of the death and burial of Christ."[58] The blood and sacrifice of Hindoo practice appeared in the form of a crucifix processed around the Catholic church. The noise of Hindoo worship also accompanied the sacrificial savior in the form of stamping with the feet, rapping with canes, and clapping of hands. The whole scene was so close to Hindoo worship that "many of the heathen were present. They feel much strengthened in their image worship by observing the same practice among Christians."[59] Another account described the specious conversion of Hindoos to Catholicism. The missionaries wrote, "but though they assumed the name of Christian, yet they have never ceased to be idolaters; for instead of their former idols, they substituted the images of saints, to which they paid a religious worship as really idolatrous as the worship paid by the Hindoos to their gods."[60] Indian Catholics also drew on Hindoo ideas to defend their practices. In addressing some "lapsed Catholics," Gordon Hall discovered "they are fast learning to use the Hindoo sophistry in defence [*sic*] of their idolatry."[61] Indian Catholic religion looked and sounded like Hindoo religion. And missionaries labeled them both as idolatry.

The bloody, lascivious, and noisy Hindoo religions of evangelical missionary reports suited the needs of missionary propagandists. The titillating scenes of unutterable eroticism offered exotic entertainment to readers. They also reinforced New England revivalist theology. As religious historian David W. Kling has convincingly argued, the ABCFM and its missionaries were "a New Divinity creation, rooted in New Divinity theology, inspired by New Divinity revivals, and staffed by a well-established New Divinity social and institutional network."[62] "Disinterested benevolence," the hallmark of New Divinity theology emphasized by Samuel Hopkins, gave meaning to the ABCFM mission in India and structured missionary constructions of Hindoo religion. According to New Divinity preachers, "true Christians are given a new disposition (or 'taste' or 'relish') for God and all things he has brought into existence, and consequently they have a love of being in general"—a disinterested benevolence toward God's creatures. The true Christian acted on this new benevolence "in unselfish acts of love and mercy (even in a willingness to die and be damned) in order to bring glory to God and further his kingdom."[63] Disinterested benevolence provided an important theological rationale for heading to the mission field. As revivalism took hold among New England evangelicals, the representations of bloody and vulgar Hindoo religion encouraged the benevolent action of giving to the missionary project. The chaotic noise of Hindoo religions described in the pages of missionary propaganda attempted to engender benevolence in Christians at home. As historian Clifton Phillips put it, "if the Calvinist image of the sinful condition of natural man made it possible to believe in the moral degradation of the heathen, the need for continuing missionary support made imperative its constant evocation."[64] The ABCFM used representations of Hindoo depravity to foster support for the missions and to increase their institutional strength.

The missionary reports also constructed a unified "Hindoo system" that could be found throughout the Indian subcontinent and even in Sri Lanka. At the heart of this pan-Indian religious system stood the idol. Pennington has described the evangelical construction of Hindoo religion qua idolatry: "stripped of all of its show and pomp, the complex and intractable mess of Hindu rite sheepishly confessed its prosaic and pitiable brute veneration of matter. . . . Hindus did not merely employ images as aids to meditation, nor did they believe them simply to house concentration of divine energy; they revered them as gods themselves."[65] The moral depravity of blood and obscenity grew out of attachment to the idol. "Unlike spirit, which was rational in nature and therefore unitary, ordered, and abstract, matter displayed no one ultimate form or reason. Each idol was a law unto itself."[66] For ABCFM missionaries and their New England readers, true religion was spiritual, rational, ordered, abstract, and systematized. Hindoo religion, as constructed by New England evangelicals, was the antithesis of true Protestant religion.

"What May Be the Effects of This Man's Labors?": Rammohun Roy's Monotheism

Some South Asians agreed with the missionaries about the problem of idols. Rammohun Roy rejected the idolatry of his countrymen. He argued that the bloody, obscene, and noisy rituals that engrossed the missionaries were anathema to true religion and to true Hindoo religion. He further believed that Hindoo religion was a monotheistic religion that called for worship of the one formless, supreme, creative deity. So, while the evangelical representation of Hindoo religion traveled from Bombay to Boston, Roy's representation of Hindoo religion began to make its way to New England from Calcutta. Roy's writings about Hindoo theism and Christianity embroiled him in controversy in the United States, Europe, and India. In India, he disputed with the English missionaries at Serampore and the brahmins in Calcutta. In Britain and the United States, his writings became part of the larger

Unitarian controversy. Americans wrote about Roy's conflict with Calvinist missionaries as if it were the second theater of theological dispute between Calvinism and Unitarianism. Roy introduced America to Vedanta philosophy and engendered interest in Sanskrit texts among religious liberals in the United States. During the years of his popularity in the American press, Unitarians and Trinitarians would use him as evidence in their own theological disputes.

Roy was born in either 1772 or 1774 in the Burdwan district of Bengal to a brahmin family. His father served the Muslim rulers and gave Roy an education in Persian and Arabic, preparing him for civil service. His mother began his Sanskrit education, preparing him for life as a scholar. Rejecting his parents' religious devotion to Vishnu at the age of sixteen, Roy was a "highly independent, precocious, troubled, but dutifully filial youth."[67] In 1797, Roy settled in Calcutta, where he first came into contact with the British East India Company by lending money to young British civil servants. It was through money lending that Roy made the contacts that landed him a place within the world of public administration. In Calcutta at the turn of the nineteenth century, Roy "may be seen as typical of the Bengali babu of the turn of the nineteenth century, an entrepreneur, a man of means, whatever his caste or background."[68] Beginning in 1805, Roy secured work for John Dibgy, the magistrate at Ramgarh. While working for Digby he improved his Western languages "by perusing all of my [Dibgy's] public correspondence with diligence and attention, as well as by corresponding and conversing with European gentlemen, he acquired so correct a knowledge of the English language, as to be enabled to write and speak it with considerable accuracy."[69] Roy also accepted Digby's offer to read Greek and Latin literature with him. While with Digby, Roy took interest in European politics, especially revolutionary France, which he saw as a rational order for society and a land of equality.[70] By 1818, an Englishman touring India remarked upon meeting Roy that "his learning is most extensive, as he is not only generally conversant with the best books in English, Arabic, Persian, Sanskrit, Bengalee, and Hindoostanee, but has even studied rhetoric in Arabic and in English, and quotes Locke and Bacon on all occasions."[71] To his European admirers, Roy was a master of Western and Eastern culture, language, and philosophy.[72]

In New England, Roy caught the attention of Protestants on both sides of the period's theological disputes. In April 1817, the Trinitarian *Boston Recorder* and the Unitarian *Christian Disciple* each extracted the introduction of Roy's *Translation of an Abridgement of the Vedant*, introducing Roy to their audiences.[73] These two American magazines took their extracts not from Roy's text itself but from an article in the British *Missionary Register*.[74] Roy addressed the introduction, "To the Believers of the only True God," which both sides assumed applied to them, and sought "to prove to my European friends, that the superstitious practices, which deform the Hindoo religion, have nothing to do with the pure spirit it dictates."[75] Furthermore, Roy argued, true Hindoo religion derived from the sacred texts of the Vedas. Roy then offered readers a brief explanation of the *Vedant*, which he had abridged and translated. The word *Vedant* came from the Sanskrit, meaning "resolution of all the Veds," and it was the book "most highly revered by all the Hindoos; and in place of the more diffuse arguments of the Veds, is always referred to as equal authority."[76] True Hindoo religion, for Roy, rejected idolatry and focused worship on a monotheistic supreme deity.

Roy invoked reason to defend his argument. As he put it, "if correct reasoning, and the dictates of common sense, induce the belief of a wise, uncreated Being, who is the supporter and rule of the boundless universe; we should also consider him the most powerful and supreme existence, far surpassing our powers of comprehension or description."[77] Such a deity would be beyond the forms and rituals of idols or images. Not only reason, but Hindoo scripture itself supported the view of a unified creative deity; "by making them [other Indians] acquainted with their Scriptures" he hoped to "enable them to contemplate, with true devotion, the unity and omnipresence of Nature's God."[78] Human reason and Hindoo scripture pointed to a unified God, not polytheistic heathenism. Roy wrote to convince European and Indian alike: true Hindoo religion, true religion, worshipped one Supreme Being.

At first Americans did not know what to make of the Bengali writer. Americans agreed that Roy was a "reformer." But what kind? The *Boston Recorder* must have agreed with the assessment in the *Missionary Register* article it borrowed from. Rather than make any editorial comments, it just reprinted the entire *Missionary Register* article, which wondered if Roy and his followers might "undermine the fabric of Hindoo superstition."[79] Yet, the magazine reminded readers of the need for missionary work. For, "reason and philosophy may not have a voice powerful enough to reach the hearts" of Hindoos, and so "the Christian Missionary, who Christ sends forth, will find a mouth and a tongue, which no man shall be able to gainsay or resist."[80] Roy might be a reformer, and a monotheistic reformer at that, but his reforms fell short of the missionary's gospel.

For their part, the Unitarians at the *Christian Disciple* used the Bengali reformer to take theological shots at Trinitarian orthodoxy. It noted that Roy had been opposed (and even had two attempts made on his life) by brahmins who disagreed with this monotheism and interpretation of the Vedas. The *Christian Disciple* represented Roy as a compatriot in the battle of true religion against despotic orthodox power. "For they [the orthodox] will very easily prove, to their own satisfaction, that *all good men* have been *orthodox* in their opinions, and that *polytheism* is *orthodoxy*."[81] In this, the article's final sentence, the subject of the pronoun "they" slipped between the orthodox on two continents. The orthodox brahmins were the same "they" as the New England orthodox. Polytheism was the same as Trinitarianism, and Roy's reform was the same as Unitarian reform. Unitarians began to make Rammohun Roy one of their own.

Both sides of New England's Protestant divide took continued interest in Roy. In March 1818, "Theology of the Hindoos, as Taught by Ram Mohun Roy," appeared in the *North American Review and Miscellaneous Journal*, a magazine that was "Bostonian, Harvardian, Unitarian."[82] The article, written by William Tudor, reviewed three English pamphlets that Roy published in Calcutta: *Translation of the Ishaopanishad*, *Translation of the Cena Upanishad*, and *A Defence of Hindoo Theism*.[83] The first two were Roy's translation of parts of the Vedas, and the final was a work of religious controversy arguing against idolatry. Once again the emphasis was on Roy's argument for a Supreme Being based on his interpretation of the Vedas. The review described how "although the Vedas taught the existence, the unity, and overruling providence of a Supreme Being, and the propriety, if not the necessity of worshipping him as being invisible and of pure intelligence; yet the Bramins carefully concealed this from the people, and insisted on the barbarous sacrifices and idols worship."[84] The review contained considerable extracts from the translations in order to make readers "somewhat acquainted with the present religious notions of the Hindoos, the pure doctrines of their sacred books, and the views and motives of the learned native [Roy]."[85] The extracts painted a picture of brahmin conniving and Hindoo ignorance conspiring to keep Indians habitually inclined toward idols. The article stopped short of labeling Roy a Christian, but granted that "the doctrine he inculcates differs very little from the christian [*sic*] doctrine respecting the nature and attributes of the Deity."[86] Finally, Tudor hoped that Roy's work and "the aide of Divine Providence" might work together to change "the moral condition" of India.

The Trinitarian editors at the *Boston Recorder* agreed on that count and reprinted an article from a Calcutta newspaper that briefly reviewed the same three works and concluded that if Roy was successful, "a reformation must take place—the power of the Priesthood, will be deprived of all its terror—reason will succeed to the dominion of prejudice; and the example of the higher classes will rapidly be followed by the mass of the population."[87] New England Protestants saw Roy as a native reformer who would pave the way for Christian progress in the country. He shared the Protestant abhorrence of idolatry and love of scripture. "He appealed to Protestant readers by casting himself as a crusader against ingrained superstition, idolatry, and priestcraft who suffered social ostracism for attempting to restore the pure religion of the Vedas."[88] Whether orthodox or Unitarian, New Englanders agreed that Roy's reform work was a good thing for India and for the progress of Christianity.

As missionary involvement in India increased, Roy turned his attention to Christianity and the impurities he saw in the evangelical Protestantism that

Britons and Americans were promulgating in India. In 1820 he published *The Precepts of Jesus, the Guide to Peace and Happiness*, a compilation of Jesus' moral teachings from the four gospels that left out any historical or miraculous material. Roy believed that separating out the moral teachings would "be more likely to produce the desirable effect of improving the hearts and minds of men of different persuasions and degrees of understandings" because "moral doctrines, tending evidently to the maintenance of the peace and harmony of mankind at large, are beyond the reach of metaphysical perversion, and intelligible alike to the learned and unlearned."[89] Roy rejected the dogmatic impurities added to the pure moral monotheism of Christianity, just as he had with Hindoo religion. The heart of Christianity for the reformer was "the law which teaches that man should do unto others as he would wish to be done by."[90] For Roy, Jesus' importance lay in his moral teachings, not his death on the cross or his place as the second person of the trinity. The British Baptist missionaries based at nearby Serampore took exception to Roy's text. Joshua Marshman replied to Roy in a series of articles in the evangelical *Friend of India*. Marshman called Roy an "enlightened heathen." He argued that Jesus' moral teachings could not be separated from his divine place as the Son of God and his atoning work on the cross. Roy wrote a series of replies to Marshman. Roy countered that the three persons of the trinity were little different from the multiple gods of Hindoo religion. According to Roy, the trinity was the real heathenism.[91]

As the controversy between Roy and Marshman played out in the printed pages of Calcutta, Americans on both sides of their own Unitarian debate took notice. In November 1821, the Unitarian *Christian Register* printed an article from its British brethren at the *Monthly Repository of Theology and General Literature* describing Rammohun Roy and "the controversy which he has so ably maintained with the English Calvinistic Baptist Missionaries." The dispute was "one of the most singular controversies which the world has ever witnessed."[92] The *Register* followed up in December with a seven-column, two-page article detailing Roy's life and the controversy with the Baptists. The article outlines the debate through various selections from Roy and Marshman. The writer concluded by declaring that Roy is "plainly a firm and zealous Unitarian," and ventures to wonder rhetorically if he could also be labeled a Christian.[93] The lengthy article introduced Rammohun Roy, the Hindu Vedanta philosopher, to New England Unitarians as an ally in the fight against Trinitarians. In the process, Roy himself became a Unitarian and possibly a Christian in the eyes of the author. One article in the *Register* even referred to the debate as the "Indian Unitarian Controversy."[94] The *Register* continued its coverage of the debate throughout the 1820s. It reprinted Roy's *Second Appeal to the Christian Public in Defence of the Precepts of Jesus* in serial in its July 5 through August 30 issues of 1822.

The Unitarian account of the Indian controversy did not go unchallenged in New England. In March 1823, the Baptist-run *Christian Watchman* reviewed Marshman's *Reply of the Baptist Missionaries at Calcutta, To Rammohun Roy*. The review extracted a portion of Marshman's argument focused on "the accuracy of various statements made by Rammohun Roy" in order to show that Roy's views were inaccurate. The editor at the *Watchman* also desired "to present this extract, as the author replied to has been praised by his friends in this country."[95] Marshman's reply argued for the doctrines of original sin, the trinity, and the atonement for sin through Jesus' death and resurrection. Then in December the *Watchman* and *Boston Recorder* reprinted a scathing article from the *New Haven Religious Intelligencer* that claimed Roy had not written his own works, but that a British Unitarian in India had penned them. "So that the whole amount of this wonderful matter is, that an [sic] Unitarian can write in India, in much the same way that an Unitarian can write in Europe." The article also smirked at "writers in this country [who] trumpet forth the praises of a man merely because he writes heresy in India."[96] New England Calvinists saw Roy as yet another heretic to be denounced, and his ideas about Jesus little different from those of their Unitarian neighbors.

The question of who counted as a Christian drove the New England Unitarian controversy. Unitarianism is heresy, claimed the orthodox, and not true Christianity. Meanwhile, Unitarians believed they had found the purest, most refined, and most reformed Christianity in Western history. Yankee Protestants pulled Roy into this question of Christian identity. In 1824, *The Missionary Herald*, true to its roots as a defender of orthodoxy, published some remarks about Roy from Rev. William H. Mill, principal of the Bishop's College at Calcutta. The *Herald*'s editor prefaced the remarks by noting how Roy "swerved first from Hindooism to Mohammedanism" and "influenced by the light, which missionaries in the first instance had been the means of introducing into Calcutta . . . became a rational Hindoo Philosopher, or in other words, a Deist." The editor also interpreted Mill as asserting that Roy was at least "an infidel." Mill himself asserts that Roy claimed to be a Christian, but it was a Christianity divested of "supernatural revelation," leaving "no reason to applaud the change." The *Christian Watchman* reprinted the comments from the *Herald* and proclaimed that Roy's "advocates may hereafter see cause to be ashamed of their prodigal encomiums." Roy's American critics echoed Marshman's "enlightened heathen" assertion.[97]

The *Christian Register* responded. The Unitarian magazine published the remarks from Mill, noting their appearance in the *Herald*, and prefacing them with the words, "It was to be expected that so able an advocate for the Divine Unity, and so powerful a opposer of the leading doctrines of Calvinism, as Rammohun Roy, would excite the enmity, and be a subject of the detraction of all who are pledged to support the *trinity* and its accompaniments." A week later, a much longer two-column article critiqued Mill for requiring Roy to accept a Christianity "disfigured and deformed by its association with the doctrines of the trinity, native depravity, &c. and with all the other human appendages" that Calvinists attached to it. The article stopped short of claiming that Roy was a Christian, but referred to him as a "friend and promoter of Christianity."[98] *The Unitarian Miscellany and Christian Monitor* showed less restraint. The magazine, published in Baltimore but circulated among New England Unitarians, claimed that Roy "not only stands foremost in the ranks of those who oppose idolatry, but has declared himself a Christian."[99] Unitarians continued to defend the Christian identity of Rammohun Roy by asserting that he was a Unitarian and that Unitarian theology was Christianity. As Unitarian clergyman Joseph Tuckerman put it, "This evidence may not satisfy his Trinitarian opponents, who refuse the name of Christian to their Unitarian brethren. But it will go far to solve the doubts of any who are themselves Unitarians."[100] Unitarians and Trinitarians continued to debate Rammohun Roy's Christian identity throughout the decade.[101] Unitarians defended their Christian identity by defending Roy's. Neither they nor Roy were the "enlightened heathens" that Trinitarians claimed them to be.

Roy's social reforms attracted Unitarian attention as much as his theological controversy. Roy had long been an opponent of sati in India, arguing that the Vedic texts did not require or endorse the practice. Roy began publishing tracts opposing sati around 1819, and his 1822 tract, *Brief Remarks Regarding Modern Encroachments on the Ancient Rights of Females According to the Hindu Law of Inheritance*, caught the interest of an English reading audience. Roy continued publishing against sati in both Bengali and English until William Bentinck banned it in the Bengal Presidency in 1829. For a decade, Roy argued that Sanskrit sacred texts required that widows inherit their husband's property and did not endorse sati or polygamy. David Reed, editor of the *Christian Register*, took great interest in sati and published multiple accounts of the practice.[102] But Reed also published Roy's work to combat sati. He published an extract of *Brief Remarks* in 1823 and then, after the abolition of sati, he credited Roy with doing much to hasten the ban and improve women's rights in India.[103] Historian Lynn Zastoupil has noted how Reed was also an avid abolitionist and argued that Reed's interest in abolishing slavery overlapped with his desire to see sati abolished as well.[104] Other American abolitionists found inspiration in Roy as well. An 1833 tract written anonymously called on Congress to abolish slavery. The tract was signed: "In closing this address, allow me to assume the name of one of the most enlightened and benevolent of the human race now living, though not a white man. RAMMOHUN ROY."[105] Indeed, after his death in Bristol, England, in 1833, Roy became a material symbol of social reform among New England liberals. Six envelopes containing locks of his hair were sold to raise money for the abolitionist cause in 1844. Those returning from the 1840 World Anti-Slavery Convention in London also distributed Roy's hair in the United States. The "Hindoo reformer" became a symbol for liberal theology and social reform among New England elites.

Rammohun Roy was a significant figure in New England religious culture for over twenty years. In 1833, Philadelphia artist Rembrandt Peale invited Roy to sit for a portrait while the two were both visiting London. The Boston Anatheum exhibited the portrait in 1834 and bought it in 1837, occasionally exhibiting it "for a community in which Rammohun Roy was well known and esteemed."[106] Contact between New England Unitarians and Roy prompted the Unitarians to attempt a missionary project in India. Though the project failed rather miserably, it strengthened the bonds between Bengali reformers and Yankee liberals.[107] Word of Roy spread beyond New England and throughout the East Coast. A bibliography of references to Roy in magazines during the period numbers over two hundred articles, spread across thirty-one different publications. His name appeared in almost 50 percent of Eastern religious journals.[108] Jackson has argued that Roy's greatest significance was his translation and explication of Hindu texts and philosophy.[109] Cultural historian Susan Bean has argued for Roy's influence on American literary culture, especially on the Transcendentalists.[110] But both of these evaluations miss Roy's important role in the New England Protestant controversy. He was part of the debate among liberal and evangelical Protestants about what constituted true Christianity and true religion. His writings emboldened Unitarians and frustrated the orthodox. The ripples of Roy's influence expand across literature, religion, and philosophy in the United States from the early nineteenth century to the arrival of another Indian reformer, Vivekananda, at the end of the century.

Hindoo Religion and True Religion in Early America

A triangle of exchange moved goods, people, texts, and ideas between America, Britain, and India. A series of relationships established and maintained this triangle. First and most obviously, Britain's imperial occupation of India and its continued rise to power in South Asia constituted the relationship between colony and metropole. Second, evangelical Christians in New England took part in a transatlantic evangelical movement that linked Britain and the United States and brought missionary intelligence about the British and American missionary movement in India to American evangelicals. Third, American Unitarians discovered an ally in their battle against orthodoxy in the person of Rammohun Roy while also maintaining contacts with their theological brethren across the Atlantic. A series of transatlantic movements also maintained this triangle. Revivalism united evangelicals across the Atlantic. Religious liberalism, rationalism, Unitarianism, and critiques of evangelicalism kept Unitarians and Indian reformers connected in New England and Bengal. These relationships shrunk the distance between places like Boston, Bengal, Andover, Bombay, and London.

It is also important to note how the Protestants along this triangle shared a common view of Hindoo religion as a system of idolatry. When evangelicals encountered idolatry, it reinforced their identity as Protestants. Missionaries overrepresented the small number of Catholic converts in India in their reports because the Catholic-Hindoo-Other reinforced the Protestant identity of the missionary and his audience. Jenny Franchot has argued that antebellum New England forged a "Protestant Way, a cultural route invoked to unify an increasingly fragmented Protestantism and to fight the threats posed by Irish and German Catholic immigration."[111] Through the Protestant Way, New Englanders constructed "a national identity that was not only oppositional but even 'negative' in its essence, for it was profoundly shaped by a rejection of and rivalry with Roman Catholicism."[112] Thus, when evangelical missionaries wrote about idolatrous Hindoos and Hindoo Catholics, they were at the same time writing against the Catholic Other at home in the United States and in their own Euro-American memory and imagination. To speak of Hindoos was also to speak of Catholics and to reinforce New England Protestant national identity. Whether Hindoo or Catholic, Protestant New Englanders labeled it idolatry all the way down.

Clearly this is the case for evangelicals, but even Unitarians believed that the vast majority of Indian religion was heathen idolatry; they only accepted Roy because he rejected idols and believed in a monotheistic godhead. Americans considered Roy a reformer in the vein of Martin Luther. He was taking on the priestly class and arguing for a pure religion. Roy's popularity in America grew because he admitted that his fellow countrymen who worshipped idols were indeed heathens, though he wanted to make the same point about Americans who believed in the trinity. At the height of his popularity, Unitarian Christians considered Roy a Christian precisely because the idea of an enlightened monotheistic Hindoo was unthinkable. If Roy believed in true religion, as Unitarians were beginning to think, then he must be a Christian.

By the 1830s, Hindoo religion had become a relatively stable category in American culture. Americans in New England and along the East Coast had two competing representations of Hindoo religion. On the one hand, Hindoo religion—or sometimes "Hindooism"—was a system of heathen idolatry found throughout the Indian subcontinent. This system consisted of priests, temples, idols, festivals, rituals, violence, blood, sex, and noise. Evangelical missionary magazines in the United States and Britain circulated these representations, and they eventually spread into the larger and fast-growing print culture of the United States. Meanwhile, other New Englanders represented Hindoo religion as a monistic, philosophical, and monotheistic religion derived from ancient Sanskrit texts, such as the Vedas. Based mainly on the example of Rammohun Roy, this representation circulated among elites and literati in the Unitarian enclaves surrounding Boston. From the 1830s forward, the Hindoo would be both heathen idolator and ancient mystic in the American imagination.

3 Hindoo Religion in American National Culture

LOOKING AT THE broad expanse of the American West, Presbyterian minister Lyman Beecher claimed a special purpose for the United States as a Christian nation. Beecher believed the United States was "destined to lead the way in the moral and political emancipation of the world."[1] That destiny was to be decided in the West. Beecher imagined a conflict in the West for America's soul and identity. It was "a conflict of institutions for the education of her sons, for purposes of superstition, or evangelical light, of despotism, or liberty."[2] As the rest of Beecher's plea illustrated, superstition and despotism alluded to the perceived evils of Roman Catholicism. But more important, Beecher argued that evangelical Protestantism was intimately linked to American liberty. According to Beecher, Protestant religion and American liberty must be maintained and extended through proper education and institutions.

In the wake of the revivalism that shaped American Protestantism during the first third of the nineteenth century, American Protestants like Beecher built a moral and cultural establishment in the United States. They believed this Protestant Way was vital to the health of the republic. During his tour of the United States in 1830, Alexis de Tocqueville noted the shared morality maintained by American Christianity: "each sect therefore adores God in its manner, but all sects preach the same morality in the name of God."[3] This morality undergirded the politics of the American republic. "I am sure that they believe it necessary to the maintenance of republican institutions. This opinion does not belong only to one class of citizens or to one party, but to the entire nation; one finds it in all ranks."[4] Religion suffused the

American republic such that "in the United States religious zeal constantly warms itself at the hearth of patriotism."[5] As historian David Sehat has observed, "for much of its history the United States was controlled by Protestant Christians who sponsored a moral regime that was both coercive and exclusionary."[6] The Americans behind this establishment believed that Protestant religion was necessary to "reinforce the moral fabric of the people, [and] was, in turn, necessary for the health and preservation of the state."[7] Protestant cultural power undergirded a coercive moral establishment that maintained the health and virtue of the republic.

The Protestant moral establishment worked through a variety of institutions, producing a national culture that united Protestant morality with American nationalism. "An increasingly nonspecific Protestantism," as religious historian Tracy Fessenden has termed it, dominated "over nearly aspect of American life, a dominance as pervasive as it is invisible for exceeding the domains we conventionally figure as religious."[8] In public schools and popular print culture, two such domains, nonspecific Protestantism and Protestant morality coalesced with American nationalism to produce a national culture that taught students and adults how to be moral, Protestant, American citizens in the republic.

As producers of American national culture, writers and editors constructed representations of Hindoo religion to entertain and educate American citizens of various ages. These representations of Hindoos reinforced notions of America as white, Protestant, civilized, and democratic by imaging India as dark, heathen, uncivilized, and hierarchical. According to these representations, Hindoo religions led to despotism, and American Protestantism led to freedom. These representations took the earlier missionary representations of Hindoo heathenism and added an explicitly nationalist rhetoric of racial and civilizational supremacy. Writers worked to inculcate Protestant morals and American nationalism in readers by representing the Hindoo Other.

Schoolbooks and the Production of American Citizens

"This extensive and populous country . . . retains its peculiar manners which have stamped the people as a peculiar race from the earliest periods of history."[9] So writes Samuel Goodrich in 1845, using the pseudonym Peter Parley, under the heading "Hindostan" in his schoolbook *Manners and Customs of the Principal Nations of the Globe*. For Goodrich, and for the children reading his schoolbook, India was quite different from America. As common (public) schools began to grow in the middle third of the nineteenth century, writers like Goodrich believed that children in the United States needed to have a global view. Schoolbook author S. Augustus Mitchell wrote in his 1840 geography book, "There is perhaps no subject of greater interest, or of more real value in education, than geography."[10] For Mitchell and other nineteenth-century educators, geography meant more than maps. "It treats, also, of the manners and customs, the moral habits and qualities, the social combinations, and the institutions of the various communities and races of men."[11] Other types of schoolbooks also took account of "manners and customs." Histories and readers joined geographies in presenting students examples of how different human beings in the world behaved and thought—a common-school anthropology of sorts.

Geography books set the standard for how students understood the differences between human beings. They presented students with a systematized approach to difference that allowed them to understand who they were and who they were not. Often, American schoolbooks sought to engender a sense of American-ness and nationalism in children through what they said about the United States.[12] But the ways in which these textbooks represented other nations and people, such as Hindoos, also reinforced American identity and cultural values. Children learned more about America by learning more about "Hindoostan."

Schoolbooks told American children who Americans were and what America was. In this way, schoolbooks were an early form of a burgeoning national culture that sought to overcome regional differences with a shared sense of the American nation. As one historian notes, "By the end of the 1820s, before the rise of wire services, nationally distributed newspapers, and mass-subscription magazines, children throughout the republic began to share the same spellers, arithmetics, geographies, and histories."[13] As an early form of nationally circulated print, schoolbooks constituted the beginnings of an American popular culture and a popular understanding of American identity.

During the first half of the nineteenth century, schoolbook authors acted less as writers and more as compilers. In the schoolbook production process, "a teacher, doctor, clergyman, or anybody might decide to write a text, do the necessary work, confer with the proprietor of a printing establishment, and a book appeared. Thus there was a new book for other compilers to contend with."[14] By 1830, Samuel Goodrich employed a salaried "professional compiler" for his Peter Parley series. The compilation process makes these schoolbooks particularly useful but also somewhat baffling for historical research. On the one hand, they reflect various strands of knowledge and discourse floating around in American and, more broadly, European culture during the period. A compiler of a geography or history text borrowed from multiple sources for each chapter or section. A compiler acted as a sort of cultural quilt maker, sewing together different accounts to make one whole text. Schoolbooks amounted to more than the writing of one author. They reflected pieces of the broad cultural discourse on a topic. But on the other hand, the schoolbook only reflected what the author chose to include. Only the material he or she found interesting or important made it into the quilt. These early schoolbooks, then, were cultural products fashioned according to individual visions of what mattered for American children.

Schoolbooks had to balance educational, moral, and civic aims in order to inculcate American values and produce children who would make good American citizens. Education historian John Nietz identified four major aims for schoolbooks: acquisition of knowledge, interest and entertainment, development of nationalism or world-mindedness, and the connection of cause-and-effect relationships.[15] While Nietz had geography books in mind, histories, readers, and other texts that offered a broad and global view of human activity shared these aims. All four aims were important to the growth of American children into citizens in the young republican nation. Most obviously, authors sought to engender nationalism in American children in order to produce loyal citizens. Second, educators believed that knowledge bred virtue, an important trait for citizens in a democracy. The acquisition of knowledge aimed not at individual betterment but at civic improvement. Likewise, an understanding of the relationship between cause and effect allowed students to grow into rational democratic citizens. Interesting, entertaining, and exotic material served to keep children's attention while reaching these other aims. In short, the schoolbooks tried to produce educated American citizens.

Faraway places, such as India, were crucial to fulfilling these educational aims. American schoolbook authors had access to a large body of English-language knowledge of the country. American missionaries, British writers, and earlier American representations provided schoolbook authors with information about India and Hindoo religion. By the middle third of the century, after decades of missionary activity, India held a special place in the American imagination and so, too, in American schoolbooks. India served as a foil against which authors could identify what counted as American. Authors created American identity through the difference of Indian Hindoos.

Nineteenth-century geography books loved classificatory systems. Roswell C. Smith's *Geography on the Productive System* (1836) began with water.[16] Water came from springs, it flowed in rivers, which then formed lakes, which were smaller than seas, which were parts of oceans. In between were waterfalls, creeks, bays, straits, and sounds. In order for a student to fully understand water, the child needed to be able to classify it correctly. Schoolbooks applied this same classificatory approach to a child's understanding of humans. Schoolbooks in antebellum America categorized people, cultures, and societies along systems that insisted on mutually exclusive categories of race, religion, and condition of society. These systems appeared in the early chapters of the book alongside lessons on longitude and latitude or geographical terms. They served as the hermeneutic through which students would understand the later chapters about specific countries. These categories gave students a grid for understanding their American identity in contrast to people in faraway cultures. They also emphasized the superiority of American culture, religion, and values. Children learned that they were different—and that they were better.

Geography books categorized people along racial lines first. For example, in his 1844 *A System of Modern Geography*, Mitchell described the human race as "differing greatly from each other in colour, form, and features."[17] These physical differences constructed race. The major divisions on the racial hierarchy were European, Asiatic, American (as in American Indian), Malay, and African. Each race corresponded with a color and a geographic area: white/Europe and America, yellow/Asia and Alaska, copper or red/America, brown/Pacific islands, and black/Africa. Texts often also included engravings to illustrate each racial group. Smith included a small engraving with each description of a race. As Figure 3.1 shows, Mitchell included one image of all five races together—the European in the center, of course.[18] The racial categories made up a loose hierarchy insofar as Europeans were the noblest race and everyone else was below them. As Mitchell put it, the European "excels all others in learning and the arts, and includes the most powerful nations of ancient and modern times. The most valuable institutions of society, and the most important useful inventions have originated with the people of this race."[19] The white American students of the book's audience—authors seemingly ignored African American and Native American students—could immediately locate themselves. The exercises in

Asiatic. Malay. European. African. American.

RACES OF MEN.

FIGURE 3.1. The races of the world, from Mitchell's *A System of Modern Geography*.

Mitchell's text even asked them to identify themselves across these categories. Such exercises assured students of their racial nobility.

These various races could then be plotted along a hierarchy of "states of society" or "conditions of man." Schoolbooks argued that some cultures had progressed further than others and had reached higher levels of civilization. "Savage" societies sat at the bottom of this hierarchy. These societies depended on hunting, fishing, and robbery; lived in caves or huts; were superstitious and bloodthirsty; and treated their women as slaves. Generally, "half-civilized" societies made up the next level of the hierarchy. These societies had established laws and religion, could read and write, and had some commerce. But, they also treated their women as slaves, and were "very jealous of strangers." Textbooks regarded most of the Asian countries, including India, as "half-civilized." Next on the social scale came the "civilized" class. It separated itself from its half-civilized competitors through its printing, scientific knowledge, and better treatment of women. But the civilized societies were also superstitious and maintained large gaps between the poor and the wealthy. Most of the examples of civilized society came from Eastern and Southern Europe, that is, Catholic and Eastern Orthodox Europe. "Enlightened" societies held the top position in the social hierarchy. These societies perfected art and science, were free from superstition (meaning they were mostly Protestant or secularized), were industrious, elevated women "to their proper station in society, as equals with, and companions for the male sex," and maintained free governments. Enlightened civilization, according to these schoolbooks, depended on the maintenance of gender roles. As expected, the United States and Western Europe exemplified these enlightened social values. Figure 3.2 presents one example of how these stages were depicted. Students in American common schools could identify themselves as part of the noblest race and the superior society, in contrast to other people they encountered in their schoolbooks.[20]

Finally, schoolbooks offered students a system for understanding religious difference. On the most basic level, schoolbooks divided religions into two categories: "true and false."[21] Smith defined true religion as "[t]he belief in, and worship of the one only living and true God."[22] Such a definition included Christianity and possibly also Judaism and Islam. In searching for a definition of true religion that skirted sectarianism, Smith left the boundaries hazy. But schoolbooks also employed a clearer set of divisions between religions. Schoolbooks divided religion into four familiar categories: Christianity—(which they subdivided into Protestant, Greek, and Catholic), Islam ("Mahomedan"), Jewish, and "Pagan or Heathen."

The first two categories maintained rather standard definitions whereby Christians believe in God, Jesus, and the whole Bible, but Jews believe in God and only the Old Testament. The schoolbooks described Muslims as followers of Muhammad and

FIGURE 3.2. Frontispiece from Mitchell's *A System of Modern Geography*, depicting the stages of society.

labeled him an imposter and false prophet. The final and lowest category, Pagans, was defined by belief in false gods, worship of sun, moon, stars, and animals, and idolatry. Mitchell took special note to mention that there were several classes of Pagans, including "Bramins, Buddhists, and worshippers of the Grand Lama, &c."[23] As Figure 3.3 shows, he included an engraving of a "pagan temple" that resembled images of temples in India that had become common in Europe. This fourfold division was roughly unchanged from the one Hannah Adams had proposed at the beginning of the century. Tomoko Masuzawa has described how this four-category taxonomy "recognizes 'Christians,' 'Jews,' 'Mohammedans,' and 'heathens,' rather

A Pagan Temple.

FIGURE 3.3. Engraving from "Religion" chapter of Mitchell's *A System of Modern Geography*, depicting a "pagan temple."

than different 'isms' that supposedly prescribe distinct spiritual cosmologies and so-called worldviews particular to each of these different people."[24] As such, the taxonomy was about religious *identity*, rather than categories of religious *systems*. Categories of religious systems, or "world religions," would come later in the century. At this point, Protestant American students could identify themselves as part of the true religion, and could identify where others they encountered fit into this early taxonomy of religion.

Mitchell and Smith published the two most popular schoolbooks of their time—Smith's geography went through over forty editions, while Mitchell's geography had the widest circulation of any in the United States before 1900.[25] But these same categories were central to other books as well. Goodrich used a similar set of categories in *A System of School Geography* (1833) and then simplified his categories down to a racial theory based solely on skin color and a division between "savages" and "gentle" people in *Peter Parley's Geography for Beginners* (1845), a book meant for much younger children, written mostly in verse.[26] Human beings were different from each other in myriad ways, but race, religion, and society held the central importance in nineteenth-century schoolbooks. Furthermore, the convergence of these major books around these three categories pointed to their central role in American culture at the time. American children needed to learn they were white, Protestant, and enlightened before they encountered others in the pages of schoolbooks. When they encountered India, they could identify Hindoos as brown, half-civilized, pagan, and inferior to themselves in all three categories. While these differences could be the engine for missionary outreach, they also buttressed children's self-understanding as white Protestant Americans.

The Hindoo Other: "A Distinct and Peculiar Nation"

"I shall now tell you of a people, who may be regarded as the most interesting of all the inhabitants of Asia, I mean the Hindoos . . . the Hindoos, in personal appearance, in disposition, in character, and in religion, are a distinct and peculiar nation," wrote Samuel Goodrich in *The Tales of Peter Parley about Asia* (1845).[27] Children would find the Hindoos interesting because they were so different from Americans—so "peculiar." As Goodrich pointed out, they looked different, lived differently, and believed in a different religion. The categories of difference outlined in the geography books determined the material that authors included about India in histories, readers, and other schoolbooks. Schoolbooks converged upon three themes in their descriptions of India: children and women, Hindoo religious practice and belief, and the British presence in India. Schoolbook authors grounded the discussion of these themes in the categories of difference outlined in the geography texts. The general systems of human difference in geographies determined the specific material about other cultures in other books.

Because they were written for children, schoolbooks often included information about Indian children in their stories and articles about India. For example, Salem Town and Nelson M. Holbrook included a dialogue between the Scottish missionary Alexander Duff and an Indian youth entitled "The Theory of Rain" in their *Progressive Third Reader* (1857).[28] The dialogue recounted Dr. Duff and an Indian boy (simply named "Hindoo") discussing where rain comes from. Hindoo claimed that it comes from the trunk of Indra's elephant because his guru told him the "shastras" say so. Dr. Duff then used various examples, such as a pot of boiling water with the lid on it, to explain how vapor rises and creates rain in clouds. The boy exclaimed, "Ah, our Shastra must be false! Our Shastra must be either not from God, or God must have written lies!" With his new view on the shastra, Hindoo was on the path toward becoming Christian.

"The Theory of Rain" played upon all three categories of difference. Hindoo was a brown, pagan, half-civilized child. From the American child's perspective, he was ignorant of science and held to a superstitious understanding of natural phenomenon. But the story erased some of the difference between the American child and the character of Hindoo. First of all, both were children—an immediate touchstone.

Second, Dr. Duff taught Hindoo and the reader. By the end, the reader and Hindoo had a scientific explanation for rain. They had the enlightened understanding of it. Finally, when Hindoo rejected the shastras and his guru, he came closer to Christianity. The introduction to the dialogue explained "how the principles of science are made the means of convincing the heathen of the falsity of their religious systems, and the truth of Christianity."[29] Dr. Duff revealed the truth of Christianity to Hindoo and reinforced it upon the reader. "The Theory of Rain" began by putting Hindoo in different categories than the reader. It then gradually brought Hindoo closer to an enlightened and Christian identity and reinforced the reader's own white, enlightened, and Christian identity. The story highlighted and then slowly effaced Indian difference as Hindoo accepted Protestant and Enlightened values. This process of gradual effacement attempted to reinforce these same American values on the young audience.

While "Theory of Rain" offered students a happy ending, some stories of children in India likely horrified child readers. Like earlier missionary reports, schoolbooks could not get over a perceived violence in Hindoo religions, a violence taken out on women and children. Mitchell's geography described Hindoo religion as follows: "The people worship images, and, under the blind influence of superstition, drown their children in the rivers."[30] Smith wrote, "Their religion is of the most degrading kind [it] even prompts widows to burn themselves on the funeral pile of their husbands."[31] Even the normally bright and jovial Peter Parley series included in its *The World and Its Inhabitants* (1856) that "the females of the two higher castes are required to burn themselves on the dead bodies of their husbands."[32] Beyond the obvious religious difference emphasized in these examples, the treatment of women and children also signaled a social difference. Hindoos who burned widows fulfilled the half-civilized expectations already set out in the texts. Enlightened societies like the United States treated their women with respect and equality and protected their children. On another level, these stories of child murder and widow suicide struck close to home. A child could immediately wonder if he would be killed had he been born in India. Reading that a child is drowned to appease the gods could have conjured up identification between the child reading and the child drowning. Also, women were key figures in the lives of nineteenth-century children. In a period where the cult of domesticity held sway, women took care of children. The image of women forced onto death fires would have profoundly horrified children. It would have signaled the end of their support structure. Because India was already a land of half-civilized pagans, according to the systems of difference, one expected to find violence against women and children in the name of religion. Schoolbook authors made sure to include this violence in their texts.

Beyond the treatment of women and children, schoolbooks emphasized a violent theme throughout Hindoo religious practice and belief. Much of this material must have been as horrifying for readers as the drowning children and burning women. Goodrich described how their religion taught the Hindoos to "allow themselves to be buried alive in the earth, tear their bodies with hooks, cut their flesh with knives, and other things like these" in order to gain favor with their gods.[33] In another text, Goodrich attributed wrestling and "the performances of the cockpit, where they exhibit spiders, bugs and quails, trained in fighting" to Hindoo religion. Goodrich then went on to give a lengthy description of the "Thuggees," which he identified as "an extensive and organized fraternity of *murderers*, which has spread itself over the whole country."[34] The Thuggees were more than just criminals, though; they were another form of religious violence. Goodrich described an extensive ritual system and system of "gooroos" that regulated and maintained a religious form of robbery. Goodrich then ended the chapter by highlighting the violence he believed to be inherent in Hindoo religion: "The same religious feeling which leads the Thugs to believe that they are performing laudable action in murdering travelers who are thrown in their way, while the auspices are favorable, causes them to be regarded without horror by the other Hindoos. They are supposed to be only doing their duty in that state of life to which God has called them."[35] For schoolbook authors, Hindoo religion required violence. Violence served as more evidence for the degraded and pagan nature of Hindoo religion, further solidifying its place at the bottom of the religion hierarchy and further distancing Hindoos from the Christian child-reader.

In addition to violence, schoolbook writers emphasized polytheistic and "idol-atrous" themes in Hindoo religion—two themes that writers believed proved the falsity and moral degradation of Hindoo religion. Goodrich argued that "[t]he Hindoos have a great many idols, and worship a great many different gods. . . . They have a great many temples, and spend a great deal of time in the various services of religion. . . . The tendency of their devotion is not to make them virtuous."[36] Goodrich tied idolatry and polytheism to moral degradation. In other places, however, Goodrich de-emphasized the idols and focused more on the pantheon of gods. In *Lights and Shadows of Asiatic History* (1844), he wrote, "Of the host of Hindoo divinities, Brahma, Vishnu, and Siva are the most exalted. Other nations have gener-ally bestowed upon one deity all power in heaven and earth; but the Hindoos have divided the creation and government of the universe among these three."[37] Similarly, in *The World and Its Inhabitants*, he outlined the same three gods and then com-mented, "these three persons are, however, but one God, and form the Trimourti, or Hindoo Trinity."[38] In these latter examples, Goodrich emphasized the existence of a trinity analogous to that of Christianity. But he immediately dispelled any ideas that India may be on the right religious track. "In India on the contrary, we behold only the vast allegoric image which represents majesty by enormous statue . . . providence by innumerable eyes, and ubiquity by innumerable bodies . . . the Hindoo seemed inspired with a sacred horror of bringing the actions of his deities within the range of human credibility . . . their fictions scorned the least approximation to truth."[39] Goodrich warned students not to take the similarity between the three Hindoo gods and the Christian Trinity as evidence of any real similarity between the two. Christianity was true; Hindoo religion was false. American children were Christians and they were different from the people of India.

Caste also stood out as a central theme in descriptions of India. Schoolbooks always emphasized a connection between caste and religion. The chapter titled "Religion of the Hindoos" in *The Tales of Peter Parley about Asia* began, "The religion of the Hindoos is very curious. By this, the people are divided into four classes or castes."[40] In his more advanced text, *Lights and Shadows of Asiatic History*, Goodrich wrote, "The plan of society and government . . . is established by divine prescription," before he explains in the next paragraph, "The first feature which strikes us, in the organization of society among the Hindoos, is the division of the people into four classes, or castes."[41] Brahmin priests, soldiers, merchants, and laborers made up the four castes, as explained in these books. Once again, caste fit into the overall understanding of India as a half-civilized land. Enlightened countries were marked by their equality and democracy, which offered freedom. On the other side, the rigid class-driven caste system described in schoolbooks fulfilled the description of half-civilized society. The half-civilized caste society was then tied to the pagan religion of Hindoos. The presentation of caste also reinforced the value of Protestantism, democracy, and freedom in the United States. Children were taught that false religion (Hindoo paganism) led to hierarchical and unenlightened society (caste) and that, conversely, American Protestantism and American democracy connected and supported one another. Hindoo religion led to a hierarchical caste system, while Protestant Christianity brought egalitarian democracy.

The British colonization of India made much of the religious and social knowledge of the country available to textbook writers. The British imperial project created a wealth of knowledge about India that drifted into the hands of schoolbook compilers, and these authors made sure to include the British in their descriptions of contemporary India and Indian history. For example, the model letter entitled "From an English Bishop in India to a Friend in England" appeared in *The Parlour Letter-Writer* (1845). The letter offered students and families a model for how one should communicate while traveling in a colonized country. The letter stated, "I am sure there is no ground whatever for the assertion, that the people are become less innocent or prosperous under British administration."[42] It then went on to claim that in Bengal "the English government is popular."[43] The model is clear—when touring an imperial colony, be sure to compliment the empire on its beneficence and defend its control.

Missionary work gave schoolbook authors another justification for British control of India. "The Theory of Rain," analyzed earlier, was one example. The imperial British control allowed the Scottish missionary to come to India, which in turn allowed Hindoo to see the falsity of his religion and the truth of Christianity. Goodrich made a similar argument in *The Tales of Peter Parley about Asia*, when he wrote, "One thing is certain, our religion is the best gift which God has imparted to man, and the diffusion of it among ignorant nations, is one of the highest and noblest enterprises, to which a man can devote himself." He followed this call to missions with: "I have told you that the British have large possessions in Hindoostan."[44] The implication was that missionary work was possible in India *because* the British had large possessions there. In both cases, religious difference—Christianity versus paganism—provided justification for imperial control. Authors presented the expansion of the British Empire as a positive and beneficial growth of Christianity among the pagans.

The treatment of Indian women and children; the violence, idolatry, and polytheism of Hindoo religion; and the benefits of British power in India recurred in the representations that schoolbooks constructed about India. As authors approached India through the grids of difference outlined in the geography texts, they decided that these themes constructed the knowledge of India that was important for American students to learn. These themes at once distanced India as a foreign Other, different from American children along racial, religious, and social categories, and reinforced the importance of Protestantism, whiteness, and American democracy.

Antebellum common schools tried to educate American children and prepare them to be good American citizens. Educators emphasized virtue and knowledge as important components of the citizenry of the new republic. To that end, geography books gave students a system for gaining knowledge about other parts of the world. Through categories of difference built around race, religion, and society, these schoolbooks tried to help students identify themselves and others. The next step was to flesh out these identities with examples. Authors did so in schoolbooks ranging from history to letter-writing. By presenting students with the horrors and immorality of India and the benefits of British control, schoolbooks reinforced the importance and value of Christianity, democracy, "civilized" society, and white imperial control. These schoolbooks reinforced American traditions and attempted to educate the next generation of American citizens by teaching students the difference of the Hindoos.

Educating Citizens: Hindoo Religion in *Harper's New Monthly Magazine*

Just as schoolbooks taught American children about American citizenship, popular magazines functioned pedagogically for literate American adults during the latter half of the century. *Harper's New Monthly* Magazine, founded by Fletcher Harper in 1850, became the most successful magazine in the country during the second half of the nineteenth century. The magazine sought to unite American citizens around a unified identity and national culture. In his 1950 speech celebrating the centennial of *Harper's Magazine*, editor-in-chief Frederick Allen narrated the national scope of the early years of his magazine. "To a family in a steepled town on the Erie Canal, or on a remote Ohio farm, the magazine was a welcome messenger from the great world, bringing information and ideas and entertainment to be devoured eagerly." Allen described the array of matter available to these scattered readers: life in the Balkans, elephant-hunting in Ceylon, the Baltimore & Ohio's railroad line, current world events, book reviews, and serial English novels. "For the first time," Allen proclaimed, "the United States had what might reasonably be called a general national monthly magazine." In the 1850s, *Harper's New Monthly Magazine* was "not only a show-place for English fiction but a mirror of American life and ideas as well."[45] Allen described *Harper's* as a magazine that reflected American culture back to American citizens.[46] This national culture, as envisioned by *Harper's*, was a Protestant, industrious, literate, and upwardly mobile America, always poised ready for the next opportunity, the latest news, or a wider glimpse of the world.

The magazine combined this national influence with a national pedagogical project. Fletcher Harper touted the magazine as a "popular educator of the general public" that would present the best of English fiction as well as a record of current events, "science articles, travel accounts . . . and an illustrated section on ladies' fashions."[47] These various genres worked together "to produce a new periodical format that was not merely eclectic and cosmopolitan, but focused and nationalistic."[48] Literary historian Jennifer Phegley has labeled *Harper's* and its pedagogy a "family literary magazine," meant to appeal especially to women readers. The magazine appealed "to women not solely through domesticity but also through literary values that the proper woman reader could use to advance the cultural status of her nation."[49] Phegley argued for the importance of "the roots of the [family literary magazine] in the nationalistic goals of the growing middles classes, who were struggling to construct a coherent identity through literary culture."[50] Placing *Harper's* within this genre of family literary magazines highlights its role in producing a national American culture for the middle classes that taught them how to be a part of the American nation-state.

The breadth of *Harper's* circulation, combined with its pedagogical and nationalist aims, made it one of the foremost producers of American national culture during the period. *Harper's* printed 7,500 copies of its June 1850 debut issue, but within six months its circulation reached 50,000. By the beginning of the Civil War the magazine had a national circulation of 200,000. As a rival magazine editor lamented in 1857, "Probably no magazine in the world was ever so popular or so profitable. There is not a village, there is scarcely a township in the land into which [it] has not penetrated."[51] Much to the chagrin of its competitors, *Harper's* had become the quintessential American magazine.

Harper's aimed to entertain and educate its audience. The advertisement for the first issue boasted that the magazine would give its audience "an immense amount of useful and entertaining reading matter" and "would seek in every article, to combine entertainment with instruction and to enforce, through channels which attract rather than repel attention and favor, the best and most important lessons of morality and of practical life."[52] Entertainment would serve to both educate and communicate a moral message to readers. This education and this moral message maintained the health of the American republic. Editors and contributors took the moral well-being of their readers very seriously and "asked readers what would become of the American republic if self-absorption caused them to abandon their loyalty to the nation, their commitment to the general welfare, and their desire to follow God's will."[53] For *Harper's*, education, nationalism, and moral uprightness worked together to maintain the republic. Furthermore, *Harper's* gendered its project of national education and moral instruction. "Harper's writers, both men and women, and its editors spelled out women's roles as guardians of Christian and republican morality. They described women as educators of their sons to the nature and importance of that morality and as protectors of family cohesion."[54] *Harper's* saw itself as a force maintaining republican morals in American households through entertaining content that would appeal to women readers.

Beyond its gendered audience, *Harper's* national project of education and moral instruction also included white supremacy and Protestant superiority. Catholic immigration increased throughout the latter part of the nineteenth century, and slavery gave way to the Civil War and Reconstruction. Throughout this tumult, *Harper's* addressed its readers as members of a superior Protestant white race. In various articles, the magazine represented Catholic immigrants as poor folks lacking the ambition and integrity to work their way out of poverty. Moreover, "readers were warned that, like the blacks and the Jews who preceded them, these newcomers were members of inferior races."[55] The magazine warned readers that these inferior races "comprised much of the city's criminal class and were a potential source of mob violence, ready to explode at any time for any reason."[56] The magazine marked non-white, non-Protestant races with poverty, urban place, poor character, and the potential for violence. *Harper's* explicitly tied religious identity to "the immigrant problem" and published feature stories deriding Joseph Smith and the Mormons, as well as Catholics and Jews—all of whom they saw as threats to the republic.[57] As it educated and instructed its white Protestant audience, *Harper's* warned of the dangers that non-whites and non-Protestants posed to the nation.

The intentions of the publishers, editors, and contributors, along with the tastes of the perceived audience and the shifts in American culture of the period, all swirled together as *Harper's* produced and maintained white Protestant American national culture. In short, the magazine sought to educate and morally instruct middle-class white Protestant US citizens. This moralistic, Protestant, white, and worldly national culture defined the horizons of meaning for many white readers in the late nineteenth-century United States. How readers decoded and found meaning in the midst of this culture remains unclear and may be inaccessible. However, what is available in the historical record is a picture of what the national culture constructed by *Harper's* looked like. It looked a lot like the Harper brothers themselves—white, literate, hardworking, internationally knowledgeable, Protestant, moralistic, and fiercely nationalistic. Representations of Hindoo religion appeared on the pages of *Harper's* as part of this national culture and the magazine's educational and instructional project. These representations entertained and educated readers as they reinforced the superiority and importance of white Protestant America.

Harper's publishers sought to entertain their audience with stories that jump-started the imagination. The magazine's earliest representation of India transported the reader to a land of enchantment and the supernatural. The first article in *Harper's* to address India immediately focused attention on enchanted spirits that were part of everyday life. "Ghosts and Sorceresses of India," published in 1853, offered *Harper's* readers several brief stories in which household and village spirits affected life in India. Functioning more as entertainment than education, the article was a series of brief stories about supernatural events that British colonial officials had observed or experienced in India. *Harper's* reprinted the article from a British magazine, but placed within *Harper's* the article became part of American national culture.

The opening paragraph of the article set the stage, "the Hindoo . . . is not haunted by the vague, indefinable terror . . . he knows very well what he dreads . . . substantial and tangible inflictions—such as a sound drubbing."[58] The article then told the story of a spirit that haunted a specific piece of farmland. One day, the farmer of the neighboring plot thought he might take control of a bit of the spirit's ground by plowing his field over the boundary line and claiming some of the unmanaged land. That night a snake bit the greedy farmer's son and his bulls became sick. The story concluded: "The smitten sinner at once rushed to the village temple, confessed his crime, and promised not only to restore the stolen land, but to build a handsome shrine upon the spot to its true proprietor. The ghost was appeased: the boy and the bullocks recovered; the shrine was built, and is the boundary-mark to this day."[59] This small part of the larger article presented the reader an India where sprits and ghosts dictate the mechanics of everyday life. Supernatural forces manipulated and enchanted property, sickness, and agriculture.

But the Hindoo was not always at the mercy of this supernatural world. Some women—and it was always women—turned these enchanted powers to their own designs. In a later section of the article, a traveler passing through a village on his way home took a chicken from an old woman without paying her. As he continued on his way home he got hungry, stopped, cooked, and ate his stolen rooster. Immediately upon getting up and continuing homeward he began to feel sick to his stomach. By the time he reached his house he was screaming in pain. His pain attracted a crowd inside his house, consisting of both natives and Europeans. While the man writhed on the floor in agony, the crow of a rooster echoed in the room. At first no one was sure what was happening, but the rooster crowed one more time. Then, "a third chant removed every particle of doubt from their minds: the cock was crowing in the man's belly! As the groans of the dying wretch grew fainter, the note of unearthly triumph swelled the fuller; till at length death put a period to his sufferings, and to the crow of the phantom cock."[60] The old woman the man victimized was able to manipulate the enchantments of India for her revenge. In this enchanted land, even the seemingly weakest person—an old woman easily robbed—could draw upon fabulous power. The story reflected a sense of anxiety that there might be native power somewhere in India that European power should fear.

The article structured the different brief stories such that the imagery in the stories built in intensity from one vignette to the next. This added to the entertainment value and slowly ratcheted up the sense of enchanted power in India. As the article moved forward, the consequences meted out by the supernatural became scarier and scarier. At first an ox died and a boy got sick but recovered. Then a large snake appeared. Next, two individuals got sick as payback for stealing, but they repented and recovered. Then the stories took a visceral and horrific turn when sugarcane turned to blood in a man's mouth. This story was followed by an account of a "sorceress" sucking a man's blood out through a stolen sugarcane so that it spilled into the street. The grand finale of horror came in the final story, in which the thief who stole the rooster died when it came back to life inside his stomach (crowing and all). The article built, narrative by narrative, toward a climax in the final story and the horrifying "Cocki-lilli-la-a-a-w!" of an undead rooster.

As it entertained with strange stories of the supernatural, "Ghosts and Sorceresses of India" also carried a gendered message about American morality. The article's narrative of how a woman becomes a sorceress in India reflected American domestic morality turned on its head. The sorceress "ministers" to her devil "by means of sacrifices, and pampers his unclean taste with livers of human beings. She makes no scruple of digging young children out of their graves, and bringing them to life . . . so that [the devil] may feast on the part he covets."[61] The moral American woman, on the other hand, was to sacrifice of herself for her husband and children, while ensuring they had clean, well-cultured tastes. Furthermore, the image of the young child brought to life from the grave represents an inversion of childbirth. The American mother brought children into the world, taught them Protestant morality, and raised them to be proper US citizens. The sorceress resurrected children to be used as food for the devil. Hindoo sorceresses thus represented the opposite of American motherhood and the difference between American and Hindoo identity. As rendered by *Harper's*, American women were good moral wives and mothers; Hindoo women were evil, bloodthirsty sorceresses. American women were the bastions of morality, and Hindoo women the propagators of evil. The sorceress of India served as a cautionary tale to American women about what would happen if they abdicated their responsibility as moral guardians. If they began to serve themselves, to sacrifice proper morals for their own power, like the sorceress, then American culture would devolve to the same state as the nameless Hindoos in the villages of India worshipping superstitious shrines.

"A Priest of Doorga," written by Phil Robinson and printed in 1885, also entertained readers through its representation of Hindoo religion. Robinson, born in India, was a journalist, writer, and son of a reverend. His work focused on life in India and was published in *Contemporary Review* and *Gentleman's Magazine,* as well as *Harper's.*[62] In this story, a group of traveling brahmins stole a young son of a cowherd, Gunga, from his family in a small village. They took him to the temple of Doorga, where they sold him to the priests as a brahmin child. Gunga learned quickly and set himself apart as a wonderful student. Meanwhile, a man-eating tiger killed his father, and his mother went mad with the despair from losing her husband and her son. The story had many twists and turns as Gunga felt despair about not having a mother or father, and his mother continued to wait for her son and husband at the village well night and day. The story ended when Gunga's mother went to the Doorga temple and died inside. Meanwhile, Gunga made a vow to Doorga that he would give his life in exchange for the end to a famine that had struck the land. As a large rain cloud moved into the area, Gunga climbed to the top of the temple roof. When the first raindrops fell to the ground, Gunga jumped to his death, upholding his vow.[63]

As with the earlier "Ghosts and Sorceresses of India," Robinson's story emphasized the supernatural powers and superstitions of Hindoos. Gunga's father, Ram

Lal, possessed magical hunting abilities that allowed him to easily kill wolves, bears, and other dangerous animals. Also, Ram Lal thought the man-eating tiger that eventually killed him was the spirit of his ancestor. Yet, this later story reflected a more detailed understanding of Hindoo religion. The description of the temple of Doorga also reflected some understanding of the centrality of the temple to Hindoo religious practice. Robinson's story also added an emotional element to the representation of Hindoos. His story invited the reader to feel the pain of Motee, Gunga's mother, when she found that her son had gone missing. In another emotional scene after Ram Lal died, Motee was left waiting at the village well. Gunga's struggle to make sense of his place in society as an orphan also was intended to tug at the reader's heart. These examples of death, widowhood, orphanhood, and loss may have occurred in a story about Hindoo characters, but they were experiences that also occurred in the nineteenth-century United States. While the setting and the religions were fantastic, the human emotions in the story were probably quite familiar to readers. Motee the Hindoo widow by the well was strange, but the mother mourning the loss of her son was common to *Harper's* readers.

Along with these stories, *Harper's* also published traveler's accounts and historical essays about religion in India. These essays represented Hindoo religion as an ancient religion of grand temples. For example, the 1857 article "Madras, In Pictures," described one traveler's visit to Madras and spent three pages describing the so-called "Seven Pagodas" of Mahabalipuram, or "Mavalipoor," as the author spelled it, south of present-day Chennai on the coast of the Bay of Bengal. It included the engraving in Figure 3.4 of one of the temples, surrounded with lush vegetation. The traveler spent most of his account on descriptions of the architecture and imagery of the temples:

> I'm not sure that I can give dimensions, and I doubt whether it would be of any use if I could. It was not the size, but the shape, the sculpting, and above all, the situation of the temple, that lent it such a profound interest in my sight. . . . The pyramidal top of the lower half, looking inland, might be about thirty, and the other that faced the sea forty feet high. As you entered the holy place of the lower temple, you saw sculpted on the back wall the four-armed god, while minor forms of "gods and bulls" looked out, dim with age from the other walls and from the side-posts. . . . But the most august aspect of the building was when you looked up from the rocks at the great door through which the sea had evidently dashed up many a time, mocking the power of man.[64]

The temple impressed the visitor with the ability of human craftsmanship and power of nature.

SCULPTURED ROCKS AT MAVALIPOOR.

FIGURE 3.4. Engraving from "Madras, In Pictures."
Courtesy of Cornell University Library, Making of America Digital Collection.

Despite all the striking descriptions and images of Hindoo temples, travel narratives and essays still represented Hindoo religion as filthy, malevolent, and superstitious. William L. Stuart's 1867 travel narrative, "Calcutta, the City of Palaces,"
described a city with a "background of everything that is repulsive and horrible,"
and where "the heavens are offended by the smoke of abominable sacrifices."[65] The
outward filth reflected the "Paganism and superstition" of Hindoo religion, a religion where "perfect evil is the summit of religious aspiration" causing "the complete
inversion of all natural and moral laws."[66] Figure 3.5 shows an engraving of "a devotee" sprawled on the ground, which accompanied Stuart's article. The account of
Madras referenced the Jewish religious elites who opposed Jesus in its criticism of
the brahmin priests as "Pharisees and Sadducees," and "pompous ignoramuses."[67]
On top of these denunciations of Hindoo religion, articles also made mention of
how caste functioned as a religiously sanctioned social structure that kept Indian
culture stratified. The representation of Hindoo religion as evil, foul, and superstitious ritual probably prompted most readers to agree with Stuart's appraisal that

A DEVOTEE.

FIGURE 3.5. Engraving from "Calcutta, City of Palaces."
Courtesy of Cornell University Library, Making of America Digital Collection.

Hindoo religion was so terrible that it forced the traveler to "turn from the luxuri-
ance of splendid tropical life about him with pious thankfulness to the comparative
barren hills of New England, where civilization was taught and chastened by the
spirit of Christianity."[68] *Harper's* writers represented Hindoo religions in ways that
tried to make American Protestants thankful of their religious identity and confident in their superiority.

The 1878 article, "Juggernaut," by a former editor of the magazine, A. H. Guernsey,
represented Hindoo religion as both an ancient religion of temples and a contemporary religion of filthy superstition.[69] The article offered a detailed account of the
Jagannath temple at Puri, India, the same temple popularized by Claudius Buchanan
decades earlier. Guernsey was a Hebrew scholar who had worked his way up to the

editor's chair by 1856 but had stepped down as editor-in-chief in 1869. [70] Though
he was a Protestant Christian, his approach to Jagannath differed from the earlier
missionary representations. To begin with, Guernsey wrote of Jagannath not as a
missionary seeking support from readers, but as a writer working to entertain and
educate. Though the title used the word "Juggernaut," Guernsey quickly informed
the reader that the proper name is Jagannath, or "the Lord of the World." He also
gave the reader a long narrative of the myth behind the founding of the temple and
the history of its construction. As with the travel accounts, the architecture and
structure of the temple itself were given central place in the article. "The central
and chief pagoda" had a tower "rising like an elaborately carved sugar-loaf, back
with time, to the height of 192 feet . . . surmounted by the mystic wheel and flag of
Vishnu."[71] An accompanying map of the temple, shown in Figure 3.6, illustrated his
physical description of the temple's various interior chambers.

But Guernsey, like the other writers in *Harper's*, also represented the worship at
Jagannath's temple as filthy superstition. He made a distinction, however, between
the older image of Juggernaut as bloody and his account of its filth. "Contrary to
what has been almost uniformly asserted," he wrote, "the worship of Jagannath is

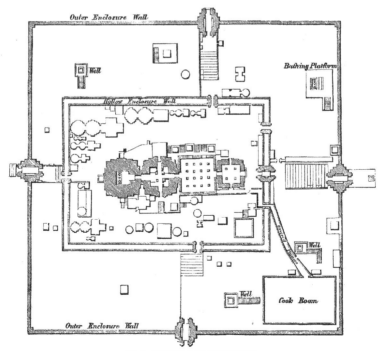

PLAN OF TEMPLE OF JUGGERNAUT.

FIGURE 3.6. Map of the Jagannath Temple from "The Juggernaut."
Courtesy of Cornell University Library, Making of America Digital Collection.

absolutely bloodless."[72] Indeed, Guernsey asserted that blood was seen as a pollut-
ant inside the temple and the real bloody worship went on at the nearby "temple to
Bimala, one of the wives of Siva, who is worshipped with midnight orgies and bloody
sacrifices."[73] While Jagannath does not claim lives in bloody worship, Guernsey still
represented his worship as filthy superstition. He described Puri as "perhaps, the
filthiest city on earth." The Ratha Yatra, the festival when Jagannath rides on his
cart through the city, occurred during the rainy season. Guernsey described how
"every lane and alley becomes a torrent or a stinking canal."[74] Furthermore, the eating of sacred rice sanctified by Jagannath "becomes a means of death" because after
"forty-eight hours it becomes a loathsome mass of putrid matter unfit for human
use—dangerous to a person in robust health, and deadly to the way worn pilgrims."[75]
The poisonous rice was doubly tragic for Guernsey because it was the one democratic moment he found in the rigid caste system of Hindoo religion. "This food is
so holy that it wipes away all distinctions of caste or sect. The highest may eat it with
the lowest."[76] According to Guernsey, the most democratic moment of Jagannath's
devotion was also its most deadly.

One article in *Harper's* stands out because of its shift in terminology. An 1869
article by then editor Henry M. Alden on the religious history of Benares described
"Hindus" and even "Hinduism." As in the other articles, Alden emphasized ancient
temples and filthy practices. He narrated the history of the city through the building and razing of temples before, during, and after its conquest by Muslims. Because
the Muslim conquerors "forbade the Hindus to build spacious temples," the article
explained, "the Hindus of the present day, blindly following the example of their pre-
decessors of two centuries ago, commonly build their religious edifices of the same
dwarfish size as formerly."[77] Despite their diminutive size, the temples of Benares
were "of elegant construction . . . delicately carved . . . [and] so lavishly ornamented
that the eye of the beholder becomes satiated and wearied."[78] Large engravings, such
as the one in Figure 3.7, depicting the temples towering over small foregrounded
Hindus, accompanied the textual descriptions, constructing the image of Hindu
religion as ancient sacred architecture on a grand scale. Alden also described Hindu
worship as filthy. He described how devotees bathe in a well that is "insufferably
foul. . . . The worshiper, descending into the water, laves his head and body in the
vile liquid, and at the same time, utters certain phrases appointed for the ceremony"
in hopes of washing away his sins.[79]

Alden took the ancient temples and filthy practices and transformed them into an
ancient religious tradition. Benares, the city of temples and practices, "is regarded by
all Hindus as coeval with the birth of Hinduism."[80] Alden imagined an ancient tradition that spans from "the clouds and mists [of] Vedic pre-historic periods" to his
own time. He constructed this ancient Hinduism by drawing on the work of British

RAJA OF AHMETY'S TEMPLE.

FIGURE 3.7 Engraving of Benares temple from "The Sacred City of the Hindus."
Courtesy of Cornell University Library, Making of America Digital Collection.

writers ranging from Warren Hastings to M. A. Sherring. By drawing on these British Orientalist sources, Alden shifted his representation from the filthy Hindoo in an ancient temple to the ancient tradition of Hinduism. In the process, India, represented by Benares, became a site for a form of comparative religion. Drawing on Sherring, Alden noted that the city was "the religious centre of Hinduism, of Buddhism, and then of Hinduism again, and for a long period as a secondary centre of Islam."[81] Alden's British sources provided him a different image of religion in India from other Americans writing in *Harper's*. His reliance on recent Orientalist sources and his interest in comparative religion transformed Hindoo religion into Hinduism. But Alden is an outlier. His representation of Hinduism prefigured the representation of a comparative world religion of Hinduism that Americans would more fully develop at the end of the nineteenth century.

Harper's blended Protestant morality with entertainment and education in hopes of attracting a broad national readership. *Harper's* consistently used Hindoos as a warning and example of a nation that lacked America's Protestant morality and democratic freedom. Superstition led to filth and death. Hindoo religion undergirded the hierarchy of caste. But Protestant Christianity gave Americans democracy, freedom, and life. Articles in *Harper's* described Hindoo religion and its destructive effect on Indian society in hopes of reinforcing the important role that Protestantism played in maintaining American society. For example, Stuart closed his article about Calcutta by remarking that "never before visiting other lands have I known how to value the principles which, to a certain extent, govern us in our own country ... measuring progress between these old kingdoms and the Western World, we may judge of the effect which pure and true religious principles can effect when grafted on human civilization."[82] *Harper's* allowed readers a similar experience—traveling to India and observing the grand temples, enchanted villages, and filthy superstitions, only to return home thankful for their life in Protestant America.

The American River Ganges: Hindoos and the Protestant Moral Establishment

Representations of Hindoo religion in schoolbooks and popular magazines converged in the 1871 *Harper's Weekly* cartoon "The American River Ganges" by Thomas Nast (Figure 3.8).[83] Drawing on the image of children sacrificed to the Ganges River popularized in missionary reports and schoolbook accounts of Hindoo superstition, Nast pivoted from Hindoo superstition to Catholic superstition. A Protestant pastor with a Bible in his coat protected the children from Catholic crocodiles crawling out of the river. The Vatican rose in the background, while on the right side the US public school crumbled. Thomas Nast used Hindoo religion to warn Americans of the dangers of Catholicism and to reinforce the power and necessity of the Protestant moral establishment. The theme of Hindoo superstition and

FIGURE 3.8 "The American River Ganges" from *Harper's Weekly*, September 30, 1871.

anti-Catholicism that began with the ABCFM's missionary reports came into full view as part of American national culture.

Representations of Hindoo religion in national culture drew upon many images and themes from previous representations, especially those of early Protestant representations. Schoolbooks relied upon a system of comparative religion similar to that proposed by Hannah Adams. Images of noisy Hindoo ritual and superstition in *Harper's New Monthly Magazine* built upon, if at times re-evaluating, missionary reports from early in the century. But while they drew on past representations from earlier in the century, the representations of Hindoo religion that spread as part of American national culture added racial and political difference to the earlier religious difference. National culture emphasized the racial difference of Hindoos that had been latent in earlier representations. Hindoos became a religious, racial, and political Other. This combination of racial, political, and religious difference made the Hindoo an apt comparison to the Catholic for Nast. Drawing in the 1870s, Nast believed that Catholics posed a threat to white democratic Protestant America. By representing Others, both at home and in India, American national culture reinforced the superiority of white, democratic, Protestant America.

4 Transcendentalism, Brahmanism, and Universal Religion

WHILE MISSIONARY AND popular representations of Hindoo religion buttressed the Protestant moral establishment in America, other Americans encountered a very different image of religion in India. The philosophical and liberal interest in India that began with Rammohun Roy in the 1820s and 1830s grew. As Protestant sects proliferated, another American religious culture grew during the period: metaphysical religions. Metaphysical religions are typified by the themes of mind, correspondence, movement and energy, and salvific healing. As religious historian Catherine Albanese has argued, metaphysical religions constituted a religious culture spanning the entire history of the United States.[1] Metaphysical writers critiqued American Protestantism through representations of religion in India. American Transcendentalism was the first metaphysical movement to construct such representations.

Early Transcendentalists imagined Hindoo religion as the soul of an essentially spiritual and mystical India, which provided a needed balance to Western materialism and Protestant practicality. Though they differed in the details, Ralph Waldo Emerson and Henry David Thoreau believed that the West, with the United States as its pinnacle, and the East, typified by India, needed each other's cultural resources. An East–West hybrid would combine American actions of materialism and industry with an Indian mind of spirituality and unity. Building on the literary work of Thoreau and Emerson, later Transcendentalist writers produced comparative religion texts and invented a religious system they called "Brahmanism," the religion of India. Lydia Maria Child, Samuel Johnson, and James Freeman Clarke produced texts that put Brahmanism into a larger model of comparative religions, meant to find universal truth across various "great religions." For the first generation of Transcendentalists, Hindoo religion was one part of the larger Orient that they imagined as the complimentary opposite of the West. Later Transcendentalists took up a more comparative model of religion. They imagined Brahmanism as a great religion with its own claims to larger universal truths that transcended any East–West divide.

The Transcendentalists are often considered the first Americans to incorporate Asian religions into their thought, writing, and practice. For both scholars and non-scholars alike, the story of "Hinduism" in the United States typically begins in Concord, Massachusetts, with Emerson and Thoreau. In his recent popular history of Vedanta and yoga in America, self-described spiritual counselor and author Philip Goldberg began the story with Ralph Waldo Emerson, "the first public thinker to openly embrace Eastern religious and philosophical precepts. . . . Because of Emerson and his direct heirs, Henry David Thoreau and Walt Whitman, millions of educated Americans have been touched by India since the mid-nineteenth century."[2] On the academic side, Catherine Albanese cited the nineteenth-century Transcendentalists, and Emerson and Thoreau in particular, as the starting point for considering the role of Asian religions and Hinduism in American metaphysical religion.[3] For "new agers," yoga enthusiasts, and historians of religion, Asian religions enter the American story at Concord.

Historians writing about Transcendentalism and Asian religions have taken a largely essentialist view. Academic attention to the encounter between Transcendentalists and Asian religions began with the work of Arthur Christy and Frederic Carpenter in the 1930s.[4] Christy described his project as explaining "*why* Concord men read the Orientals and to *what end*; and most important of all, the *sources* from which they took Oriental ideas and ornamentation for some of the classic pages of American literature."[5] Thus began a tradition of searching Transcendentalists' journals and published works for references to Asian texts, symbols, and theologies. Some studies, such as Christy's, argued strongly for the influence of Asian religions on the Transcendentalists and tried to match up the public and private writings of Thoreau or Emerson with Asian texts they had read as proof.[6] Other studies took a slightly different tack and argued that Asian religions provide the key to the "real" meaning of many Transcendentalist works.[7] Arthur Versluis's *American Transcendentalism and Asian Religions* maintained this essentialist approach as late as 1993. In that book, he treats the "discovery" of Asian religions by Transcendentalist writers and relies on the "world religions" discourse for his understanding of Asian religions.[8] In all of these studies, scholars assumed that "the Orient," "Hinduism," or "Asian religions" were stable categories that either influenced the Transcendentalists or were the keys to understanding them. The influence moved in one direction—from a real Orient to the mind and work of the authors.

By focusing on influences and decoding journals and published works, scholars have assumed the same essentialist view of Hindu religions held by their Transcendentalist subjects. For example, Arthur Christy's point that "the religious aspect [of Indian literature] stands in the foreground, for the Indian mind is essentially of this temper" could just as easily come from Thoreau's pen.[9] Likewise, Versluis argued, "the center of the entire American Transcendentalist movement was the encounter with the world religions."[10] By focusing on influence, scholars constructed an essentialist "Hinduism," "Asian religions," "world religions," or "Orient" that somehow influenced the Transcendentalist writers. This essentialist approach missed the ways in which the Transcendentalists imagined and constructed Asia as they read ancient Indian texts for literary resources and spiritual inspiration. As Albanese noted, "we need not subscribe to an essentialism that posits a one true reading of Asia to notice that Americans were creating an Asia to their own visionary requirements."[11] Finding influences and connections with Indian texts in Transcendentalists' published or private writings was only the first step toward understanding the Transcendentalist encounter with religion in India. The next step is an analysis of how these connections and influences led to the construction of the Orient, the Hindoo, and Brahmanism in Transcendentalist imaginations. The Transcendentalists did not discover India, they constructed it.

"Transcendentalism, Thy Name is Brahme!"

In 1822, Mary Moody Emerson wrote to her young nephew Ralph Waldo and encouraged him to search for his muse in the scriptures of the East. Young Ralph Waldo seemed intrigued but intimidated. He wrote back, "I am curious to read your Hindoo mythologies. . . . When I lie dreaming on the possible contents of pages as dark to me as the characters on the seal of Solomon, I console myself with calling it learning's El Dorado."[12] He thought it natural that "literature at large should look for some fanciful stores of mind which surpassed example and possibility."[13] The "Hindoo mythologies" suggested by his aunt were, like the mythical city of El Dorado, full of riches but perhaps impossible to mine. Emerson seemed skeptical that studying them would ever pay off. He did, however, find value in the figure of Rammohun Roy. He wrote to his aunt: "I know not any more about your Hindoo convert than I have seen in the *Christian Register*." But he was glad the Unitarians had "one trophy to build up on the plain where the zealous Trinitarians have builded a thousand."[14] Though at the age of nineteen Emerson had little to write to his aunt about her "Hindoo mythologies," between 1836 and 1856 he read many classic Sanskrit texts in part or in whole, including the Vedas, the Upanishads, the Bhagavad Gita, the Vishnu Sarma, and the Vishnu Purana.[15]

These texts fostered a view of India and its religion that continued the El Dorado trope of his earlier letter. India became part of "Asia," a land of unity and contemplation. Emerson imagined Asia as passive, religious, contemplative, unifying, and feminine. He used the pet name "Mine Asia" for his wife Lidian Emerson. Like his wife, Asia held a feminine attraction. They both represented the mysterious and fascinating opposite of his Western male mind. When Emerson imagined Asia, he imagined its essence in Indian philosophy and the Hindoo mind. Through his encounters with Sanskrit texts and his construction of India as the mind of Asia, Emerson imagined Hindoo religion as the complementary opposite of America, the essence of the West.[16]

Emerson made the East–West contrast central to his argument in his essay "Plato, or the Philosopher," part of his 1850 book *Representative Men*. In the essay, Emerson argued that resolving the distinction between oneness and otherness was the central problem of philosophy. He laid out the problem:

> Two cardinal facts forever lie at the base [of philosophy]; the One; and the two. 1. Unity or Identity; and 2. Variety. We unite all things by perceiving the law which pervades them, by perceiving the superficial differences, and the profound resemblances. But every mental act,—this very perception of identity or oneness, recognize the difference of things. Oneness and Otherness. It is impossible to speak, or to think without embracing both.[17]

Unity, identity, and oneness defined Asia for Emerson. The tendency for "raptures of prayer and ecstasy of devotion" and losing "all being in one Being . . . finds its highest expression in the religious writings of the East, and chiefly in the Indians scriptures, in the Vedas, the Bhagavat Geeta, and the Vishnu Purana."[18] To prove his point, Emerson paraphrased Krishna from the Vishnu Purana. "'You are fit,' (says supreme Krishna to a sage,) 'to apprehend that you are not distinct from me. That which I am, thou art, and that also is this world, with its gods, and heroes, and mankind. Men contemplate distinctions, because they are stupefied with ignorance.'"[19] Asia, and India most of all, contemplated unity in all things and comprehended the one within the many.

Emerson opposed Oriental contemplation and unity with Western action and diversity. He wrote, "If speculation tends thus to a terrific unity, in which all things are absorbed,—action tends directly backwards to diversity."[20] He then constructed a detailed list of qualities broken along the East–West divide: the one/the many, being/intellect, necessity/freedom, rest/motion, power/distribution, strength/pleasure, consciousness/definition, genius/talent, earnestness/knowledge, possession/trade, caste/culture, king/democracy, escapism/executive deity. Emerson pointed out the social effect of these philosophical differences. Asia's delight in unity led to a belief in "the idea of a deaf, unimplorable, immense Fate," made manifest in the caste system of India, while "the genius of Europe is active and creative" and produced culture, art, trade, and freedom. The central problem of the "two cardinal facts" played out in the national and social differences between India and the United States.

Emerson considered the West superior to the East, but he did not set up a distinctive hierarchy. Rather, he sought a synthesis of the two, and he found such a synthesis in the person of Plato. In Plato "a balanced soul was born, perceptive of the two elements." He was the man "who could see two sides of a thing." Emerson praised how Plato came to join "the unity of Asia and the detail of Europe, the infinitude of the Asiatic soul and the result-loving, machine-making, surface-seeking, opera going Europe."[21] For Emerson, Asia and Europe, East and West, needed each other and could not be separated, just as the one was made manifest in diversity.

The theme of Asian unity extended into Emerson's poems as well. In his 1847 volume *Poems*, Emerson published "Hamatreya," a poem that represented the synthesis of Eastern unity and Western action that he desired. H. H. Wilson's translation of the Vishnu Purana, which Emerson read and copied extracts from into his notebook in 1845, provided inspiration for the poem. The section of the Vishnu Purana on which Emerson based the poem features the goddess Earth explaining the folly of kings who seek to conquer great kingdoms and yet ignore their own mortality. As Emerson copied into his notebook, "How great is the folly of princes who are endowed with the faculty of reason, to cherish the confidence of ambition when they themselves are but foam upon the wave."[22] The king's sense of individual ambition was an illusion, for in truth his life was a brief moment of foam on the great unified wave of being.

Emerson used this warning to Indian kings as a jumping-off point for his own critique of Yankee landlords. The first section of the poem named and described landlords from great families around Concord, Massachusetts, and how they believed their ownership of the land to be absolute. "Each of these landlords walked amidst his farm/Saying, 'Tis mine, my children's, and my name's.'"[23] Yet, the poem's speaker asked, "Where are these men? Asleep beneath their grounds."[24] Like the kings of the Vishnu Purana, they failed to remember they were mortal. And so "Earth laughs in flowers, to see her boastful boys."[25] In the second section of the poem, with the subtitle "Earth-Song," the Earth, as she does in the Vishnu Purana, rebuked the Yankee kings:

They called me theirs,
Who so controlled me;
Yet every one
Wished to stay, and is gone.
How am I theirs,
If they cannot hold me,
But I hold them?[26]

The Earth swallowed up the bodies of the dead New England landlords in an image
that unites Eastern unity and Western action, each balancing the other. The active
will of the Yankee landlord must not go unchecked, and so the eternal and universal
voice of Earth reminded the reader that life is short and flees "like the flood's foam,"
an image taken directly from the Vishnu Purana.[27]

The poem reflected Emerson's belief that the East and West needed each other
through its use of a Sanskrit text to critique the folly of New England landlord families. It is unclear why Emerson altered the name "Maitreya" of the Vishuna Purana to
the "Hamatreya" of his poem's title, yet the title remained an allusion to the Sanskrit
text. The noticeable shift from the Indian-sounding title to the first line of the poem
(a list of New England family names: "Bulkley, Hunt, Willard, Hosmer, Meriam,
Flint") fused together East and West.[28] The poem also used the text to make a moral
point about New England society. The final quatrain of the poem, following the
"Earth-Song" section, reflected the speaker's moral and emotional response to the
Earth's rebuke:

When I heard the Earth-song,
I was no longer brave;
My avarice cooled
Like lust in the chill of the grave.[29]

The Earth, the voice of the East, effected a change in the speaker. The avarice and lust
of his Western activity cooled. The grave became a reminder of the folly of his activity. The spiritual mind of the East thus balanced the industrial passion of the West.

Emerson expressed Asia's unifying principle in another poem with a Sanskrit
name, "Brahma," which first appeared in an 1857 issue of the *Atlantic Monthly*. In
this poem the speaker was unity itself, the One.

If the red slayer think he slays,
Or if the slain think he is slain,
They know no well the subtle ways

I keep, and pass, and turn again.
Far or forgot to me is near;
Shadow and sunlight are the same;
The vanished gods to me appear;
And one to me are shame and fame.
They reckon ill who leave me out;
When me they fly, I am the wings;
I am the doubter and the doubt,
And the hymn the Brahmin sings.
The strong gods pine for my abode,
And pine in vain the sacred Seven;
But though, meek lover of the good!
Find me, and turn thy back on heaven.[30]

The poem was one long meditation on unity, drawing on Hindu texts. It had influences and paraphrases from the Vishnu Purana, the Laws of Manu, and the Katha Upanishad.[31] In the poem, Brahma spoke and outlined its own fullness, exceeding any sense of difference or differentiation. Near and far, shadow and sunlight, shame and fame, all melted together in the great unity. This unity was the unity of Asia, specifically of the Hindus, whose "Brahmin sings" and whose "gods pine." As Carpenter wrote about "Hamatreya" and "Brahma," "the two deal with different aspects of the same Hindu idea. 'Hamatreya' expressed the feeling for the identity of matter under its various appearances in spite of the 'magical illusions of reality'—the identity of earth and the human body. 'Brahma' expressed the feeling for the identity of energy—of the human soul and the life-process."[32] Carpenter was right to identify the shared theme of identity and unity in the two poems. However, like Emerson, Carpenter saw these as "conceptions which were essentially Hindu."[33] Rather than essentially Hindu, these concepts were the essential components of Emerson's own construction of an "Asia" imagined through Orientalist translations of certain Sanskrit texts. Emerson was not inspired by Hindu concepts. He forged an imagined "Asia" out of bits and pieces of translated Sanskrit texts.

Emerson often befuddled readers and reviewers with his representations of India and Asia. With tongue planted firmly in cheek, the reviewer in the *North American Review* noted that in Emerson's first book of poems, which include "Hamatreya," "sometimes, an uncouth Sanscrit, Greek, or German compound word stands as the title of a few verses, and answers the poet's object to puzzle his readers quite delightfully. The contrivance is ingenious and shows how highly obscurity is prized, and that a book of poetry may almost attain the dignity of a child's book of riddles."[34] Both the title and the contents of the poem baffled the reviewer. The reviewer confessed lacking the knowledge or time to search encyclopedias "for a solution of the enigma."[35] "Brahma" also inspired bemused mockery from reviewers. In an article headed "Emerson Travestie," the *New York Times* called "Brahma" "an exquisite piece of meaningless versification, that no sooner is it read than the desire to parody it becomes irresistible." The newspaper wryly praised Emerson because "a poem in which no one can find a meaning, must be acknowledged a very great success. None but a man of genius could have produced such an exquisite piece of no-nothingism."[36] Indeed, "Brahma" inspired many popular parodies, one printed in the *Times* a few days later, entitled "Mutton," which turned the red slayer into a butcher, the slayed into lamb, and, in the final line, asked readers to turn their back on pork.[37]

At least a few readers grasped the theme of unity in the poem, however. The *Boston Herald* published a poetic response to "Brahma" with lines reflecting that the writer grasped Emerson's meaning: "And I am God, for God is but the whole, / Of which all souls form each an equal part."[38] Writing in *Graham's American Monthly Magazine of Literature, Art, and Fashion*, the editor claimed that the poem "consists almost entirely of the characteristic and leading points" of the Bhagavad Gita. For the reviewer, the overall theme of the Gita was "God is all things, one being and one substance, or all beings and all substances," and the poem was an attempt to exemplify this by offering pictures of opposites and declaring them identical.[39] The review then goes through a line-by-line reading of the poem, matching each of Emerson's lines with passages from the Gita. Whereas these writers understood and appreciated Emerson's image of unity, *The Christian Watchman and Christian Reflector*, possibly remembering earlier critiques of Rammohun Roy, found Emerson's *Representative Men* to be "Oriental Pantheism" and rejected it outright. The Baptist magazine identified the theme of unity that Emerson associated with Asia and believed it to be a dangerous heresy.[40] Representation of Asia as the land of unity and the One seemed to resonate with those who were sympathetic with Emerson or had some prior experience with religion in India, either in the form of the Bhagavad Gita or the writings of Rammohun Roy.

Emerson's use of Sanskrit texts reflected his desire to balance East and West. His vision of East and West relied upon a notion of essential difference between the people, religion, and culture of each. That difference made fusion possible, but it also allowed for comparison—hence the long list of qualities divided between the two in "Plato." The desire for fusion and the reliance on comparative difference continued throughout Transcendentalist representations of India and the East.

Emerson's friend Henry David Thoreau took a similar essentialist view of East and West, but he went further than Emerson, and more of his published work dealt directly with texts and ideas from India. Thoreau also praised the East more than Emerson. He used the East–West contrast to critique New England Protestant Christianity. In two of Thoreau's major works, *A Week on the Concord and Merrimack Rivers* (1849) and *Walden* (1854), he picked up the basic East–West essentialism of Emerson and expanded on it.

Thoreau imagined Asia as a land of contemplation, unity, and ancient wisdom. As he and his brother reclined by the river and ate melons in the "Monday" chapter of *Week*, he described the two of them as "more or less, Asiatics" who "give over all work and reform."[41] Their thoughts "reverted to Arabia, Persia, and Hindostan, the lands of contemplation and dwelling places of ruminant nations."[42] But for Thoreau, India was the center of Asia and the heart of the Orient. Later, in "Monday," Thoreau compared Eastern and Western philosophy and religion through a comparison of the Bhagavad Gita and the New Testament. The Gita recounted the god Krishna encouraging the warrior Arjuna to fulfill his duty as a warrior and enter battle against his estranged family members on the enemy's side. Thoreau praised Krishna's advice as "a sublime conservatism; as wide as the world, and as unwearied as time; preserving the universe with Asiatic anxiety, in that state in which it appeared in their minds."[43] For Thoreau, Hindoo philosophers "dwell on the inevitability and unchangeableness of laws. . . . The end is an immense consolation; eternal absorption in Brahma. Buoyancy, freedom, flexibility, variety, possibility, which also are qualities of the Unnamed, they deal with not."[44] Here Thoreau, similarly to Emerson, imagined an Asia typified by Indian philosophy, unity, passivity, absorption, and lacking action, freedom, and diversity. Once again, India was the land of the One.

Thoreau took a step further than Emerson, though, and made explicit comparisons between Hindoo religion and Christianity. Where Hindoo religion encouraged contemplation and represented a divine unity, "Christianity, on the other hand," he wrote, "is humane, practical, and, in a large sense, radical." Then, in a remarkable passage, Thoreau connected Hindoo religions and Christianity, while at the same time presenting their differences:

So many years and ages of the gods those eastern sages sat contemplating Brahm, uttering in silence the mystic "Om," being absorbed into the essence of the Supreme Being, never going out of themselves, but subsiding further and deeper within; so infinitely wise, yet infinitely stagnant; until at last, in that same Asia, but in the western part of it, appeared a youth, wholly unforetold by them,—not being absorbed into Brahm, but bringing Brahm down to earth and to mankind; in whom Brahm had awaked from his long sleep, and exerted himself, and the day began,—a new avatar.[45]

Thoreau presented a new Christology and history for Christianity. Jesus emanated from the same God, the same Brahm, that the Eastern sages contemplated. But while the sages contemplated, Christ reformed. Christ took action. The difference between Christ and the Hindoo emerged in their texts. The New Testament "furnishes the most pregnant and practical texts" and "is remarkable for its pure morality; the best Hindoo Scripture, for its pure intellectuality."[46] While the Christian busily reformed evil, the Hindoo resorted to ascetic attempts to "patiently starve it out."[47] Thoreau supported this claim through an extensive set of quotes from Charles Wilkins's translation of the Bhagavad Gita, discussing "the forsaking of works."[48] For Thoreau, action marked the difference between East and West, Hindoo and Christian: "The former has nothing to do in this world, the latter is full of activity."[49]

Thoreau universalized the East–West difference beyond merely essential national characteristics: "There is a struggle between the oriental and the occidental in every nation; some who would be forever contemplating the sun, and some who are hastening toward the sunset. The former class says to the latter, When you have reached the sunset, you will be no nearer to the sun. To which the latter replies, But we so prolong the day."[50] There were Orientals and Occidentals everywhere, even in Concord, and the tension between those who sought contemplation and those who sought action typified society generally. Throughout "Monday," Thoreau praises the Gita and the Laws of Manu for their philosophy, contemplation, and understanding of universal truths. Thoreau aligned himself with the contemplative Orientals. He took the trope of Eastern contemplation and Western action—the same trope that Emerson had unified in Plato—and applied it to the society around him and to people universally. But unlike Emerson, for Thoreau the East and West were not geographically far apart. They could be found anywhere, even in Massachusetts.

In a similar vein, Thoreau played with the common image of Indian heathenism: he turned it upside down. In the "Sunday" chapter of *Week*, Thoreau inverted traditional themes of work/rest and Christian/heathen in a critique of New England Protestantism. Thoreau recounted how he had been reprimanded by a pastor for heading on a hike up a mountain instead of attending church on a Sunday. For Thoreau, the Protestant emphasis on keeping the Sabbath was superstition.

> The country is full of this superstition, so that when one enters a village, the church, not only really but from association, is the ugliest looking building in it, because it is the one in which human nature stoops the lowest and is most disgraced. Certainly, temples as these shall ere long cease to deform the landscape. There are few things more disheartening and disgusting than when you are walking the streets of a strange village on the Sabbath, to hear a preacher shouting like a boatswain in a gale of wind, and thus harshly profaning the

quiet atmosphere of the day. You fancy him to have taken off his coat, as when men are about to do hot and dirty work.[51]

Thoreau's image of the pastor on Sunday used the same tropes as the missionary accounts of popular Hindoo practice found in the *Panoplist* or *Missionary Herald*. The pastor was loud and profane. The church became a temple. The town was a village. The scene was "disheartening and disgusting." Thoreau also used the noisy and profane image of the Hindoo temple or festival to critique New England Protestantism as superstition. He compared New England superstition with Hindoo superstition, calling Sabbath keeping "pagoda worship" and "like the beating of gongs in a Hindoo subterranean temple."[52] Just as Thoreau used the elements of Hindoo religion he found admirable to praise the "Orientals" of all nations, he used the parts of Hindoo practice he found objectionable, the "superstitions," to critique the Protestant practices he saw around him. For Thoreau, the superstitious held to their creeds too tightly. The superstitious failed to contemplate and they failed to seek after truth. Instead, the superstitious held up in their churches and temples, preached, and beat gongs. The contemplatives, meanwhile, could be found in the Gita and Manu or on top of a mountain. As he put it, "A man's real faith is never contained in his creed, nor is his creed an article of his faith. The last is never adopted."[53] The superstitious, Yankees and Hindoos alike, reduced the greatness of their faith to creeds and ceremonies.

In *Week*, Thoreau used notions of Oriental difference to critique society around him, but in *Walden* he began to apply his reading in Indian texts to his own life and practice. In the first chapter of *Walden*, "Economy," Thoreau claimed his "purpose in going to Walden Pond was not to live cheaply nor to live dearly there, but to transact some private business with the fewest obstacles."[54] In the chapter titled "Where I Lived, and What I Lived For," he explained his business in a famous passage:

> I went to the woods because I wished to live deliberately, to front only the essential facts of life, and see if I could not learn what it had to teach, and not when I came to die, discover that I had not lived . . . I wanted to live deep and suck out all the marrow of life, to live sturdily and Spartan-like as to put to rout all that was not life, to cut a broad swath and shave close, to drive life into a corner, and reduce it to its lowest terms, and if it proved to be mean, why then to get the whole and genuine meanness of it, and to publish its meanness to the world; or if it were sublime, to know it by experience, and be able to give a true account of it in my excursion.[55]

Here Thoreau emphasized living and acting. "Living deliberately" meant taking control of himself and his actions: living "deep," living sturdily, driving life, reducing, cutting, shaving, publishing, and, most important, experiencing. This was no Emersonian essay on the nature of philosophy or a poem on the One. Thoreau would apply his reading of Indian texts to himself and his actions. Emerson pulled East and West together to produce a balanced poem. Thoreau sought to draw on the Orient and produce a balanced life.

Some scholars have read Thoreau's experience and practice at Walden Pond as the first American experiment with yoga. Christy argued that "the fact remains that Thoreau *did* think of himself as a Yogi, and more than once affirmed it."[56] Christy cites a letter Thoreau wrote to H. G. O. Blake in 1849 in which he remarked, "even I am a yogi," and a September 1, 1841, entry in Thoreau's journal as corroborating evidence.[57] Religious historian Shreena Gandhi argued that Thoreau used "the Bhagavad Gita and the practice of yoga to deal with the alienation of modernism (and capitalism)."[58] Meanwhile, religious historian Alan D. Hodder linked Thoreau's yoga with his experiences of ecstasy. For Hodder, Thoreau's yoga operated "as a kind of spiritual model and imaginative construct, zealously distilled from his Eastern reading and thoughtfully elaborated, for the calculated purpose of representing to himself and his would-be readers authentic experiences of ecstasy."[59] Hodder saw three themes in Thoreau's yoga: celestial sounds, literary organicism, and asceticism.[60] It is the third theme, asceticism, that I find most convincing and useful for considering how Thoreau represented and applied Indian religious culture in *Walden*.

The deliberate living Thoreau strived for at Walden Pond and described in *Walden* was a life of control, achieved through ascetic practice. In the chapter "Higher Laws," Thoreau quoted and expanded on Rammohun Roy's *An Abridgement of the Vedant*:

> "A command over our passions, and over the external sense of the body, and good acts, are declared by the Ved to be indispensable in the mind's approximation to God." Yet the spirit can for the time pervade and control every member and function of the body, and transmute what in form is the grossest sensuality into purity and devotion.[61]

By controlling one's passions, one's body, and one's actions, one could achieve spiritual devotion and purity. Furthermore, this devotion need not take extreme forms, but could be found in a sacralization of the everyday. "Our whole life is startlingly moral," wrote Thoreau.[62] And he found sanction for this idea in Hindoo texts. "Nothing was too trivial for the Hindoo lawgiver, however offensive it may be to modern taste. He teaches how to eat, drink, cohabit, void excrement and urine, and the like, elevating what is mean, and does not falsely excuse himself by calling these things trifles."[63] For Thoreau, Hindoo texts required bodily control, and he used the ascetic control of the body to reach God.

Thoreau used this image of the Hindoo's bodily control to once again critique New England Protestantism. "What avails it that you are a Christian, if you are not purer than the heathen, if you deny yourself no more, if you are not more religious? I know many systems of religion esteemed heathenish whose precepts fill the reader with shame, and provoke him to new endeavors, though it be to the performance of rites merely."[64] As with the comparison in *Week*, Thoreau flipped the usual Christian/heathen dichotomy. The heathen is pure because he denies himself, and his religion prompts acts of denial that lead to purity. Thoreau ended the chapter with a brief story of John Farmer, an everyman who sat on his porch thinking at the end of a workday. He heard the notes of a flute, perhaps an allusion to Krishna the flute-playing god, and then a voice inside him asked, "Why do you stay here and live this mean moiling life, when a glorious existence is possible for you?" Farmer came to a conclusion: "All that he could think of was to practice some new austerity, to let his mind descend into his body and redeem it, and treat himself with ever increasing respect."[65] Ascetic denial and bodily control were not just for Hindoos and hermetic writers, they were for all the John Farmers in New England, Thoreau claimed. Yankees like John Farmer could live a "glorious existence" by turning to the austerity of the East.

Just as Emerson imagined a union of East and West in Plato, Thoreau had his own vision of unity that connected the Orient and Occident. As with his image of Hindoo asceticism, Thoreau came at this vision through experience and Hindoo texts. In his chapter "The Pond in Winter," Thoreau began with a description of men working to harvest ice from Walden Pond that would be shipped around the world. He then launched into a vision that united New England and India. He started by noting how many townsfolk considered Walden Pond to be bottomless. He wrote, "I am thankful that this pond was made deep and pure for symbol. While men believe in the infinite some ponds will be thought to be bottomless," signaling the potential the pond held for representing larger truths.[66] As he watched the men cutting and loading the ice, he began imagining where the ice would be shipped:

> Thus it appears that the sweltering inhabitants of Charleston and New Orleans, of Madras and Bombay and Calcutta, drink at my well. In the morning I bathe my intellect in the stupendous and cosmogonal philosophy of the Bhagavat Geeta, since whose composition years of the gods have elapsed, and in comparison with which our modern world and its literature seem puny and trivial; and I doubt if that philosophy is not to be referred to a previous state of existence, so remote is its sublimity from our conceptions. I lay down the book and

go to my well for water, and lo! There I meet the servant of the Brahmin, priest of Brahma and Vishnu and Indra, who still sits in his temple on the Ganges reading the Vedas, or dwells at the root of a tree with his crust and water jug. I meet his servant come to draw water for his master, and our buckets as it were grate together in the same well. The pure Walden water is mingled with the sacred water of the Ganges. With favoring winds it is wafted past the site of the fabulous islands of Atlantis and the Hesperides, makes the periplus of Hanno, and floating by Ternate and Tidore and the mouth of the Persian Gulf, melts in the tropic gales of the Indian seas, and is landed in ports of which Alexander only heard the names.[67]

In this passage, Thoreau began with the image of the East and India as distant, eternal, textual, and contemplative. The ice from Walden was headed to a land of exotic books like the Gita and exotic people like the brahmin. But when Thoreau went down to the well, he found, surprisingly, that India was not so far away. The economic connections that send Walden ice to India mirrored the spiritual connections established by texts like the Gita. Thus, Thoreau's bucket clanked in the pond alongside the bucket of the brahmin's servant. The water of Walden and that of the Ganges were not separate. A union between East and West not only existed, it was central to Thoreau's spiritual experience.

Moving from *Week* to *Walden,* Thoreau's use of Hindoo texts and his representations of Hindoo religion shifted from India as a land of contemplation to India as a land of ascetic practice and control. In *Week*, Thoreau disparaged the Brahman for "starving out" evil, but in *Walden* he aimed for his own ascetic control and purity. As he spent more time in his Indian sources, Thoreau discovered that there was action in the East. He read about the everyday acts of control found in the Laws of Manu or the fruitless action of the Bhagavad Gita. Yet, for Thoreau, both contemplation and everyday action functioned to give the mind access to experiences of unity. The contemplation Thoreau admired in the texts of India and the sacralized everyday actions Thoreau recommended to Yankees like John Farmer fired his vision of Walden Pond's universal waters and the unity between Concord and Calcutta. Thoreau represented Hindoo religion as a religion that praised contemplation and controlled action. These were things that Americans needed for their own spiritual experiences and that American Protestantism had failed to give them. Thoreau lamented Hindoo superstition, as he did Christian superstition. Still, he believed the Hindoos had superior abilities of contemplation and control. And he believed too many Americans lacked these qualities.

Contemporary critics more readily grasped Thoreau's use of Hindoo texts than they did Emerson's. But, as with Emerson, they roundly rejected Thoreau's praise of

Hindoo religion. George Ripley, a Transcendentalist and founder of the Brook Farm commune, identified Thoreau's philosophy as "Pantheistic egotism vaguely characterized as Transcendental."[68] Ripley took particular offense at Thoreau's "misplaced Pantheistic attack on the Christian Faith" in *Week* and found Thoreau's comparison between Hindoo religions and Christianity to be "revolting alike to good sense and good taste."[69] Poet and critic James Russell Lowell echoed Ripley's critiques when he described Thoreau's "intelligent paganism" that "might absorb the forces of the entire alphabetic sanctity of the A.B.C.F. M."[70] Thoreau flummoxed Lowell with his desire for a sentence "which no intelligence can understand!" and Lowell thought "it must be this taste that makes him so fond of the Hindoo philosophy, which would seem admirably suited to men, if men were only oysters."[71] For these critics, Thoreau's use of Hindoo texts was at best unintelligible and at worst an attack on the truth of Christianity.

Yet Thoreau found at least one sympathetic reader. Edwin Morton, a Harvard student writing in *Harvard Magazine*, praised Thoreau's turn Eastward and proclaimed "Transcendentalism, thy name is Brahme!"[72] Morton went on to temper his praise of Thoreau: "There are many very wise things in those books.... Yet [Thoreau] plays too long upon that one string,—we get too much of that heathenish music, when we have good or better of our own."[73] For Morton, the Vedas were "all very good in their way" but "that sublime life of Christ" was a better religion "with less obscurity."[74] Morton's assessment showed how even the most sympathetic readers resisted Thoreau's critiques of Christianity. Thoreau's inversions of heathenism fell on deaf ears, and reviewers ignored his admiration for the control and asceticism he found in the Gita and the Laws of Manu. When Thoreau's contemporaries recognized representations of Hindoo religions in his work, it was only as a defect in his writing.

Emerson and Thoreau built on New England's long history with India when they imagined the contemplative Orient. Like the East India Marine Society, these two Transcendentalists imagined the Orient as an exotic land altogether different from the West and, also like the EIMS, they imagined India to be its best example. But these early Transcendentalists also drew on the Vedanta of Rammohun Roy. Mary Moody Emerson recommended the Bengali reformer to her young nephew. Thoreau read and quoted from Roy's English translations of Vedic texts. Both American writers accepted the Vedic Hindoo religion that Roy championed in the United States and Britain, founded on the ancient Sanskrit texts. Earlier religious liberals, such as the Unitarians, had turned Rammohun Roy into a Christian to protect the exclusive truth of Protestant religion. But Thoreau and Emerson imagined true religion as something bigger than any one sect. Thus, Emerson imagined a unity between the One of the East and the many of the West—between Mind and Nature. Thoreau took it a bit further and used the contemplation and asceticism of the Hindoo to critique the overly practical and industrious American Protestant. Both men sought out true religion, and neither was afraid to look to India in his search.

Ethnical Scriptures, Brahmanism, and the Search for a Universal Religion

In their published prose and poetry, Emerson and Thoreau imagined a division between the East and the West, but their work in the pages of *The Dial*, a magazine for Transcendentalist thought and literature, showed the beginnings of a more nuanced comparative approach to religion. After taking editorial control of *The Dial* in 1842, Emerson decided to begin printing a series of "Ethnical Scriptures" in the magazine. These scriptures included excerpts of ancient texts from around the world, including two Indian texts, the Laws of Manu and the Vishnu Sarma. In the introduction to portions of the Vishnu Sarma, Emerson argued that "each nation has its bible more or less pure; none has yet been willing or able in a wise and devout spirit to collate its own with those of other nations."[75] Emerson hoped to do something of the sort with the "Ethnical Scriptures" and believed that it was necessary to drop the "civil-historical and the ritual portions" of texts and keep only the "grand expressions of the moral sentiment in different ages and races, the rules for the guidance of life, the bursts of piety and abandonment to the Invisible and Eternal."[76] He further believed that these various texts from around the world contained truth about the "Invisible and Eternal" and that removing their differences and comparing their similarities would reveal universal religious truth. This was not merely a literary exercise. It was a work "to be done by religion and not by literature."[77] It was the search for universal religious truth through literary comparison. [78]

Two Sanskrit texts appeared in the "Ethnical Scriptures." Emerson began the series with the portions of the Vishnu Sarma taken from Charles Wilkins's translation. But, as Arthur Versluis has pointed out, Emerson dropped the narrative portions of the text, and so what he published in *The Dial* was a series of aphorisms devoid of any context.[79] From Emerson's perspective, he was simply getting rid of the unnecessary "civil-historical" portion so as to make the truth within the text more accessible. The resulting list of aphorisms had no cultural fingerprints and read with a certain universalized tone. For example, the first aphorism was "Whatsoever cometh to pass, either good or evil, is the consequence of man's own actions, and descendeth from the power of the Supreme Ruler."[80] There was nothing obviously Hindoo about the phrase. Further down the list, "Of all men thy guest is the superior" sounded like common manners.[81] The obviously exotic Sanskrit title of

"Veeshnoo Sarma" contrasted starkly with the decontextualized aphorisms. In printing the extracts, Emerson transformed the Vishnu Sarma from an Indian Sanskrit text to a universal scripture containing truth that transcended cultural context.

While Emerson pared down the cultural context of the Vishnu Sarma, Thoreau used the contextual details of the Laws of Manu to point toward universal truths when he reprinted it as part of the "Ethnical Scriptures." In his introduction to the text, Thoreau gave a brief history of the Laws of Manu taken from William Jones's preface to his 1794 translation of the text. Quoting Jones, Thoreau described the Laws of Manu as "being believed by the Hindoos 'to have been promulgated in the beginning of time by Menu, son or grandson of Brahma,' and 'the first of created beings.'"[82] Rather than strip the Laws of Manu of any cultural context, Thoreau kept the references in the text to the Vedas or various deities, and reorganized the text around themes he felt important. He used the cultural details in the text to point toward higher universal truths. Thoreau reorganized the text around the following: Custom, Temperance, Purification and Sacrifice, Teaching, Reward and Punishment, The King, Woman and Marriage, The Brahmin, God, Devotion.[83] Throughout these various sections, Thoreau's selection of passages emphasized bodily control, asceticism, and contemplation. For example, under "Purification and Sacrifice" he placed the passage, "Bodies are cleansed by water; the mind is purified by truth; the vital spirit, by theology and devotion; the understanding, by clear knowledge."[84] Again, under "The Brahmin" he put "not solicitous for the means of gratification, chaste as a student, sleeping on the bare earth, in the haunts of pious hermits, without one selfish affection, dwelling at the roots of trees;—for the purpose of uniting his soul with the divine spirit."[85] Thoreau believed these specific injunctions about purity or the proper conduct of a brahmin pointed toward universal truths for all people in search of purity and divinity. In his selections for the "Ethnical Scriptures," Thoreau universalized the themes of the Laws of Manu without stripping them of their cultural context. He imagined transcendent universal truth that lay behind the cultural specifics of the text.

The "Ethnical Scriptures" imagined Hindu religion as a religion of texts, ancient wisdom, contemplation, and asceticism that could be mined for transcendent and universal truth. Thoreau and Emerson assumed that universal religious truth should be found in texts and that those different texts distinguished different religions. To find a religion greater than these "civil-historical" differences, Emerson and Thoreau argued, one must take the best of all of them, the universal truths hidden within the cultural differences. Through the work of the proper editor, religious difference could be collated into universal truth.

The "Ethnical Scriptures" took the first steps in a larger project of comparative religion that engaged religious liberals for the rest of the nineteenth century.

Transcendentalists constructed taxonomies of comparative religion to identify and compare religions in hopes of discovering a universal core of Mind, Truth, or Religion that could unite mankind. Transcendentalist writers surveyed world religions in the quest for the universal. In the process, they constructed a religious tradition they named "Brahmanism" that stood as the religion of India and could be compared with other religions. Three major works during the latter half of the nineteenth century took this comparative approach to religions and Brahmanism: Lydia Maria Child's *The Progress of Religious Ideas Through Successive Ages* (1855), James Freeman Clarke's *Ten Great Religions* (1871), and Samuel Johnson's *Oriental Religions and Their Relation to the Universal Religion: India* (1873). These writers broadened the four-part taxonomy of religions used earlier by Hannah Adams. They believed that each religion in the taxonomy contained partial truth and, when compared, these religions would reveal universal and transcendent religious truth for all people. Within these taxonomies of religions, authors represented Brahmanism as the religious system of India. As imagined by the Transcendentalists, Brahmanism originated in the ancient Sanskrit texts. Its theology was pantheistic and spiritual, and it resulted in a degraded society organized by caste.

Published a year after Thoreau's *Walden*, Lydia Maria Child's *Progress of Religious Ideas* was the earliest of these comparative texts and served as a bridge from the earlier comparative work of Hannah Adams and the later works of Transcendentalist comparative religion. Child did not acknowledge Adams's earlier work, and in fact claimed she was not aware that anyone had ever before attempted to account for the various religions of the world.[86] Nonetheless, she shared Adams's frustration with sectarianism and schismatic Protestantism, desire to render religions in their own words and logic, and theory that religious truth progresses through history. For Child, Universal Religion meant getting rid of the divisive and exclusive claims of theology and doctrine and focusing on shared reverence and worship of God in various cultural forms. She used a musical metaphor to describe it: "*Unison* of voice was the highest idea *theology* could attain to; but when *religion* can utter itself freely, worshippers sing a *harmony* of many different parts, and thus make a music more pleasing to the ear of God, and more according to the pattern by which he created the universe."[87] Child's work was meant to be accessible by common readers, but she made use of many elite Orientalist sources, including the works of William Jones, Rammohun Roy, and Joseph Priestley. Reviewers criticized Child for not treating Christianity preferentially in her account of religions. "She appears to regard [the Christian Scriptures] as little better than the writings of Confucious, or the Shasters of the Hindoos," wrote a reviewer in the *New-York Observer*.[88] Yet, Transcendentalists and other religious liberals, most notably Samuel J. May and Theodore Parker, applauded Child's work as an important step in liberal religion and theology.[89]

Like Child, James Freeman Clarke claimed he was offering an unbiased and empirical account of religions, a science he dubbed "Comparative Theology," in his *Ten Great Religions*.[90] Writing fifteen years after Child, he mentioned her work in his introductory chapter. He noted that it was well done considering the scarce sources available at the time. However, Clarke arrived at a very different conclusion from Child. He argued that an unbiased, empirical, and scientific survey of the world's great religious traditions proved that only Christianity could serve as a Universal Religion for all humankind. That said, Clarke's idea of Christianity was a liberal, Transcendentalist, and mystical one. For Clarke, Christianity was uniquely "catholic" and "therefore, capable of adapting itself to every variety of the human race."[91] Though he gave Christianity the privileged place in his comparative taxonomy, Clarke did take an overall positive view of the other religions in his study:

We shall find them always feeling after God, often finding him. We shall see that in their origin they were not the work of priestcraft, but of human nature; in their essence not superstitions, but religions in their doctrines true more frequently than false; in their moral tendency good rather than evil. And instead of degenerating toward something worse, they come to prepare the way for something better.[92]

Clarke's text was widely read and available in the late nineteenth century. It began as a series of articles serialized in *The Atlantic*, and the book itself went through thirty editions between 1871 and 1893, becoming a popular text among religious liberals.[93] Clarke shared the approach to comparative religion used by Joseph Priestley earlier in the century. Both were Unitarians, both believed Christianity to be the apex of religion, and both tried to prove this through a careful and empirical process of comparison.

If Child's project shared similarities with Hannah Adams and Clarke's with Joseph Priestley, then Samuel Johnson was most similar to John Adams. Just as John Adams spent his late years searching through Orientalist literature to discover true religion, Johnson turned to Orientalist accounts of Asian religions to discover Universal Religion. Johnson's use of the spelling "Hindu" reflected his reliance on British Orientalist sources that had made the "oo" to "u" switch and the distance between his work and Clarke's more popular book. Yet, it is important to note that Johnson did not describe *Hinduism*, but rather, described Brahmanism, the religion of the Hindus.

Johnson was born and raised in Salem, Massachusetts. In his memoir of Johnson, Samuel Longfellow wondered if Johnson had spent time at the East India Society museum and if the artifacts there had inspired Johnson's turn to the Orient later in life.[94] Johnson's work spanned three volumes of *Oriental Religions and Their Relation to the Universal Religion*, one each on India, China, and Persia. For Johnson, Universal Religion could be found only through a careful and thorough examination of all the religions of the world. "Universal Religion, then, cannot be any one *exclusively*, of the great positive religions of the world. Yet it is really what is best in each and every one of them; purified from baser inter-mixture and developed in freedom and power."[95] The volume on India appeared in 1872 and was given "slight recognition" despite favorable reviews in a few papers, such as the *North American Review* and the *New York Tribune*.[96] At the time of its publication, Johnson's text was the most extensive treatment of Indian religious history produced by an American, even though it lacked the accessibility of Child's and Clarke's. He combined a Transcendentalist vision of a Universal Religion inherent within human religious imagination with in-depth discussions of philosophy, philology, and history drawn from elite Orientalist sources. As such, he produced a text at that was inaccessible to common readers.

Despite the differences in their texts, all three of these Transcendentalist writers invented a religion they called Brahmanism to account for the religion of India. Child, Clarke, and Johnson characterized Brahmanism as a religion of spiritual contemplation. Child described Hindoos as having "a temperament more inclined than others to veneration and mysticism" and Clarke described Brahmanism as a religion of "pure spiritualism" with a God who is "an intelligence, absorbed in the rest of profound contemplation."[97] Johnson built his entire appraisal of "Oriental religions" around the belief that the Hindu mind was the "Brain of the East." He described "the Hindu mind" as "subtle, introversive, contemplative. It spins its ideals out of its brain substance, and may be properly called *cerebral*."[98] Both Clarke and Johnson, fulfilling the vision of Emerson and Thoreau, connected the cerebral and contemplative Hindoo/u mind to Euro-Americans through a theory of language drawn from the philological work of F. Max Müller. Using Müller's study of Indo-European languages, they connected the Aryans and their Sanskrit Vedic texts with Europeans as one common nation. As Clarke wrote, "The study of the Sanskrit language has told us a long story concerning the origin of the Hindoos. . . . It has given us the information that one great family, the Indo-European, has done most of the work of the world."[99] Thus, Brahmanism was not only the Brain of the East; it was also the contemplative and spiritual ancestor of Euro-America.

Brahmanism, as imagined by the Transcendentalists, consisted of Sanskrit texts and complex systems of philosophy. As with the "Ethnical Scriptures," Transcendentalists argued that Sanskrit texts held the central theology and philosophy of Brahmanism. All three writers discussed the Vedas, epics, Laws of Manu, Bhagavad Gita, Brahmanas, and Puranas. Johnson and Clarke also spent considerable space discussing three major schools of Indian philosophy. Clarke devoted a whole section of his chapter on Brahmanism to three schools of philosophy: Vedanta, Sankhya, and Nyasa. For his part, Johnson gave Vedanta and Sankhya philosophy each a full chapter. Contemplative Brahmanism relied on ancient texts to produce complex systems of philosophy.

All of these texts and philosophical systems pointed toward Brahmanism's theology of pantheism and unity of being, according to the Transcendentalists. For example, Child claimed that Brahm was the central god of Brahmanism and described how Hindoos believed "God [was] in all things, and all things in God" and that "all life, whether in essence or form, proceeds constantly from Brahm, through a variety of mediums." [100] Similarly, Johnson praised the pantheism of Brahamanism and its "Hindu dreamers." Hindu pantheism suited his Transcendentalist vision of a unity of Being:

> In its nobler forms it is essentially of the spirit and rests, as its name imports, on these principles: that Being is, in its substance, one; that this substantial unity is, and must be implicated in all energy, though indefinably and inconceivably,—as Life, all-pervading, all-containing, the constant ground and ultimate force of all that is; and that the recognition of this inseparableness of the known universe from God is consistent with the worship of God as infinitely transcending it. [101]

Clarke summed up the Transcendental understanding of Brahmanism's unified, pantheistic, and spiritual theology: "Brahmanism teaches the truth of the reality of spirit, and that spirit is infinite, absolute, perfect, one; that it is the substance underlying all existence." [102] The Transcendentalists characterized Brahmanism as a pantheistic religion that contributed a recognition of unity and pure being to the Universal Religion.

When these Transcendentalist writers shifted from accounts of ancient philosophy and pantheism to discussions of religion in contemporary India, they used a narrative of declension, often using the example of caste. Child's narrative of decline was representative of the later texts and reminiscent of Hannah Adams, Joseph Priestley, and Rammohun Roy:

> Many causes have been at work to produce a gradual degeneracy in the manners, customs, and opinions of the Hindoos. Knowledge of the Vedas is confined to the learned, and few ever heard of such a doctrine as the unity of God. The great mass of the people are neglected by the Bramins, who are either taken up with the acquisition of temporal power, or striving to obtain spiritual

elevation for themselves, by contemplation and penances. Such instruction as the populace do receive, rather serves to confuse their moral perceptions.[103]

A failure to properly educate the common people in Vedic theology led to social decline. The result of this moral confusion is a backward society where "thefts, perjury, or murder" can be atoned for through ritual practices officiated by brahmins but "killing a cow, selling beef to a European, offending a Bramin, or being converted to a foreign religion" results in the death penalty or social excommunication through loss of caste.[104] Indeed, caste itself stood as a powerful example of Hindoo decline. Caste "narrow[ed] the sympathies and imped[ed] the progress" of Hindoos.[105] Samuel Johnson described a similar narrative of declension and the evils of caste, comparing it with American slavery.[106] For all that Transcendentalist writers found to praise in the unity and spiritualism of Brahmanism, they believed the failure of Brahmins to spread correct theological knowledge to the masses had resulted in a socially backward India.

Transcendentalists turned to comparative religion as a tool for finding religious truth—be it in James Freeman Clarke's liberal and mystical Christianity, Lydia Maria Child's religious liberalism, or Samuel Johnson's Universal Religion. Brahmanism, the religion of Hindoo India, played an important role in these comparative projects. It provided the spiritual, cerebral, contemplative, and pantheistic aspect of religion. More than that, drawing on Müller's theory of the Indo-European family, this contemplative and spiritual religion shared historical connections with European Americans. Reversing the usual declension narrative of Hindu religion, Samuel Johnson claimed Brahmanism provided "a new dawn after centuries of comparative death and night" in Western religion.[107] Brahmanism reached "its spiritual hands across the seas of race and mind—just as electric wire is encircling the material globe, just as all the relations of trade and science and politics are becoming ecumenical" to give an escape from "the Christian and the Judaic dogma . . . upon the ground of those inherent, inalienable, and immutable relations that unite Man with God."[108] For Johnson, Western religion was in decline and India could save it. Within taxonomies of comparative religion, where every religious tradition offered its own pieces of truth, Brahmanism gave American Transcendentalists contemplative, pantheistic spirituality.

Transcendentalist India and Metaphysical Religion

Beginning with the Oriental mind of Emerson's Plato and carrying through Johnson's image of Brahmanism as "the Brain" of the East, the contemplative aspects of Hindoo religion attracted Transcendentalist attention and aligned with the metaphysical tradition's emphasis on the mind. Albanese has pointed to Emerson's *Nature* as "the early proclamation of Transcendental good news" and in her reading she finds "an American gospel of divinization."[109] This gospel relied upon a process of self-fashioning and interior work of the mind. "The result suggested that the restoration of the world meant its subjection to an enhanced ego-self, an ego-self that used the power of higher spiritual energies to advance this-worldly projects and delights."[110] The contemplative Hindoo mind provided Transcendentalists a model of how one could fashion such an ego-self. The Oriental mind of Plato, Thoreau's reading of the Bhagavad Gita, and the contemplative philosophies of Brahmanism provided spiritual resources for fashioning the self through the mind.

Likewise, the Transcendentalists returned to the unity and pantheism of Hindoo religion or Brahmanism again and again because of their own metaphysical theory of correspondences. Transcendentalists theorized a connection between microcosm and macrocosm that resonated with the pantheism they saw in Hindoo religion. Again, Albanese described how "Emerson was connecting human will to a higher source of will and desire, and he was arguing for the release of self into that vastness."[111] She also connected the emphasis on mind with the theory of correspondence in Transcendental thought: "In the Transcendental version of creating one's own reality, the deep recesses from which intuition willed were also the deep recesses that connected people with one another. The human cosmos, like the natural one, was a grand collective of the spirit."[112] Looking at the world with a vision that connected the individual to the cosmos through a shared spirit, it is no surprise that the Transcendentalists would praise the pantheism they saw in Brahmanism. Hindoo religion allowed Transcendentalists to crystallize and articulate their ideas of unity, pantheism, and contemplation as "the Orient" or Brahmanism. Yet these articulations were just the first step toward a larger project of discovering true or Universal Religion. For all the resources Transcendentalists found in India, and for all the ability it gave them to articulate an alternative religious vision to American Protestantism, Hindoo religion and Brahmanism were never an end in themselves. That said, Indian religion did prove to be an important source for Transcendentalist renderings of American metaphysical religion.

Images of India as the "mystic East" did not begin with the Transcendentalists, as the East India Marine Society museum shows. Yet, in recognizing metaphysical themes of mind and correspondence in Indian texts and imagining the religion of Brahmanism, typified by contemplation and unity, the Transcendentalists were the first to turn to India for viable religious resources. Unitarians, the liberal Protestant grandparents of the Transcendentalists, imagined Rammohun Roy as a Unitarian in order to deploy his arguments. But Emerson rebuked Yankees through the voice of a goddess, Thoreau could imagine himself a yogi on the Ganges, and Samuel Johnson could find the mind of Universal Religion in India. It is true, as many have argued, that the Transcendentalists were the first Americans to appreciate Indian religion. More important, they were also the first Americans to imagine a metaphysical India of contemplation and unity—an image that remains in American culture well into the twenty-first century. Yet, as the following chapter reveals, Transcendentalist Brahmanism was not the only metaphysical approach to Indian religion.

5   The Theosophical Quest for Occult Power

WHILE THE TRANSCENDENTALISTS compared religions and imagined "Brahmanism" in and around Boston, another metaphysical movement emerged from a chance meeting at a farmhouse in Vermont. Henry Steel Olcott noticed that when Madame Helena Blavatsky showed up, the spirits who visited the Eddy home changed. In 1874 two brothers, Horatio and William Eddy, began summoning spiritual manifestations in their home in Chittenden, Vermont. Before Blavatsky's arrival, the spirits that visited had been Native Americans, Euro-Americans, or Europeans.[1] These were figures from a Western past, whether native to the New World or the Old. But when Blavatsky arrived at the house on the October 14, 1874, the fraternal mediums summoned spirits beyond the continents of Europe and America. On the first evening of Blavatsky's stay in Chittenden, her soon-to-be friend and confidant Olcott described how "spooks of other nationalities came before us. There was a Georgian servant boy from the Caucasus; a Mussulman merchant from Tiflis; a Russian peasant girl. . . . A Kourdish cavalier armed with scimitar, pistols, and lance; a hideously ugly and devilish-looking negro sorcerer from Africa."[2] But not all of the spooks could be so easily identified. On another evening during Blavatsky's visit, a more curious visitor appeared at the séance, "one who seemed to be either a Hindoo coolie or an Arab athlete. He was dark-skinned, of short statue, a lean, wire, active form, with no more superfluous fat on his frame than has a greyhound in working condition."[3] The Eastern visitor "came to visit Mme. de Blavatsky, and made her a profound obeisance: but she failed to recognize him."[4]

Though they did not know it at the time, the night the ambiguous Hindoo-Arab appeared in the Eddy's parlor prefigured the future for Colonel Olcott and Madame Blavatsky as religious innovators and friends. The Hindoo-Arab spirit that materialized before Blavatsky and Olcott was an ambiguous figure from the East—maybe from India or Palestine or Egypt or somewhere else—but, whoever he was, he represented an Oriental Other, different from the Western spirits that had been frequenting the Eddy's séance circle. In a similar vein, as the founders of the Theosophical Society, Blavatsky and Olcott mined religious cultures from Kabbalah to Egypt to India to construct their Theosophical religion of ancient wisdom. Theosophy, like the ambiguous Eastern spirit, looked like Egyptian religion at one point and Hindoo religion at another, but it was always an Oriental Other and an alternative to American Christianity. Beginning with Blavatsky, Theosophical writers imagined the religion of India in different ways throughout the late nineteenth century, but Theosophical constructions all shared the idea that Indian religion held esoteric truths, and associated these truths with metaphysical energy and powers.

The meeting between Blavatsky and Olcott in Vermont began a lifelong relationship and led to the formation of the Theosophical Society in New York in the fall of 1875. Olcott and Blavatsky shared an interest in the occult, spiritualism, and various forms of religious liberalism that were gaining popularity in the nineteenth-century United States. Occultism, Mesmerism, Rosicrucianism, Swedenborgianism, Freemasonry—in short, metaphysical religions—attracted Americans who were dissatisfied with American Christianity. A group of such disaffected American seekers assembled in Blavatsky's apartment in New York on September 7, 1875, to hear a lecture from George Felt, himself a Mason and student of the Kabbalah, on "The Lost Canon of Proportion of the Egyptians." During Felt's lecture, Blavatsky passed a note to Olcott: "Would it not be a good thing to form a Society for this kind of study?"[5] Olcott agreed, and after the lecture he announced the formation of a new society for investigating the occult and esoteric.

Writing in his history of the Theosophical Society years later, Olcott remembered, "it was to be a body for the collection and diffusion of knowledge; for occult research, and the study and dissemination of ancient philosophical and theosophical ideas."[6] But it was also a society meant to save Americans from what the founders saw as an anemic religious culture, repressed by Christianity on one side and science on the other. In his inaugural address as president at the first meeting of the Society on November 17, 1875, Olcott identified the role of the Society in rejuvenating American religion. "If I rightly apprehend our work, it is to aid in freeing the public mind of theological superstition and a tame subservience to the arrogance of science."[7] Using the analogy of slavery, Olcott described the oppressive nature of American Christianity and scientific materialism: "we see the people struggling blindly to emancipate their thought from ecclesiastical despotism. . . . They struggle from an irrepressible desire to be free from shackles which bind their limping reason after their volant intuitions have outgrown them."[8] Scientists "invite them to an apotheosis of matter" while "the clergy hold them back and hiss warnings and anathemas in their ears."[9] The current state of religion in the United States required action. "Society has reached a point where *something* must be done; it is for us to indicate where that *something* may be found."[10] It could be found in ancient religious texts, especially "the primeval sources of all religions, the books of Hermes and the Veda—of Egypt and India respectively"—books from the lands of that ambiguous Hindoo-Arab spirit.[11]

Theosophical Comparative Religion: The Origins of the Ancient Wisdom Religion

In the wake of the Theosophical Society's founding, Madame Blavatsky wrote and published the first major work of Theosophical thought in 1877, *Isis Unveiled: A Master-Key to the Ancient and Modern*. Blavatsky divided *Isis Unveiled* into two volumes, Science and Theology, representing her two main targets of criticism. Blavatsky identified a fissure between science and religion in modern Western culture, "a death-grapple of Science with Theology for infallibility."[12] Blavatsky saw "a bewildered public, fast losing all belief in man's personal immortality, in a deity of any kind, and rapidly descending to the level of a mere animal existence."[13] The solution to the quarrel, she argued, was not to choose one over the other, but to unite them. Blavatsky believed that science and religion should work together. Furthermore, she argued that the two were incomplete on their own and must work together in order to find truth. This cooperation could be achieved through a return to "the anciently universal Wisdom-Religion, as the only possible key to the Absolute in science and theology."[14] To find religious and scientific truth, modern society needed the wisdom religion of the ancients, which originated in the Orient. Theology and science would continue to falter until "these pretended authorities of the West go to the Brahmans and the Lamaists of the far Orient, and respectfully ask them to impart the alphabet of true science."[15]

Science had developed a tragic myopia, according to Blavatsky. Materialism had limited the scientist's field of study. "As it is claimed to be unphilosophical to inquire into first causes, scientists now occupy themselves with considering their physical effects. The field of scientific investigation is therefore bounded by physical nature."[16] For Blavatsky, the boundaries of physical nature excluded phenomena that the scientist must consider. True science, she argued, rejected boundaries. "For a man of science to refuse an opportunity to investigate any new phenomenon, whether it comes to him in the shape of a man from the moon, or a ghost from the Eddy homestead, is alike reprehensible."[17] By cordoning off the natural world, modern science had abdicated its responsibility to investigate spiritual phenomena. But this had not always been the case. Blavatsky argued that among ancient civilizations, science was broader, bigger, and was not held captive to materialism. She believed that the findings of modern science had been anticipated by the great ancient civilizations. "In the *Vedas*, for instance, we find positive proof that so long ago as 2,000 B.C. the Hindu sages and scholars must have been acquainted with the rotundity of our globe and the heliocentric system."[18] Blavatsky saw a return to the ancient science, the science of the wisdom religion, in the offing. She proclaimed, "the day is approaching when the world will receive the proofs that only ancient religions were in harmony with nature, and ancient science embraced all that can be known."[19] *Isis Unveiled*, then, was her attempt to restore that ancient wisdom religion that would renew and expand science to its true role in society as inseparable from theology. She was on a quest for absolute truth.

As strongly as she critiqued modern science, her criticisms of religion in American society had an added bite. For example, she offered this overview of Protestantism in the United States:

> The God of the Unitarians is a bachelor; the Deity of the Presbyterians, Methodists, Congregationalists, and the other orthodox Protestant sects, a spouseless Father with one Son, who is identical with Himself. . . . We will not mention the multitude of smaller sects, communities, and extravagantly original little heresies in this country which spring up one year to die out the next, like so many spores of fungi after a rainy day.[20]

But it was not just the various sects of American Protestantism that Blavatsky attacked. She saved her harshest language for Christianity writ large as a bloodthirsty world religion. "There has never been a religion in the annals of the world with such a bloody record as Christianity. All the rest, including the traditional fierce fights of the 'chosen people' with their next of kin, the idolatrous tribes of Israel pale before the murderous fanaticism of the alleged followers of Christ!"[21] According to Blavatsky, this bloodshed flowed from the Christian church's goals of squashing Gnostic and Neo-Platonist heresies throughout history. Meanwhile, Blavatsky argued that the priests from the early church forward engaged in their own forms of "*sorcery* for the ages."[22] So, for Blavatsky, Christianity, and particularly the Roman Catholic Church, had on the one hand viciously opposed and marginalized the truth of the ancient wisdom religion and, on the other hand, had run it underground and concealed it within itself in order to maintain church power and religious dogmatism.

Echoing the arguments made by Henry David Thoreau decades earlier, Blavatsky's critique of contemporary American Christianity flipped the Christian/heathen distinction on its head. She particularly rejected the violent image of Indian religion promulgated by evangelical missionaries. She complained, "there is scarcely a report sent by the missionaries from India, Thibet, and China, but laments the diabolical 'obscenity' of the heathen rites." Furthermore, she countered that Christianity had its own obscenities. "When a religion which compelled David to cut off and deliver two hundred foreskins of his enemies before he could become the king's son-in-law (1 Sam. xviii, 25–27) is accepted as a standard by Christians, they would do well not to cast into the teeth of heathen the impudicities of their faiths."[23] For Blavatsky, the Christianity of the Protestant and Catholic churches—which she referred to as "exoteric forms" or "external religious form of worship"—was "pure heathenism," and Catholicism "with its fetish-worshipping, [was] far worse and more pernicious than Hinduism in its most idolatrous aspect."[24] Blavatsky labeled Christianity as the real heathenism, an idolatry of church dogma that falsified the esoteric truths of the wisdom religion. Rather than comparing Hindu religion with Catholicism, as the evangelicals did, she argued that the church was far more idolatrous than the heathen.

It is important to note that Blavatsky's comparison between Christianity and Indian religion gives rise to her use of "Hinduism" in the preceding quote. Just as the Transcendentalists invented "Brahmanism" within their own schemes of comparison, here Blavatsky used "Hinduism" alongside Catholicism, heathenism, and other "-isms." But it is equally important to note that Blavatsky's "Hinduism" is not the same as what most Americans or Indians think of when they use the term today. Blavatsky used a host of terms to refer to religion in India. Reflecting later Orientalist scholarship, she turned to the "Hindu" spelling. She rarely used the term "Hinduism" in her work. "Brahmanism" appears in the index to *Isis Unveiled* and represented the ancient Sanskritic religion that Blavatsky valued most in India. So, whether she called it "Hinduism," "Brahmanism," or just "Hindu," Blavatsky imagined the religion of India to be ancient, philosophical, and esoteric, and the basis for the ancient wisdom religion.

Blavatsky argued that the wisdom religion could unite science and theology and that it was the absolute truth undergirding every major religion in history. She wrote, "What we desire to prove is that underlying every ancient popular religion was the same ancient wisdom-doctrine, one and identical, professed and practiced by the initiates of every country, who alone were aware of its existence and importance."[25] The wisdom religion, though found in every religion, had been entrusted to "initiates" and "sacerdotal castes who had the guardianship of mystical words of power."[26] The wisdom religion was secret, and divulging its secrets meant a death penalty for the initiate. But most important, its origins lay in Hindu religion. "The Eleusinian and Bacchic Mysteries, among the Chaldean Magi, and the Egyptian hierophants" contained the wisdom religion, but it was "with the Hindus from who they were all derived."[27] Though widespread throughout the ancient world, the wisdom religion began in India.

Indeed, for Blavatsky, all civilization traced back to India. She asserted "that it is to India, the country less explored, and less known than any other, that all the other great nations of the world are indebted for their languages, arts, legislature and civilization."[28] Blavatsky constructed a history through which the esoteric wisdom religion was handed down from civilization to civilization:

> It is on the strength of such circumstantial evidence—that of reason and logic—that we affirm that, if Egypt furnished Greece with her civilization, and the latter bequeathed hers to Rome, Egypt herself had, in those unknown ages when Menes reigned, received her laws her social institutions, her arts and her sciences, from pre-Vedic India; and that, therefore, it is in that old initiatrix of the priests—adepts of all the other countries—we must seek for the key to the great mysteries of humanity.[29]

It was in ancient India—the India older than its oldest Vedic texts—that one would find the origins of the great mysteries of esoteric truth. In another passage, Blavatsky tied the Hebrew book of Genesis to the Chaldeans and the Akkadians, and then argued that "the Akkad tribes of Chaldea, Babylonia, and Assyria" were "cognate with the Brahmans of Hindostan."[30] These Akkadians, according to Blavatsky, "were simply emigrants on their way to Asia Minor from India, the cradle of humanity, and their sacerdotal adepts tarried to civilize and initiate a barbarian people."[31] Blavatsky had one answer for the origins of the wisdom religion buried in all the world's religions: "It was imported from India, and the importers were Brahmanical Hindus."[32] All esoteric roads led to India.

Blavatsky's theory that brahminical Hindu religion was the source of the esoteric wisdom religion relied upon a form of comparative religion. Blavatsky's Theosophical comparative religion used analogy in order to find the common root that various religious cultures shared. Rather than a comparative religion that emphasized difference, Theosophical comparative religion focused on similarities, connections, and esoteric meanings. By comparing religions, Blavatsky sought to find the shared core, the wisdom religion, buried deep within the variety of religious texts in the world. For example, through a series of analogies, identifications, and connections, Blavatsky found the origins of the biblical patriarch Abraham in the Mahabharata:

> Now we have to remember that Siva and the Palestinian Baal, or Moloch, and Saturn are identical; that Abraham is held until the present day by the Mohammedan Arabs as Saturn in the Kaaba; that Abraham and Israel were names of Saturn; and that Sanchoiathon tells us that Saturn offered his only begotten son as a sacrifice to his father Ouranos, and even circumcised himself and forced all his household and allies to do the same, to trace unerringly the Biblical myth to its source. But this source is neither Phoenician nor Chaldea; it is purely Indian, and the original of it may be found in the Mahabharata.[33]

In another section, Blavatsky uses three columns to compare the "Indian Pantheon," "The Chaldean," and "The Ophite" to prove that they all share the same tripartite theology of "THE GREAT FIRST CAUSE," "THE DOUBLE–SEXED DEITY," and "the creative Principle—the SON."[34] She then used another diagram to show how these three-part theologies became the Christian trinity. Ancient Hindu religion held a special place in Theosophical comparative religion as the origin of the esoteric wisdom religion that engendered all the other religions of humanity.

Beyond her own brand of Theosophical comparative religion, Blavatsky also rebuked the new field of comparative theology that was emerging during the period. She called comparative theology "a two-edged weapon." On the one hand, there were Christian apologists (perhaps she was thinking of James Freeman Clarke) who "unabashed by the evidence, force comparison in the serenest way" in order to prove that "while [Christianity] teaches us the existence, powers and attributes of an all-wise, all-good Father-God, Brahmanism gives us a multitude of minor gods, and Buddhism none whatever."[35] But the other side of the sword shows how "despite missions, despite armies, despite enforced commercial intercourse, the 'heathens' find nothing in the teachings of Jesus—sublime though some are—that Krishna and Gautama had not taught them before."[36] For this reason, argued Blavatsky, the missionaries to Asia had failed in their quest for converts. Blavatsky argued that comparative theology could as easily prove the superiority of the Hindu as it could the truth of the Christian. "Comparative theology works both ways," she warned.[37]

For Blavatsky, Hindu religion not only provided the origins of the wisdom religion, but also the terms necessary for describing the wisdom religion. She articulated the wisdom religion by repurposing terms derived from Sanskrit sources. Near the end of the introduction to the first volume of *Isis Unveiled*, Blavatsky presented a glossary of terms she employed throughout the work in order "to avoid confusion that might easily arise by the frequent employment of certain terms in a sense

different from that familiar to the reader."[38] Many of the terms were typical for mid-
to late nineteenth-century metaphysical religion: "alchemist," "hermetist," "materi-
alization," "spirit." Other terms Blavatsky took from Sanskrit without changing the
meaning, such as "fakir" and "mantra." But others were Sanskrit words that Blavatsky
put toward her own metaphysical and Theosophical ends. *Âkâsa*, the Sanskrit word
for "sky," becomes, in Blavatsky's hands, "the *occult* electricity; the alkahest of the
alchemists in one sense, or the universal solvent, the same *anima mundi* as the astral
light."[39] Similarly, *Soma*, both the name of a Vedic god and a mystical drink used in
Vedic sacrifices, had its own esoteric meaning: "According to the exoteric explanation the soma is a plant, but, at the same time it is an angel. It forcibly connects the
inner, highest 'spirit' of man, which spirit is an angel like the mystical soma, with
his 'irrational soul,' or astral body, and thus united by the power of the magic drink,
they soar together above physical nature, and participate during life in the beatitude
and ineffable glories of Heaven."[40] Again, making the sort of analogies common in
her thinking, Blavatsky notes that soma "is mystically, and in all respects, the same
that the Eucharistic supper is to the Christian."[41] Because the wisdom religion had its
origins in India, Blavatsky turned to the Sanskrit language for the terms with which
to articulate it.

Of all the terms Blavatsky repurposed in her construction of the wisdom religion,
pitris held an especially important role. The term traditionally referred to dead ancestors venerated in India, but Blavatsky used it to transition from a Western spiritualist understanding of metaphysical power to the ancient wisdom religion grounded
in India. Noting the usual meaning of *pitris* as "spirits of our direct ancestors," she
observed that Hindu "fakirs, and other Eastern wonderworkers, are *mediums*" in
the same manner as the Eddy brothers or other Western spiritualists. But such an
understanding, for Blavatsky, got at only the exoteric meaning and missed what was
really going on. The *pitris* were, in her view, not direct ancestors, but "those of the
human kind or Adamic race; the spirits of *human* races which, on the great scale of
descending evolution, preceded our races of men, and were physically, as well as spiritually, far superior to our modern pigmies."[42] Thus, when mediums—whether an
American in Vermont or a Hindu fakir in Calcutta—produced phenomena, these
were not the spirits of the dead, but rather the spirits of beings farther along the path
of spiritual evolution.

Throughout *Isis Unveiled*, Blavatsky worked to move beyond the spiritualism
that brought her and Olcott together. Her concept of *pitris* pushed spiritualist phenomena beyond the bounds of Western ideas about communing with the dead. For
Blavatsky, mediums did not know the depths they were diving when they summoned
spiritual manifestations. The spirits materializing were so much more than those of
the dead. Spiritualism, as it had been conceived, lacked the philosophy, theology,

and science necessary to fully account for what was going on. Spiritualist phenomena were "wholly misunderstood by themselves. . . . Ignoring the teachings of the past, they have discovered no substitute. . . . In its modern aspect, it is neither a science, a religion, nor a philosophy."[43] Blavatsky went back to the teachings of the past and found a philosophical and religious explanation for the spiritualist's phenomena, the *pitris*. The *pitris*, the evolved race that worked for the medium, explained the "different modes of expressing the yearning of the imprisoned human soul for intercourse with supernatural spheres" that Blavatsky saw in the society around her.[44] For Blavatsky, American religion and spiritualism were turning to India and "the worship of the Vedic *pitris* is fast becoming the worship of the spiritual portion of mankind."[45] Blavatsky redefined a term for Indian ancestral worship to offer a robust explanation for American spiritualism and its relation to the ancient wisdom religion.

Blavatsky's background in spiritualist phenomena turned her attention to those Hindus consistently represented as having metaphysical powers. Throughout *Isis Unveiled* she recounts the remarkable feats of the Hindu fakirs, jugglers, and sanyasins. For Blavatsky, the fakir was the first-level initiate into the occult powers of the wisdom religion. He was "a man who, through the entire subjugation of the matter of his corporeal system, has attained to that state of purification at which the spirit becomes nearly freed from its prison, and can produce wonders."[46] These wonders included producing spiritualist style specters, taming wild tigers, and sleeping with dangerous alligators.[47] The fakir's power worked by channeling magnetic fluid through his body or through the power of the *pitris*.[48] In either case, Blavatsky argued, the power of the fakir and the Western medium shared the same origins. In contrast to the pure fakir stood the "jugglers" who were "neither pure in their modes of living nor considered holy by anyone. . . . *They are generally FEARED and despised by the natives*, for they are *sorcerers*; men practicing the *black art*."[49] These jugglers used their powers of mediumship for making money or other nefarious goals. The third and highest class of metaphysical wonder worker Blavatsky described was the "sanyasin." He was a "living adept" who had achieved a superior level of purity such that he had complete control over the various spirit beings summoned by fakirs and jugglers. He was "a saint of the second degree or initiation, the most holy as the most reverend of them all."[50] Furthermore, the sanyasins served as gurus for the fakir. The fakir exercised his power "under the direct mesmeric influence of a living adept, his *sanyâsin* or guru."[51] The sanyasin–fakir relationship prefigured Blavatsky's later theory of enlightened Mahatmas who took initiates under their auspices and even worked through the bodies of their pupils. More generally, the fakirs, jugglers, and sanyasins contributed to Blavatsky's overall representation of India as a land of occult powers and wonder workers.

Blavatsky's description of the occult power of India in *Isis Unveiled* jumped from religious text to religious text across time and space. At one point she described this method as "the enchanted carpet of the historian."[52] The text was a hodgepodge of Western esotericism and Asian religious sources, held together by Blavatsky's central argument that one primitive and original esoteric wisdom religion united science and theology. Blavatsky's Theosophical comparative religion emphasized similarity, a common core, instead of difference, and quilted together disparate religious cultures through analogy and formal resemblance. All roads led to the wisdom religion. In *Isis Unveiled*, Blavatsky represented India as the cradle of civilization from which the wisdom religion emerged in prehistory and endured in the Sanskrit texts. Sanskrit terms held their own esoteric meanings distinct from their traditional Hindu understandings. But whatever original claim Hindus may have had on the wisdom religion, Blavatsky insisted that it had spread to the rest of the world, East and West. The wisdom religion derived from India, but it did not belong to Hindus. There was no place for exclusivism in Blavatsky's Theosophical vision.

Wisdom Religion or Hindu Sect? The Theosophical Society and the Arya Samaj

Isis Unveiled reflected the growing interest the founders of the Theosophical Society took in India and the ways they imagined and repurposed Indian religion to fit their concept of the ancient wisdom religion. Blavatsky's and Olcott's interest in Hindu religion prompted them to reach out and make contact with religious leaders in India, but their idiosyncratic imagining and repurposing of Indian texts and ideas also ignited conflict between the American Theosophists and their Hindu conversation partners. Blavatsky represented Hindu religion as the origin for a wisdom religion that was much bigger than any one tradition and was found in every religion. Theosophical comparative religion sought to remove boundaries of difference and focus on a shared esoteric core within all religions. But the Theosophical representation of India as cradle of a universal wisdom religion conflicted with a growing reform movement within India that constructed Hindu religion as the pinnacle of spiritual truth. When Theosophical comparative religion encountered Hindu religious reform, conflict ensued.

Olcott and Blavatsky had been hoping to find contacts in India. As Olcott described it, "Our two hearts drew us towards the Orient, our dreams were of India, our chief desire to get into relations with the Asiatic people."[53] Through a chance encounter, Olcott found a relationship with one such person in 1877: Hurrychund Chintamon, president of the Bombay Arya Samaj. After corresponding with him, Chintamon eventually put Olcott into contact with the head of the Arya Samaj,

Swami Dayanand Saraswati. According to Olcott, he described the views of the Theosophical Society to Chintamon "as to the impersonality of God—an Eternal and Omnipresent Principle which, under many different names, was the same in all religions," and Chintamon identified the principles of the Arya Samaj to match those of the Theosophical Society such that the two should join forces.[54] At first blush, it appeared that the conclusions of Theosophical comparative religion echoed those of the Arya Samaj's Hindu religion.

The connection with Saraswati excited Olcott and Blavatsky. Olcott had become fascinated with Vedic philosophy and regarded Saraswati as both a scholar and a religious reformer, describing him as "a great Sanskrit pandit and actually playing the part of a Hindu Luther."[55] The comparison to Luther echoes the statements by Unitarians about Rammohun Roy half a century earlier. Americans consistently looked for the man who would reform Hindu religion. Blavatsky, meanwhile, proclaimed that an adept from the Himalayan Brotherhood inhabited Saraswati's body and that he was well known to that special class of teachers guiding the Society's work. Saraswati was everything the Theosophical twins could hope for in a Hindu contact: a Vedic expert, a religious reformer, and, whether he knew it or not, already a part of their esoteric network of enlightened adepts. In May 1878 the Theosophical Society passed a vote to unite with the Arya Samaj and changed their name to "The Theosophical Society of the Arya Samaj."

No sooner was the merger approved than fissures between the two groups began to appear. When Olcott received an English translation of the Arya Samaj's rules and doctrines, he was shocked to discover that maybe the two groups did not share the same views of God. As he wrote to Chintamon in September 1878, "Either we have been especially unfortunate in misconceiving the ideas of our revered Swami Dayanand, as conveyed to us in his valued letters to me, or he teaches a doctrine to which our Council, and nearly all our Fellows, are forced to dissent."[56] The rules outlined a theology and approach to Hindu texts that the Theosophists found too exclusive and narrow. They declared, "the four texts of the Vedas shall be received and regarded as containing within themselves all that is necessary to constitute them an extraordinary authority in all matters relating to human conduct."[57] The rules also outlined a set of texts that provided an authoritative interpretation of the Vedas. Theologically, according to Olcott's reading, the rules and doctrines posited a personal God "to be adored in set phrases," who must be conciliated or else displeased, something quite different from the broad theology of the Theosophical Society.[58] The personal godhead and supremacy of the Vedas chafed against the Theosophical Society's broad comparative religion that elided difference and celebrated the wisdom religion at the core of all religions.

In December 1878, Olcott and Blavatsky took a ship to India, their "holy land." Face-to-face encounters with Saraswati did not solve the problems. Meeting at Meerut in 1880, Olcott and Saraswati agreed to maintain the independence of the Society and the Samaj but to view each other as allies, nonetheless.[59] The more time Olcott and Blavatsky spent touring India and Ceylon, however, the more skeptical of them Saraswati became. By 1882, Saraswati became so disillusioned that he wondered whether the two groups should even be allies. In March of that year he gave a lecture denouncing the Theosophical Society, and he later published a tract in Hindi summarizing his lecture, titled "Humbuggery of the Theosophists," which presented nine points against the Theosophical Society, Blavatsky, and Olcott.[60] Saraswati claimed that Blavatsky and Olcott had approached him because they "were coming to India to accept the eternal Vedic Faith and become pupils of Swami Dayanand Saraswati" but that they "did neither of these things. They do not believe in any religion, nor do they desire to study any religion."[61] Mirroring Olcott's concerns about Samaj theology, Saraswati claimed that the Theosophists had claimed they believed in God in their letters, but "later, in Meerut, contrary to this, in the presence of Swamiji and other gentlemen, both of them denied that they believe in God."[62] He also accused them of claiming to be atheists and Buddhists at different points. Saraswati went after Blavatsky's Mahatma, Koote Hoomi Lal, "a person nobody has seen or heard of," and labeled all the assertions and phenomena attributed to the Mahatma as falsehoods. Of Blavatsky herself, Saraswati claimed that she had no real knowledge of yoga, but rather her phenomena were the trickery of the mesmerists and jugglers.[63] The Vedic Hindu reformer pulled no punches in his outright rejection of the Theosophists and their attempts to include him in their comparative approach to the wisdom religion.

Olcott responded in *Theosophist*, the Theosophy Society's Indian publication. His response took on Saraswati point by point and argued that it was the swami who had misled him. Printing numerous extracts from their correspondence, Olcott argued that Saraswati had narrowed his theology and that his repudiation of the Theosophists contradicted many of his earlier statements, especially those that confirmed Blavatsky's yoga practice and abilities. Writing about the whole episode between himself and Saraswati in 1895, Olcott stated, "it was evident that the Samaj was *not* identical in character with our Society, but rather a new sect of Hinduism— a Vedic sect accepting Swami Dayanand's authority as supreme judge as to which portions of the Vedas and Shâstras were and were not infallible."[64] The Arya Samaj appeared to Olcott as a "defined sect, a sect of Hinduism, a sect based on the lines traced by its founder." The Theosophical Society had been founded to move beyond sectarianism, dogmatism, and all forms of religious exclusivism, Hindu or otherwise.

It is important to note that the term "Hinduism" Olcott employed in his 1895 retelling of the conflict does not appear in his writings from the 1878–1882 period of the Arya Samaj relationship. Rather, when trying to describe the differences between the breadth of the Theosophical Society and the narrowness of the Arya Samaj, he compared the Arya Samaj to the "Unitarian" Brahmo Samaj, founded by Rammohun Roy, or simply claimed that the Arya Samaj believed in a personal God. In the early 1880s, the idea of Hinduism as a world religion comparable to other world religions and internally divisible into sects had yet to occur to Olcott. In the 1880s, Olcott relied upon Theosophical comparative religion that emphasized sameness. It was only later, after events like the World's Parliament of Religions, when a new model for comparative religion that emphasized difference arose, that he could look back and use the language of sectarianism and the label Hinduism.

Nonetheless, Olcott's problem with Saraswati came down to the difference between Olcott's Theosophical comparative religion and Saraswati's project of Hindu religious reform. Saraswati refused to accept Theosophical comparative religion and the dissolution of religious difference. The Vedas held truth, exclusive truth, and not some truth that all religions shared. As religious historian Stephen Prothero has put it, in Olcott's eyes the blame for the failed relationship between the Society and the Samaj "fell entirely on the shoulders of Saraswati, and that failure consisted essentially in the Swami's refusal to see his religion (as Olcott demanded it be seen) as one among many and his scripture's truths as shared rather than unique."[65] Prothero has also pointed out that Olcott shared a similar approach to Hindu religion as the Christian missionaries he so often criticized. Olcott's ideology of the equality of all religions and the missionary emphasis on religious difference both "refused to recognize the Buddhist and Hindus of India as full human subjects. . . . Thus Olcott's seemingly empathetic embrace of both Buddhism and Hinduism shared with missionary Christianity and British colonialism an imperial thrust."[66]

The "imperial thrust" of Olcott's attempt to fold Saraswati and the Araya Samaj into the wisdom religion ran aground on Saraswati's refusal to let Olcott represent Hindu religion as anything but an authentic and exclusive religion of the Vedas. Furthermore, Saraswati's denunciation of the Theosophists also served as a denunciation of their comparative religious project. Indeed, it is the first resistance to American religious comparativism to emerge in this book. The Protestant comparative religion of Hannah Adams and Joseph Priestley had no space for any Indian voices of resistance. Similarly, the Transcendentalist comparative work of Lydia Maria Child, James Freeman Clarke, and Samuel Johnson went unchecked. The only criticisms these American writers faced came from conservative Protestants working to protect the exclusivity of their truth claims. But because the Theosophists went to India and sought contacts in the East, both in the form of the Mahatmas and the

Indians they met face to face, their comparative project and their representations of Hindu religion were opened to Indian critique.

The Mahatmas: Imagining India's Occult Power

Blavatsky and Olcott did not publicly articulate the existence of the Mahatma Koot Hoomi that Saraswati derided until after their arrival to India in 1879, but, according to Olcott, the Mahatmas had been a part of the Theosophical Society since its founding. Referred to as Adepts, Masters, Masters of Wisdom, or Mahatmas, these men— and they were always men—had reached the highest levels of human and spiritual evolution. According to the Theosophists, Madame Blavatsky's phenomena derived from the Mahatmas' power; they guided her writings, they communicated their doctrines of spiritual evolution and occult power to their initiates, and they authorized the leaders of the movement. Holed up in the inaccessible heights of the Himalayan Mountains, they were the source of all that was powerful in Theosophical wisdom religion. The development of Theosophical thinking about the Mahatmas during the first twenty years of the movement reflected the movement's turn from Western spiritualism to an Eastern occultism. The movement imagined India as the source of religious power, personified by the Mahatmas and their Great White Brotherhood in the Himalayas.

The transition from spiritualism to the Theosophy of Himalayan Ascended Masters began with John King. John King had been appearing at séances in the United States since the 1850s and was often thought to be the earthbound soul of the pirate Henry Morgan. In 1874 John King and another spirit, his daughter Katie King, began to manifest at the home of Jennie and Nelson Holmes in Philadelphia. The mediums would climb into a large cabinet, and the heads and hands belonging to the two spirits would appear in two large windows cut in one side of the cabinet.

On January 4, 1875, Olcott, accompanied by Blavatsky, who lived in Philadelphia at the time, began to test and research the truth of the King manifestations at the Holmes' séance. On his first night in Philadelphia, Olcott himself conversed with John King through rappings. This was not their first encounter. Olcott claimed to have met John King in 1870 in London and, further, that Blavatsky had earlier encountered him in 1861 in Russia, as well as in India and Egypt. John King's rap was "peculiar and easily recognizable from others—a loud, sharp, crackling report," and so Olcott was sure it was him once again in Philadelphia.[67] Two nights later, John King produced two copies of a note that Olcott had stowed in his portfolio. John King closed out the night by offering to forge a check of any national bank with the name of any president, cashier, or other official. Olcott declined, citing that the police did not yet believe in spiritualism. On the morning of January 13, during one of Olcott's unannounced test séances, a faceless John King appeared in the cabinet window wearing a turban, prefiguring the Orientalized John King that was to come.[68] After completing a series of test séances with the Holmes, Olcott decided to move on to investigate another medium at Havana, New York. In one of his last conversations with John King at Philadelphia, the spirit told him he would soon see "a phase of manifestation entirely new to this country," manifestations that "for many ages, have been confined to the temples and pagodas of Egypt and Hindostan."[69] As Olcott's interest shifted from spiritualism to Eastern esotericism, he proved John King right.

In his initial account of John King in the 1875 *People from the Other World*, Olcott did not connect John King to any idea of Mahatmas, Masters, or Adepts. In passing, he mentioned that Blavatsky wore "upon her bosom the mystic jeweled emblem of an Eastern Brotherhood."[70] But what that brotherhood was or what connection Blavatsky had to it remained unclear. Looking back on the events in Philadelphia in his 1895 *Old Diary Leaves*, Olcott decided that John King was no human spirit, but rather "a humbugging elemental" worked by Blavatsky to assist him in his education and initiation. "He was first, John King, an independent personality, then John King, messenger and servant—never the equal—of living adepts, and finally an elemental pure and simple, employed by H.P.B. and a certain other expert in the doing of wonder."[71] Blavatsky herself claimed later that John King's phenomena were the work of one of the Mahatmas through her, the "certain other expert" Olcott described. She wrote, "I went to the Holmeses, and, helped by M. and his *power*, brought out the faces of John King and Katie King from the Astral Light."[72] According to Olcott, Blavatsky was sent by the Mahatmas to transition America from the "cruder mediumism" of spiritualism to "Eastern Spiritualism, or Brahma Vidya," that is, the right knowledge of Brahma.[73] Blavatsky would turn Olcott and America toward the wisdom religion of India.

The Masters made their first contact with Olcott on March 9, 1875, but these first Adepts did not originate in India. Olcott received a letter written in gold ink on green paper, addressed to him as "Brother Neophyte." The letter claimed "Brother 'John'" had brought three Masters to observe Olcott and encouraged him to take care of and watch over "Sister Helen." The letter was signed "TUITIT BEY." A letter from Blavatsky arrived in the same batch of mail, saying that she had been ordered by the Universal Mystic Brotherhood to instruct Olcott in esoteric knowledge. Thus, through Blavatsky, Olcott became an initiate in the Brotherhood of Luxor, the Egyptian section of the Universal Mystic Brotherhood.[74]

Olcott's tutelage under the Egyptian Master did not last long. One night, when Olcott and Blavatsky had finished their night's work on *Isis Unveiled*, Olcott sat in his room reading. A white gleam in the corner of his eye caught his attention.

He turned and dropped his book out of astonishment. "An Oriental clad in white garments, and wearing a head-cloth or turban of amber-striped fabric, hand-embroidered in yellow floss-silk" stood over him. Under his turban the man had long raven-black hair, "his black beard, parted vertically on the chin in the Rajput fashion, was twisted at the ends and carried over the ears; his eyes were alive with soul-fire . . . the eyes of a mentor and a judge, but softened by the love of a father who gazes on a son needing counsel and guidance."[75] Olcott bowed his head and bent his knee. The Master sat in the chair across from him. The two talked about Olcott, Blavatsky, and "the great work that was to be done for humanity," in which Olcott was to take part.[76] A bond had now been established between the Master and Olcott—"a mysterious tie"—that could not be broken.[77] The Master then rose and untwisted the turban on his head, leaving it for Olcott as proof that he had not been "psychologically befooled," saluted him farewell, and was gone. Olcott had found his Master, but even more, he knew that his quest for religious truth would lead him to India. "This visit and his conversation sent my heart at one leap around the globe, across oceans and continents, over sea and land, to India."[78] Soon Olcott and Blavatsky would set sail for the land of their Mahatmas.

In India, Blavatsky's metaphysical phenomena attracted attention and brought her and Olcott into contact with Alfred Percy Sinnett, an Anglo-Indian newspaper editor. Sinnett wanted to know the secret to Blavatsky's abilities. Blavatsky attributed it to the Masters, the Mahatmas. Sinnett wanted access to these Mahatmas and their esoteric wisdom. Blavatsky obliged. A correspondence of mysterious letters thus began between Sinnett and the Masters. Letters from the Mahatmas reached Sinnett through the mail, appeared inside other letters, or even dropped from the ceiling. Based on these letters, Sinnett published *The Occult World* in 1881, the first major description of the Masters and their teachings.[79]

In *The Occult World*, Sinnett described the Masters, whose religious devotion had allowed them to acquire "unusual powers in the nature of such as Europeans would very erroneously call supernatural."[80] The power of the Mahatma was not supernatural, according to Sinnett, but came from occult knowledge of natural laws. Just as modern science had discovered the circulation of blood in the body, "occult science understands the circulation of the life-principle," and this understanding empowered the Masters.[81] These Mahatmas lived secluded lives and could only be accessed by candidates determined to be acceptable for occult training. Sinnett claimed contact with two Masters, Koot Hoomi Lal Sing, or simply K. H., and a more mysterious M.; Sinnett provided little biography of M., who he claimed had been Blavatsky's Master and "occult guardian" since her childhood.[82] However, Sinnett offered a biography of Koot Hoomi, his more intimate Master, as a Punjabi who had been interested in the occult since childhood, went to Europe for his education, and "since then has been fully initiated in the greater knowledge of the East."[83] Koot Hoomi Lal Sing was his "Tibetan Mystic name," taken on after his initiation as an occultist. Along with the phenomenally appearing letters, Koot Hoomi produced other phenomena, such as materializing a brooch of Sinnett's wife insider her picnic cushion. For Sinnett, Koot Hoomi represented the occult power available to the initiate—a power that, like Olcott's turbaned visitor, was represented as Indian and Hindu.

The Mahatmas, as described by Sinnett, introduced Americans to a representation of Hindu religion as an occult power wielded by holy Indian men. Such an image had its roots in earlier missionary literature reports of fakirs and yogis performing remarkable physical feats and in the Transcendentalist representation of Eastern mysticism and contemplation. Blavatsky's description of the fakirs, jugglers, and sanyasins in *Isis Unveiled* also prefigured the image of the powerful and turbaned Mahatma. But, as Kirin Narayan has noted, the Mahatmas signaled a change in American conceptions of Hindu holy men. "With these masters as guides, Hindu holy men were allowed the symbolic freedom to leave their beds of nails and take off for the spiritual heights of the Himalayas."[84] The Mahatmas paved the way for later images of Hindu holy men in American culture and for gurus who would come to the United States in the flesh at the end of the century. Koot Hoomi paved the way for later American images of Hindu mystical power such as Hadji, the snake-charming Calcutta orphan in the 1960s television cartoon *Jonny Quest*.

Thus, Koot Hoomi prefigured a twentieth-century American cultural image that Jane Iwamura has dubbed the "Oriental Monk." As Iwamura described him, the Oriental Monk was defined by "his spiritual commitment, his calm demeanor, his Asian face, his manner of dress, and—most obviously—his peculiar gendered character."[85] But more important than this Oriental Monk's image was his function. "Oriental wisdom and spiritual insight is passed from the Oriental Monk figure to the West through the *bridge figure* of the child. Ultimately, the Oriental Monk and his apprentice(s) represent future salvation of the dominant culture—they embody a revitalized hope of saving the West from capitalist greed, brute force, totalitarian rule, and spiritless technology."[86] As identified by Iwamura, the Oriental Monks suited the needs and fears of the twentieth-century United States. Similarly, Rammohun Roy was an Oriental Monk bringing wisdom to the debates among early nineteenth-century New England Protestants. The Mahatmas served the needs of the late nineteenth century, especially the need to unite science and religion. Through the bridge figures of Blavatsky, Sinnett, Olcott, and other Theosophists, their occult science and wisdom religion reached the West. The Mahatmas were Hindu Oriental Monks for America: turbaned men from India, secluded in their mystical Himalayan Lodge, who sent forth ageless wisdom religion through their initiates that would solve the conflict between science and religion and save Western culture.

The Esoteric Path of Raja Yoga

The Mahatmas represented an esoteric power buried deep in India and accessible to only a select few, but the Theosophists also presented an esoteric path toward spiritual evolution that was more widely available: yoga. Blavatsky and American Theosophical writer William Quan Judge presented two different forms of yoga: a superior esoteric yoga that served as a path toward spiritual development, and an inferior exoteric yoga of fleshy body postures and self-denial. In their published writings Blavatsky and Judge warned Theosophical seekers of the danger of exoteric hatha, or postural, yoga and praised the higher raja forms of yoga practice. Theosophists represented Hindu religion as a source of religious power and spiritual development, but one had to turn to the proper resources. Hindu power could be dangerous.

Blavatsky published *The Secret Doctrine*, which historian Bruce Campbell has called her "masterwork," in 1888. In the two-volume text, Blavatsky shifts noticeably from the form of comparative religion that framed *Isis Unveiled*. While in *Isis*, India represented the origin of the wisdom religion in a pre-Vedic esotericism, in *The Secret Doctrine* the wisdom religion no longer originates in India and the Vedas. Rather, Blavatsky turned to a different ancient text, one that had been revealed to her and her alone: the Book of Dzyan. In *The Secret Doctrine*, Blavatsky presents stanzas from the Book of Dzyan followed by commentary. Blavatsky described the Book of Dzyan as one "utterly unknown to our Philologists" but whose "main body of the Doctrines given is found scattered throughout hundreds and thousands of Sanskrit MSS" and "are in every instance hinted at in the almost countless volumes of Brahminical, Chinese, and Tibetan temple-literature."[87] This book, revealed to Blavatsky alone, provided a new origin for the wisdom religion and displaced Indian religious texts as the origin.

While the Vedas no longer held pride of place as the origin of the wisdom religion, now termed the "Secret Doctrine" in its eponymous text, yoga became a path of esoteric wisdom for the occultist drawn from Indian religious sources. For example, in the text Blavatsky outlined a septenary division of the human constitution. She gave a chart that broke down the seven terms for the seven different "principles of man" into three columns: Esoteric Buddhism, Vedantic, and Taraka Raja Yoga.[88] Each of these three occult systems contained the same basic truth of the Secret Doctrine. Yoga was one esoteric path among many.

The goal of yoga, according to Blavatsky, was secret wisdom and knowledge of the higher spiritual self, attained through experiences of ecstasy. In her 1889 practical manual *The Key to Theosophy*, Blavatsky argued for the necessity of such ecstatic experience for true spiritual self-knowledge. She also linked this ecstasy to yoga. Such ecstasy "is, indeed, identical with that state which is known in India as *Samadhi*. The latter is practiced by the Yogis, who facilitate it by the greatest abstinence in food and drink, and mentally by an incessant endeavor to purify and elevate the mind."[89] Blavatsky emphasized, however, that one must engage in the proper forms of yoga for spiritual progress. She distinguished between hatha yoga, the yoga of bodily postures, and raja yoga. She insisted that the would-be occultist stick to raja yoga and not tamper with hatha yoga. "The *Hatha* so called was and still is discountenanced by the Arhats. It is injurious to the health and alone can never develop into Raj Yoga."[90] Blavatsky did not outline the practical contents of raja yoga, but rather consistently defined it in contrast to the physical postures of hatha.

William Quan Judge, an influential leader of the American branch of the Theosophical Society, fleshed out Blavatsky's distinction between raja and hatha yoga by connecting raja yoga to the second century B.C.E. Indian sage Patanjali and his Yoga Sutras. In 1889 Judge published an "interpretation" of Patanjali's Yoga Sutra, titled *The Yoga Aphorisms of Patanjali*. The work was an interpretation, rather than a translation, meant to "interpret it to Western minds unfamiliar with the Hindu modes of expression, and equally unaccustomed to their philosophy and logic."[91] For Judge, Patanjali presented a yogic path toward knowledge and virtue. He granted that Patanjali's text made reference to postures and breathing practices typical of hatha yoga, but cautioned that these practices were "for the purpose of extenuating certain mental afflictions or for the more easy attainment of the concentration of mind."[92] The central component of Patanjali's system, and of raja yoga more generally, was concentration. The first aphorism of Judge's interpretation read: "Assuredly, the exposition of Yoga, or Concentration, is now to be made."[93] For Judge, yoga meant the attainment of " 'one-pointedness,' or the power to apply the mind, at any moment to the consideration of a single point of thought, to the exclusion of all else."[94] Postures and breathing techniques distracted from the mental and spiritual goal. True yoga, beneficial yoga, focused on the development of the metaphysical mind. As he wrote elsewhere, "the true student of Rāja Yoga knows that everything has its origin in MIND; that even this Universe is passing before the Divine Mind of the images he desires to appear."[95] Judge used Patanjali's text to build on Blavatsky's earlier contrast between raja and hatha yoga. He represented raja yoga as the superior practice of concentration, leading to knowledge of the Divine Mind.

Despite these arguments from Blavatsky and Judge, American Theosophists continued to show interest in hatha yoga, as evidenced by the number of answers to questions about hatha practice that Judge published in various Theosophical journals. Judge presented three main arguments against hatha yoga for his Theosophical readers. First, Judge ruled that hatha yoga was inferior because it was not about concentration leading to spiritual development, but instead resulted in "psychic development at the delay or expense of the spiritual nature."[96] It was a "physical practice for physical results," while raja yoga "aims at changes of the Inner Nature."[97] Second, Judge argued, Western students faced "racial difficulties" in the pursuit of hatha yoga that would limit their abilities. As he wrote, "partial concentration of mind, even—the first step for any practical use of the recondite laws of nature—is conspicuously absent from our people."[98] Drawing on a long-standing American view of the Hindus as a race that was naturally more mystical than Americans, Judge argued that the Hindu's racial essence prepared him for the physical and psychic practices of hatha yoga in ways that the American lacked. American postural yoga was, in a sense, unnatural. Finally, hatha yoga was downright dangerous for Americans. In an 1891 circular to the correspondence group within the Eastern School of Theosophy, Judge described an experiment he had recently performed where a doctor tracked the pulse of a person as he practiced hatha breathing techniques. The experiment found a reduction of the pulse by 20 beats in 14 minutes, "an enormous alteration which might if persisted in be very injurious."[99] This experiment is in some ways a nineteenth-century precursor to the meditation studies and brain scans of the twenty-first century. It is also an inversion of current arguments for the physical benefits of yoga postures and breathing techniques. The medical experiment led Judge to conclude that such practice required a guide and regulations for avoiding such physical effects, neither of which was available in America. Thus, "there is great danger and no benefit in pursuing hatha yoga without a guide."[100] Hatha yoga represented the dangerous side of the Theosophical turn to India.[101]

Theosophical warnings against hatha and postural yoga set the tone for the introduction of yoga in the United States. Swami Vivekananda would arrive on the heels of Judge's writings about yoga and publish his own yoga text, *Raja Yoga*, in 1896. Like Judge, Vivekananda also identified raja yoga with the sutras of Patanjali. Historian Elizabeth De Michelis has pointed out that there is nothing in Patanjali's text connecting it to raja yoga, and that this misidentification between the two "betrays a cognitive confusion which causes a typically esoteric variety of yoga (further occultized by Vivekananda and his followers) to be understood not only in terms of mainstream yoga, but as the most important and universally applicable form of yoga."[102] Building on De Michelis, historian Mark Singleton has argued that hatha practice was taboo for English-speaking yoga gurus after Vivekananda until well into the twentieth century.[103] Theosophical representations of yoga shaped larger American understandings of hatha yoga as dangerous and raja yoga as spiritually progressive.

Such representations of hatha yoga built on earlier missionary images of self-inflicted tortures of the fakir and hook-swinger. Meanwhile, raja yoga represented the esoteric path to wisdom, and Patanjali's text served as a Hindu guide to self-realization.

Hindu Religions and Occult Power in the United States

From the appearance of the Hindu or Arab man in Chittenden, Vermont, through William Q. Judge's warnings about the physical effects of hatha yoga, Theosophists continually imagined Hindu religions as a source of occult and esoteric power. Powerful agents carried marks of Oriental-ness and often specifically Hindu-ness: the turbaned Hindu-Arab spirit that visited Chittenden, the turbaned John King, the Rajput Mahatma that visited Olcott, Master Koot Hoomi, and the dangers of hatha yoga. Though a variety of representations of Hindu religions emerged in Theosophical circles from the 1870s through the 1890s, they all shared a common assumption that esoteric and occult power resided in India and Hindu religious culture.

American Theosophists represented Hindu religion and India as mystical, otherworldly, and detached from social and political realities. Though the Theosophical Society played an important role in Indian politics during the early twentieth century, American Theosophists, on the other hand, did not imagine India as a colonial territory or Hindu religion as a nationalist force. The writings of the first generation of Theosophists imagined Hindu religions as mystical, individual, and esoteric. As historian of religions Richard King has argued, "from within this interpretive paradigm one becomes predisposed to interpreting mystical doctrines, texts, traditions, and authors in a manner that makes them appear antisocial and otherworldly in orientation" and leads to "a characterization of 'mystics' as largely uninterested in or antithetical to social, ecclesiastical and political authority."[104] Theosophical representations of Hindu religion played a major role in rendering Hindu religion and India as mystical in this sense. The Theosophical representations of Hindu religion and yoga also paved the way for other esoteric and occult representations that followed in the early twentieth century, for example, the Tantrik Order in America, founded by Pierre Bernard and Ida Craddock's Church of Yoga.[105]

The rendering of Hindu religions as mystical constructed a contrast between the mysticism of Hindus, on the one hand, and the rationalism of Americans, on the other. As King has pointed out, "the association of religions such as Hinduism and Buddhism with mysticism and the stereotype of the navel-gazing, antisocial and otherworldly mystic has come to function as on the most prevailing cultural representation of Indian religion and culture in the last few centuries."[106] The mystical

Hindu could not be a political or social actor. Until Gandhi shattered this image in the twentieth century, Hinduism could not be connected with political change in the minds of Americans. The division between mystical India, with its Hindu religions, and rational America, with its Protestantism, structured understandings of American national identity that imagined American-ness in contrast to the Hindu Other throughout the latter half of the nineteenth century.

6   Putting the "Religions" in the World's Parliament of Religions

THE COLUMBIAN LIBERTY Bell tolled ten times. Each tone symbolized one of the "ten chief religions of the world": Christianity, Judaism, Islam, Buddhism, Hinduism, Jainism, Zoroastrianism, Taoism, Shintoism, and Confucianism. At ten o'clock on September 11, 1893, a parade of the world's religions walked down the aisle of the Hall of Columbus inside the Art Palace in downtown Chicago. The "stately column [was] composed of men of many tongues, of many lands, of many races: disciples of Christ, of Mohammed, of Buddha, of Brahma, of Confucius, in the name of a common God for the glorification of the Eternal Father." Observers noted the "strange robes, turbans and tunics" that revealed how "peculiar modes of dress were indicative of different religions." Despite their differences, all the members of this sacred cavalcade were part of "a grand intermingling of religions . . . a gathering under the star of Christianity, whose steady beaming draws wise men of the East to the unfading brightness and growing splendor of the Prince of Peace."[1] Like the schoolbooks and magazines of American national culture, the Parliament reinforced the American Protestant establishment. The optimistic, colorful, and grand opening of the World's Parliament of Religions set the tone for the rest of the meetings. The themes condensed into this opening ceremony—themes of difference (religion, language, dress, etc.) and the superiority of white American Christianity—echoed through the Parliament for the rest of its seventeen-day existence.

Organized as part of the World's Columbian Exposition, the Parliament brought representatives of religious cultures from around the world together in an attempt "to unite all Religion against all irreligion."[2] As such, the Parliament offered a unique opportunity for foreign non-Christian religions to represent themselves on American soil to an American audience. But the Parliament has also become a cipher for scholars of religion in America and historians of religious studies. Religious historian Kathryn Lofton has noted that, in the Parliament, "every thread of subsequent historiography may be and has been read." The list is quite long:

> The mystique and manipulations of pluralism; the pervasive persistence of American Protestantism; the inclusivity, exclusivity, decline, and fall of liberalism; the optimism of ecumenism; the appeal of the East; and the classifications of the West. Through the expository format and missionary advocacies of the Parliament, through its exhibitions and exoticism, its formalism and Midwestern populism, the World's Parliament becomes the right pivot for its contemporaneous advocates and for its subsequent historians, signaling the change over time every historian of U.S. religion needs in their plot to plot modern religious experience.[3]

To paraphrase Jonathan Z. Smith, like the category of "religion" itself, this does not mean that the Parliament cannot be defined, but rather that it can be defined in any number of ways.[4]

Historians have invested the World's Parliament of Religions with a variety of meanings and interpretations because it was an event that, despite its rhetoric of unity, exhibited a variety of conflicting understandings of what "religion" was and what it was supposed to do. Even historian of religions Richard Hughes Seager, who has most often read the Parliament as the dawn of religious pluralism in America, admitted that "taken as a whole, the proceedings displayed an elliptical quality, with visions of unity and claims of uniqueness alternately seizing the spotlight. . . . As the drama unfolded, the Parliament's overall significance remained ambiguously— some would later say dangerously—protean and obscure."[5] The Parliament papers present an archive so vast, wide, and conflicting that a scholar may find any number of historical significances. Like the category of "religion," the Parliament is best approached as an invention whose meaning is always up for grabs—now and in 1893. It was a cacophony of voices attempting to articulate the definitions, categories, and boundaries of what counted as religion in the United States and the world. Thus, when representations of religion in India emerged on the floor of the Parliament, they were always invested in this question of whether they were real "religion" or not. Speakers at the Parliament sought to differentiate Hinduism, a world religion with universal value, from what they described as superstitious, idolatrous, and degrading forms of religion in India.

The Boundaries of the Parliament

The Parliament was an argument about the nature of "religion" that took place within a specific institutional context. That context included and excluded some voices from the start. Christian voices held the most powerful place in the Parliament, beginning with the initial planning stages. Church historian Martin E. Marty described the organizers of the Parliament as "theological modernists" who "were male members of the privileged subculture, almost all of them Protestant."[6] Marty marked a "cosmopolitan habit" across American Protestantism that sought "a universal outlook, to overcome the provincialism that they thought afflicted religion."[7] The Parliament was one expression of this Protestant cosmopolitan habit.

Charles Carroll Bonney represented the most liberal wing of those involved in the organization of the Parliament. Bonney was a member of the Swedenborgian church, and Marty described him as "an essentialist who believed that there were common essentials by which everyone may be saved, in all the religions."[8] In the summer of 1889 Bonney came up with the idea for "a series of congresses for the consideration of the greatest themes in which mankind is interested, and so comprehensive as to include representatives from all parts of the earth."[9] He argued that the coming World's Fair of 1893 would be the perfect event at which to hold these congresses. The fair ought to be more than an exhibition "of the material triumphs, industrial achievements, and mechanical victories of man.... Something higher and nobler is demanded by the progressive spirit of the present age."[10] These congresses were to cover topics such as government, finance, literature, science, education, and religion and to be "more widely representative of all peoples and nations and tongues than any assemblage which has ever yet been convened."[11] For Bonney, the coming World's Fair needed to represent culture, as well as exhibit material and technology.

Lyman J. Gage, president of the World's Columbian Exposition, as the fair came to be known, picked up Bonney's plans and made Bonney chairman of the World's Congress Auxiliary of the World's Columbian Exposition in 1890. The Auxiliary set up a series of congresses as part of the Exposition that covered twenty different departments, including women's progress, the public press, temperance, medicine, music, literature, and, of course, religion. Two hundred distinct congresses were held as part of the various departments, and the proceedings were so extensive that a single volume including all of their programs numbered 160 pages.[12]

Bonney appointed Rev. John Henry Barrows, a Presbyterian minister, as chairman of the General Committee on Religious Congresses of the World's Congress Auxiliary. Barrows represented the conservative wing of the Parliament's organizers. Whereas Bonney saw truth in all religions, Barrows believed Christianity to be the only truly universal religion. He also saw the Parliament as a chance to prove the superiority of American Christianity over the rest of the world's religions. It was America's privileged position as a Christian nation that made the Parliament possible. As he proclaimed in his welcoming speech,

> You agree with the great mass of Christian scholars in America in believing that Christendom may proudly hold up this Congress of Faiths as a torch of truth and of love which may prove the morning star of the twentieth century. There is a true and noble sense in which America is a Christian nation. . . . This does not mean, of course, that the church and state are united. In America they are separated, and in this land the widest spiritual and intellectual freedom is realized.[13]

Barrows ambivalently imagined the Parliament as a project of religious unity and as a place to exhibit the triumph of Christianity. Joining Barrows was a committee of clergymen that included one Jewish rabbi, one Catholic priest, and fourteen Protestant ministers from different church denominations. Under Barrows's leadership, the Parliament became "the crowning glory of the great series of ecumenical councils" that made up the Religious Congresses. For some, the Parliament was the crowning achievement of the whole Exposition. As one observer noted, "the World's Parliament of Religions will stand out in history as the greatest event of the World's Columbian year."[14]

Barrows and the committee composed a preliminary address that outlined goals for the Parliament. This address offered the first glimpse into the boundaries of what would count as religion at the Parliament. The address began,

> Believing that God is, and that he has not left himself without witness; believing that the influence of Religion tends to advance the general welfare, and is the most vital force in the social order of every people, and convinced that of a truth God is no respecter of person, but that in every nation he that feareth him and worketh righteousness is accepted of him, we affectionately invite the representatives of all faiths to aid us in presenting to the world, at the Exposition of 1893, the religious harmonies and unities of humanity, and also in showing forth the moral and spiritual agencies which are at the root of human progress.[15]

Four aspects of religion, as the committee imagined it, appeared in this first sentence. First, religion involved belief. Second, it involved a monotheistic God. Third, religion brought about social order. Fourth, religion motivated people toward some sort of work of "righteousness" or some other good works. So, for the Parliament organizers, religion was monotheistic belief that organized society and that motivated people to do good works. They also imagined that this sort of religion could be found everywhere in the world and that there were some harmonies or unities that related the different forms of religion. The remainder of the address noted that religion is also important for promoting "Temperance and Social Purity," has a "harmony with true Science," has "dominance in the higher institutions of learning," and values "the weekly rest-day on religious grounds."[16] This "religion," with its monotheism and its focus on belief and social reform work, harmony with science, and Sabbatarianism, was founded on the assumptions and model of late nineteenth-century American liberal Protestantism.

The committee sent the preliminary address to over three thousand religious leaders around the world and began the process of assembling delegates from various religious traditions. The organizers on the committee chose to seek out delegates individually, rather than through ecclesiastical bodies or organizations, in order to secure delegates "whose breadth of view, catholicity of temper, full confidence in the power of truth to bear full light of day, and hopeful faith that the Spirit of God . . . naturally made them friends of an effort to bring into amicable conference the religious leaders of mankind."[17] Despite some holdouts—the archbishop of Canterbury and the sultan of Turkey each refused to participate or lend any assistance to the Parliament—the committee was able to secure delegates from each of their ten "world religions" throughout the world.

Liberal Protestant assumptions marked the selection of who would come to the Parliament. Mormons and Native Americans had no representation at the Parliament—the former because of strong anti-Mormon sentiments among American Protestants and the latter because their form of religious life was considered "tribal." Many conservative Protestants did not attend, and evangelical preachers A. C. Dixon and Dwight Moody actively denounced the Parliament. In terms of Asian delegates, contemplative Zen Buddhism was represented at the Parliament, while more ritualistic Tibetan Buddhism was not. Swami Vivekananda represented "Hinduism" through his monotheistic Vedanta philosophy, but *bhakti* devotionalism had no Parliament representative. In short, Parliament organizers selected delegates who matched the rational, logocentric, socially minded, intellectual, and scientifically commensurate ideals of American Protestantism and ignored more ritualized, popular, or mystical forms of religions.

The weekend before the opening of the Parliament, Henry Barrows invited the Buddhist delegates and the Greek Orthodox archbishop of Zante to the service at his First Presbyterian Church. Barrows described a baptism, the reception of three Chinese converts, and an address by the archbishop "as if the Parliament had already opened beneath the splendor of the Cross."[18] From Bonney's idea for a set of cultural congresses through Barrows's and the committee's selection of the delegates, the Parliament emerged through an American Protestant understanding of what counted as religion. The organizers believed that the Parliament would find the unity or "religion" among the plurality of religions in the United States and around the world. It was an attempt at pluralism. But the pluralism the Parliament sought remained distinctly Protestant in its definition of religion.

Putting the "Religion" in "Unite all Religion"

As Charles Carroll Bonney put it (cited earlier), the Parliament would "unite all Religion against all irreligion." Yet, throughout the Parliament it was never clear precisely what that "Religion" was. What was clear was that whatever religion was, it included Christianity. Parliament speakers articulated a variety of definitions of religion on the floor of the Parliament, but they all revolved around the relationship between Christianity and its others. These definitions and the relationship between Christianity and rest of the religions set the ground rules within which South Asian delegates would present themselves and their own religions.

For many Christian delegates, religion meant Christianity and Christianity only. These exclusivists often sought to separate the category of religion into subcategories in order to champion Christianity as the only true religion.[19] Joseph Cook, an evangelical preacher from Boston, offered one clear example of the exclusivist position. Barrows described Cook's "distinguished" orthodoxy before the preacher took the platform to deliver his address.[20] Cook quickly proved his orthodoxy by describing true religion as love of God as Lord and Savior and salvation from "the love of sin and its guilt." Using lines from Lady Macbeth as a metaphor for human sin, Cook asked of various non-Christian religions, "Can you wash our red, right hands?"[21] Cook finally argued for the only religion that can cleanse Lady Macbeth and everyone else. "How am I to keep peace with myself, my God and my record of sin except by looking on the Cross?"[22] For Cook, only Christianity offered God as "Savior and Lord" and could cleanse away sin. Only Christianity counted as religion.

Cook also argued that Christianity could lay exclusive claim to the title "religion" because it coalesced with modern science. He was deeply concerned that religion be able to answer science. As he said, "The world expects to hear from us in this

Parliament no drivel, but something fit to be professed face to face with the crackling artillery of the science of our time."[23] Cook understood religion as consisting of both Christianity and science: "If I were called upon to select watchwords for a universal religion, they should be these two: 1. Self-Surrender to the Self-Evident in Science and Scripture 2. Imitation of the Mind that was in Christ."[24] For Cook, religion was Christ in harmony with science.

Congregationalist minister Lyman Abbot showed a more gracious, if equally exclusivist, side of Christian thought about other religions in his address. Abbot argued that human beings are essentially religious. In his view, there was a Universal Religion at the source of all religions. As he put it, "Religion is the mother of all religions, not the child. . . . And the temples and priests and rituals that cover this round globe of ours have not made religion; they have been born of the religion that is inherent in the soul."[25] He then described this religion: "It is such a perception of the infinite as produces an influence on the moral character and conduct of man."[26] With his definition of religion in general deployed, Abbot made moves similar to those of Cook. He argued that Christianity offered the only complete perception and understanding of the infinite.

Near the end of his address, he welcomed the delegates from various religions all around the world. He said how glad he was to "believe that they have been seeking to know . . . the Divine" and that "we are glad to know what they have to tell us, but what we are gladdest of all about is that we can tell them what we have found in our search, and that we have found the Christ."[27] This led him to his point that "we believe no other revelation transcends and none other equals" Jesus Christ and that "we find in Christ one thing that we have not been able to find in any other of the manifestations of the religious life of the world." [28] For Abbot, then, religion was the human longing for the divine, and this longing brought with it morality and certain kinds of conduct. Christianity alone fulfilled this longing perfectly through Jesus.

William C. Wilkinson, professor at the Chautauqua School of Theology, used the lives of Jesus and the apostle Paul to argue that what is "fundamental, central, in religion, any religion, all religion, [is] namely, its undertaking to *save*. Whatever religion fallaciously offers to save is, unless I have misunderstood him, according to Jesus a false religion."[29] Wilkinson affirmed that only Christianity offered salvation and, therefore, all other religions were not religion at all but only "pathetic and partly successful, gropings after God . . . gropings downward, not upward."[30] By centralizing salvation as the earmark of religion and then holding on to the death and resurrection of Jesus as the only source of salvation, Wilkinson immediately placed the "ethnic religions," as he called them, in a category of "erring religions" or "false religion." He concluded that "men need to be saved *from* false religion; they are in no way saved *by* false religion."[31] Real true religion, capital-R "Religion," saved people, and only Christianity could do that.

Wilkinson's address infuriated Julia Ward Howe, a religious liberal, friend of James Freeman Clarke, and author of "The Battle Hymn of the Republic." She immediately rose to reproach him for his exclusiveness. Wanting to broaden the category of religion beyond only Christianity, she outlined her own definition of religion. "I think you will say that [religion] is aspiration, the pursuit of the divine in the human; the sacrifice of everything to duty for the sake of God and of humanity and of our own individual dignity."[32] Howe was clear to distinguish magic from religion: "In some countries magic passes for religion, and that is one thing I wish, in view particularly of the ethnic faiths, could be made very prominent—that religion is not magic."[33]

Magic, for Howe, involved priests fooling people into thinking charms or rituals would bring them good luck, prosperity, or immortality. She then moved on to decry the Muslim pilgrimage to Mecca for spreading disease. "This scourge is generated by a pilgrimage which pious Mohammedans—there may be some present—are led to suppose is for the benefits of their souls . . . this pilgrimage is not religion; a pilgrimage which poisons whole continents and sweeps away men, women and children by thousands has nothing to do with religion at all."[34] Howe also labeled anything that "puts one individual absolutely over others," especially one gender over the other, or anything "which sacrifices women to the brutality of men" as "no religion."[35] Religion for Howe was equalitarian, progressive, theistic, and demanded sacrifice for the greater good. Anything hierarchical, ritualistic, traditionalistic, or misogynistic could not be rightfully labeled religion.

While Howe focused mostly on what was not religion, other more inclusive Christians, such as the Unitarian Thomas Wentworth Higginson, tried to label what was shared across all religions. In his address, Higginson labeled this common denominator of religions the "sympathy of religions." Higginson had been working on this argument since 1870 and had much in common with the search for Universal Religion that animated Samuel Johnson, Lydia Maria Child, and James Freeman Clarke.[36] For Higginson, "their point of sympathy lies in what they have sublimely created through longing imagination. In all these faiths are the same alloy of human superstition . . . all seek after God, if haply they might find him."[37] Christianity is not excluded from this "alloy of superstition." Rather, Higginson argued, Christianity's claims to exclusive truths were wrongheaded. The final line of his address stood as a motto for the generations of religious liberals to follow: "give us God's pure air, and teach us the broadest religion is the best."[38] Higginson's sympathy of religions plowed down the hierarchy created by speakers like Wilkinson and Cook and left a level playing field in its wake, wherein every religion was one form of the human attempt to reach the divine. However, a deep monotheism—a God—still sat at the center of Higginson's sympathy of religions.

Higginson held a radical inclusive position, but George T. Candlin, a missionary to China, presented a more conservative inclusive view. Echoing James Freeman Clarke's argument in *Ten Great Religions*, Candlin argued that all religions held some truth, but only Christianity held the complete truth. He claimed that "all religion whatever in any age or country is in its essential spring good and not evil."[39] The problem came when religion was "burdened with never so much error, with never so much superstition."[40] Despite the flaws of superstition, religion was "the root of all morality," "the spring of every philosophy," "the incentive to every science," and the "animating soul of every civilized nation."[41] While Candlin admitted that Christianity held some error and superstition within it, he quickly pointed out the places where it is the worst. "India may be as bad as you please under the reign of Brahmanism; China, Thibet, and Corea as degraded as you choose under that of Buddhism and Confucianism; Arabia and Turkey as cruel and lustful as you can imagine under Mohammedanism; Africa as savage as you care to suppose with its dumb, dark fetichisms [*sic*]; all would be worse without these."[42] Religion was the only bright spot in these otherwise dark nations. Candlin's religion was a rational, theistic, scientific, and civilizing religion.

All of these Christians shared commonalities in their definitions of religion. First of all, they were all monotheistic. There was a God to which humans were striving, connecting, chasing, or somehow reaching, and this God, if gendered, was male. Second, morality was central to most of these speakers. Religion brought with it a moral code for evaluating the world and human behavior. Howe, Abbot, and Candlin also saw religion as generating social action through this moral code. Third, for Candlin and Cook, religion cooperated with science. Religion was rational and intellectual, and it confirmed the findings of science. Finally, all of these Christians constructed outside categories against which religion was defined. "Ethnic religion," "erring," "false religion," "superstition," and "magic" were all words that marked the limits of religion. These non-religions were characterized by ritual, mysticism, traditionalism, and hierarchy. While Asian and other non-Christian traditions were lumped into this category, the real target of this rhetoric was American Catholicism. At this time, Catholicism was an ethnic religion of Poles, Italians, Germans, and French, and while there were assimilationist Irish Catholics at the Parliament, the latest ethnic immigrants were not represented. Catholicism was also associated with hierarchy and ritual—two other aspects of the categories of "non-religion." So, like the assumptions guiding the Parliament's organization, the definition of religion constructed by a variety of Protestants on the floor of the Parliament reflected Protestant assumptions. As the majority of the organizing committee and the dominant delegation to the Parliament, Protestants authorized a definition of religion as monotheistic, rational, scientific, moral, socially progressive, egalitarian, and socially organizing. When they rose to speak at the Parliament, South Asians would have to find ways to engage this authorized definition if they wished to be heard.

The Religion of Young India

The stated goal of the Parliament was unity—an erasure of difference. However, to erase difference on one level required the highlighting of difference on another. Speakers at the Parliament revealed the unity among a plurality of religions by erasing difference and fitting all religious culture into a Protestant definition of religion. "Uniting all Religion against irreligion" meant deciding whether non-Christian beliefs and practices were religion or something else—some form of irreligion. In the case of India, Christian missionaries from India as well as Indian themselves constructed a difference between Hinduism, a religion in India that fit the authoritative Protestant model of religion, and beliefs and practices in India that were not "real" religion. These other religions, or irreligions, fell into the categories of idolatry, magic, superstition, heathenism, ethnic religion, or Brahmanism. Thus, Hinduism, as the world religion of India, emerged at the Parliament through a process of distinguishing what aspects of Indian culture were *really* religion and which were not. Speakers, both Hindu and Christian, united Hinduism against all irreligion.

Missionary to India Robert A. Hume saw the difference between Hindus and Christians in terms of inherent differences of mind. Drawing on themes that dated back to the Transcendentalists, Hume described how "the Hindu mind is supremely introspective" and has "an intense longing for comprehensiveness," whereas the Western mind "is practical and logical." So, Hume asked, "how then, could a mind which first and foremost is practical, logical, and executive, understand and repeat a mind which cares nothing for external facts or for consistency; which does not think it may act, nor act as it thinks?"[43] Like Emerson and Thoreau before him, Hume saw the West and the Hindu as having something to offer one another. The Hindu would teach the West to be introspective and holistic, while the West would give Hindus the skills of rationality. It was Emerson's Plato all over again.

Despite his vision of an East–West exchange, Hume still found plenty of problems in Hinduism. Hume described "Hinduism at its worst. Polytheism, idolatry, a mythology explained by the Hindus themselves as teaching puerilities and sensualities in its many deities, caste rampant, ignorance widespread and profound."[44] He delineated this "popular" Hinduism from "the educated Hindu [who] now believes in the scientific spirit of the West . . . dissatisfied with the mechanical and unethical teachings of popular Hinduism."[45] These new Hindus had benefited from colonial contact with Christians and the history of Hinduism that Christians had given them. "Fifty years ago neither Hindu nor Christian could give a comprehensive and rational account of the history of Hinduism. For more than half a century western thought has been studying by the scientific method the origin and growth of religious ideas and practices in India." Hume argued that this Western study had uncovered "how idolatry and caste and the superstitions of modern Hinduism had their roots in better things."[46] Hume drew on the declension narrative that had characterized representations of Indians throughout the century. He argued that the West gave Hindus a history, and with it the understanding that contemporary superstition had its roots in ancient religion. Hume believed that Hinduism and Protestant Christianity shared these roots. The two religions had ideas such as "an Infinite Being," the revelation of this being as "Word," "prayer, as intercourse of man with God," sacred books, and ethics in common. Hume made a distinction between Hindu superstition and idolatry and a privileged Hinduism that shared key concepts with Protestantism.

Another missionary, L. E. Slater, from the London Missionary Society, made a similar argument to Hume's in his address on "The Present Religious Outlook of India." Spending less time on the superstitious religion of India than Hume, Slater argued that it was a time of transition in Indian religion. There were two Hinduisms. "On the one hand the old Hinduism—the masses of people under the dominion of the priesthood, all sunk in the grossest superstition. On the other hand, there is 'Young India,' the new thought and feeling of the country reflected in the men trained at colleges in the highest western thought."[47] Slater then gave three examples of "Young India," the Arya Samaj, the Brahmo Samaj, and the Christo Samaj, all of which pointed to the demise of superstition and the rise of Christianity. Two of these three examples, the Arya Samaj of Swami Dayanand and the Brahmo Samaj of Rammohun Roy, had already attracted American attention earlier in the century.

The Arya Samaj was a "Vedic and monotheistic Hinduism. . . . It holds that when purified from error Hinduism can hold its own against every other form of faith. It stands for Indian theism as against foreign theism, and enlists on its side the patriotic preference for Indian literature and thought."[48] The nationalist theism of the Arya Samaj stood against the same superstitions that Christian missionaries decried. Similarly, the Brahmo Samaj was "the organized Theistic Church of India" that "started with the Vedas, but has gradually been approaching Christianity."[49] The capstone, though, was the Christo Samaj, which Slater noted was housed in Calcutta and only required members to take on the title of Christian, believe in the Apostle's Creed, and live a consistent Christian life. Slater drew the line of difference between the old superstitious Hinduism and the new theistic Hinduism that was slowly approaching closer and closer to Christianity. When this transition from old India to Young India was complete, superstitious Hinduism would be completely overwhelmed by the new monotheistic Hinduism.

Protap Chunder Mozoomdar, author of *The Oriental Christ* (1883), came to Chicago to represent Young India and the Brahmo Samaj. In his address, Mozoomdar described the Brahmo Samaj, the Hindu reform movement founded by Rammohun Roy in the early part of the nineteenth century. Mozoomdar's representation of Brahmo Hinduism followed the model of inclusive Protestants. He began by citing the difference between the Brahmo Samaj and other Hindu religions through the narrative of the Samaj's founder. Echoing the American Board of Commissioners for Foreign Missions missionaries, he described how earlier in the century Bengal had been "full of mighty clamor. The great jarring noise of a heterogeneous poly-theism rent the stillness of the sky. . . . Amid the din and clash of this polytheism and so-called evil, amid all the darkness of the times, there arose a man, a Brahman, pure bred and pure born, whose name was Raja Ram Mohan Roy."[50] Mozoomdar then outlined how Roy proved "the falsehood of all polytheism and the truth of the existence of the living God."[51] Mozoomdar reconstructed the difference between false polytheistic superstition and true monotheism. However, like the distinction made by Slater, this time the difference was not between Hindu and Christian, but between two different types of Hindus. Seventy years after Protestants invoked Rammohun Roy to separate Unitarians and Calvinists, Mozoomdar invoked him again to separate superstitious Hindu religion and Hinduism.

Mozoomdar outlined the basic contours of the Brahmo Samaj's Hinduism. These contours fit the Protestant model of religion operating in the Parliament. Brahmos had a monotheistic theology rooted in "the one true living God." This theology was scriptural because "the Brahmo Samaj founded this monotheism upon the inspi-ration of the Vedas and the Upanishads." The Brahmos also focused on morality and reform. As Mozoomdar asked, "What is theology without morality? . . . The Brahmo Samaj, therefore, next laid its hand upon the reformation of society."[52] Finally, Mozoomdar turned to the moderate inclusivist argument, but instead of all religion finding its perfection in Christianity, "the Brahmo-Somaj accepts and harmonizes all these precepts, systems, principles, teachings, and disciplines, and makes them into one system, and that is his religion."[53] Where Protestants had put Christianity, as the perfection of religious truth, Mozoomdar put Brahmo Hinduism. With its monotheism, scripture, reform, and claims to universalism, the Brahmo Samaj looked an awful lot like liberal Protestantism. It was Brahmo Hinduism that could truly provide the unity of religion against irreligion.

The response to Mozoomdar in a local newspaper revealed how effectively he was able to overcome the difference between Hindu and Christian by offering a

Hinduism that fit the Protestant model. "The zeal with which this distinguished scholar advocated the fatherhood of God and the brotherhood of man carried the Christian of the new world back to India for a genuine specimen of a true Christian faith."[54] By presenting a Protestantized Hinduism, Mozoomdar was able to erase the difference between his Hinduism and the Protestant Christianity that dominated the Parliament. But his Hinduism was not received as Hinduism, but rather, as the newspaper called it, as "true Christian faith." Religion was Christianity, so when Hinduism became religion, it became Christian. Like the Brahmo founder Rammohun Roy, Americans labeled the Hindu Mozoomdar a Christian.

Not all Indian delegates sought to align themselves so closely with Protestants. One Indian, who was not Hindu but Jain, offered a response to the missionary attacks on Indian religion. When evangelical missionary George Pentecost attacked the morality of Brahmanism and claimed that Indian temples housed "hundreds of priestesses who were known as immoral and profligate" and who were "prostitutes because they were priestesses and priestesses because they were prostitutes," a Jain delegate, Virichand Gandhi, responded the next day.[55] Gandhi explained that there were no priestesses or prostitutes at temples but rather, there were women dancers who danced in the outer passages of the temples and that their morality was no better or worse than any other woman's. He then used a story to reject the marginalization of so-called superstitious Brahmanism by Protestants like Pentecost.

He told a story about a boat full of Muslims captured by the Portuguese during Akbar's reign in India. The Christian Portuguese hung all the copies of the Qur'an found onboard the ship around the neck of dogs and had them tramped through the streets. Ironically, this same ship was later captured by Akbar's men. Akbar's mother, furious over the earlier treatment of the Qur'an, wanted Akbar to treat the Bibles onboard the ship similarly. Akbar's reply to his mother was Gandhi's reply to the Christian missionaries, "Mother, these ignorant men do not know the value of the Koran, and they treated it in a manner which is the outcome of ignorance. But I know the glory of the Koran and the Bible both, and I cannot debase myself in the way they did."[56] Gandhi's reply rejected the difference that placed a moral and rational Christianity above a superstitious and immoral Brahmanism. In his story the morality and rationality belong to Akbar—and metaphorically to Indians. The story, told by a Jain with a Muslim main character, responded in the mode of unity and religious liberalism that appealed to the liberal Protestant audience at the Parliament. Barrows noted that "Mr. Gandhi's remarks were followed by expressions of sympathy from among the audience."[57] Gandhi had managed to reverse, for a brief moment, the difference between Western Christian and Indian Hindu by arguing for Indian rationality and the ignorance of Christianity.

Swami Vivekananda held the most ambivalent relationship to Protestant Christianity of any of the Indian delegates. Seager heralded Vivekananda as "beyond question the most popular and influential man in the Parliament ... [who] on all occasions ... was received with greater enthusiasm than any other speaker, Christian or 'Pagan.' "[58] Vivekananda may have been the person closest to Emerson's Plato of anyone in the century. He had the advantage of a Western education at Presidency College and then the General Assembly's Institution, where he was attracted to Western philosophy and struggled with the thought of the Utilitarians. But he had also devoted himself to the *bhakti* and tantric guru Ramakrishna.[59] He spoke English well, dressed like a Hindu monk, and could speak to Western philosophy and the intricacies of Vedanta. He was Young India—a balance of East and West.

Vivekananda not only defended Hinduism against Protestant attacks, but also represented a Hinduism that fit the Protestant model of religion. He even went on the offensive against Christianity. At the end of one afternoon session, Vivekananda gave a short speech in which he chastised American Christians for sending missionaries to India to preach, instead of helping feed the starving and impoverished in the country. He declared, "It is an insult to a starving people to offer them religion, it is an insult to a starving man to teach him metaphysics. In India a priest that preached for money would lose caste, and be spat upon by the people. I came here for aid for my impoverished people and I fully realized how difficult it was to get help for heathens from Christians in a Christian land."[60] Here, as with Gandhi, the terms of difference switched. It was the Christian who lacked morality and social reform, while the Hindu pleaded for food for his people. In his history of the Parliament, Barrows seemed to ignore the force of Vivekananda's statement. He only commented, "He concluded his speech by a few remarks on the Hindu doctrine of reincarnation."[61]

There were other criticisms of Protestant Christianity that Barrows did not include in his history at all. While Henry Barrows's authoritative history of the Parliament and Walter Houghton's alternative collection of Parliament papers each included Vivekananda's address titled "Hinduism," neither volume contains his extemporaneous opening remarks to that address. In these remarks, Vivekananda condemned Christianity for its intolerance. He said,

We who come from the East have sat here on the platform day after day and have been told in a patronizing way that we ought to accept Christianity because Christian nations are the most prosperous. We look about us and we see England, the most prosperous Christian nation in the world with her foot on the neck of 250,000,000 of Asiatics. We look back into history and see that the prosperity of Christian Europe began with Spain. Spain's prosperity began with the invasion of Mexico. Christianity wins its prosperity by cutting the throats of its fellow men. At such a price the Hindoo will not have prosperity.

I have sat here today and I have heard the height of intolerance. I have heard the creed of the Moslem applauded, when today the Moslem sword is carrying destruction into India. Blood and the sword are not for the Hindoo, whose religion is based on the law of love.[62]

In his remarks Vivekananda sharply condemned Christianity and rejected the subordination of Asian religion and Asian civilization to Western Christianity. According to Vivekananda, Christianity led to immorality, and only the Hindu held to a religion of love. Vivekananda indicted modern Western prosperity. It was not built from the mind of Western progress or Protestant morals, but from the "necks of 250,000,000" and the bloody throats of fellow men. The authoritative historians of the Parliament failed to record these words. Yet the newspapers did, and they reported that the crowd in the Hall applauded the young monk. Another newspaper reported that this great crowd consisted mainly of women. "Great crowds of people, the most of whom were women, pressed around the doors leading to the Hall of Columbus . . . for it had been announced that Swami Vivekananda, the popular Hindoo monk who looks so much like McCullough's Othello, was to speak."[63] It is no wonder, then, that the conservative white Presbyterian minister Henry Barrows could not bring himself to print the sharp critique of his own religion by a dark-skinned Hindu and its roaring approval by a room full of Christian laywomen.

Vivekananda's paper titled "Hinduism" exemplified a more ambivalent relationship to Protestantism than his fiery opening remarks. In the address, Vivekananda took a few jabs at Christianity. He reminded Christians who associated widow burning with Hinduism that one could also associate witch burning with Christianity. However, the Hinduism he presented in the paper fit into the liberal Protestant model of religion dominant at the Parliament. For Vivekananda, Hinduism was monotheistic, scientific, and socially progressive. Further complicating things, unlike Mozoomdar he did not construct a difference between popular image worship, which others had called idolatry or superstition, and some rarified true Hinduism. Rather, he argued that temple practices in India only seemed polytheistic. Below the surface lay a deep monotheism. The images helped people realize the underlying unified deity. As he asked, "But if a man can realize his divine nature with the help of an image, would it be right to call it a sin?"[64] Image use in worship could be reconciled with a monotheistic God and rational belief. Rather than parse between an ignorant old Hinduism of superstition and a new Hinduism of rational monotheism, Vivekananda folded them together.

Vivekananda took his defense of Hindu images a step further by comparing their use to Christian practices. Just as other delegates separated out good contemplative Indian religion from bad superstitious Indian religion, Vivekananda pointed to superstitious Christianity. "Superstition is the enemy of man, bigotry worse. Why does a Christian go to church, why is the cross holy, why is the face turned toward the sky in prayer? Why are there so many images in the Catholic church, why are there so many images in the minds of Protestants when they pray?"[65] The practices labeled "superstition" could be found in all religions, Vivekananda argued, even Christianity. One needed to look past these differences in practice or moments of superstition to the true Religion that united all religions.

Like the Christian speakers at the Parliament, Vivekananda's speech was an attempt to answer the question of what counted as religion and what would unite all the delegates against the various forms of irreligion. In the opening of his speech he asked, "Where then, the question arises, where is the common center to which all these widely diverging radii converge; where is the common basis upon which all these seemingly hopeless contradictions rest? And this is the question I shall attempt to answer."[66] His answer was Hinduism. Hindus, he argued, understood that "every religion is only an evolving a God out of the material man; and the same God is the inspirer of all of them ... the contradictions come from the same truth adapting itself to the different circumstances of different natures."[67] Hinduism provided the Universal Religion—the Religion to unite all religion.

Vivekananda also argued that the United States held a special place in the quest for a Universal Religion: "It was reserved for America to call, to proclaim to all quarters of the globe that the Lord is in every religion."[68] In the final paragraph of his speech, Vivekananda outlined a kind of millennialist vision of Universal Religion in America:

> May he who is the Brahma of the Hindus, the Ahura Mazda of the Zoroastrians, the Buddha of the Buddhists, the Jehovah of the Jews, the Father in Heaven of the Christians, give strength to you to carry out your noble idea. The star arose in the East; it traveled steadily toward the West, sometimes dimmed and sometimes effulgent, till it made a circuit of the world, and now it is again rising on the very horizon of the East, the borders of the Tasifu, a thousand-fold more effulgent than it ever was before. Hail Columbia, mother-land of liberty! It has been given to thee, who never dipped her hand in her neighbor's blood, who never found out that shortest way of becoming rich by robbing one's neighbors, it has been given to thee to march on at the vanguard of civilization with the flag of harmony.[69]

America was the land where Universal Religion, born in the East, would come to rest and flourish. There was an irony in Vivekananda's vision, however. He was quick to critique Spanish and British colonialism and their violence in the name of prosperity and Christianity. Yet, he completely ignored the violence against Native Americans that made the very city of Chicago possible and that was ongoing in the West.

The common narrative has hailed Vivekananda as the star of the Parliament and has lionized the Parliament as the place where Hinduism came to America. But that story has oversimplified the Parliament and its role in American encounters with India. As with previous representations of religion in India, Hinduism emerged at the Parliament within the context of a protracted debate about religion. As delegates from a variety of backgrounds met in Chicago to unite all religion against irreligion, they each offered up their own definition of "religion."

The Parliament serves as a fitting end to this book because it was one big argument about religion and America that summarized all the arguments of the previous century. The ten religions represented at the Parliament signaled a change from the "Jewish, Heathen, Mahometan, Christian" of Hannah Adams's *A Dictionary of All Religions*. Yet, Christians like George Pentecost still argued for Christianity as the only true religion, while rehearsing the tropes of Indian heathen licentiousness. Thomas Wentworth Higginson's search for the sympathy of religions continued James Freeman Clarke and Samuel Johnson's quest for a Universal Religion. Protap Mozoomdar even represented the same Brahmo Hindu religion that Boston Unitarians deployed against their evangelical rivals. Vivekananda turned the argument from religion to America, as he tasked the United States with a special role in the quest for religious harmony. Indeed, the long argument about religion that was the Parliament took place within the Columbian Exposition's celebration of America. Arguing about what counted as religion, as *real* Religion, was an American pastime.

Arguments about the definitions of America and religion always required an outside. There has to be something or someone over there that is "not it," against which "it" is identified. Throughout the nineteenth century, India provided the "not it," as Americans debated religion and Americanness. Heathens, Hindoos, and Hindus provided the representations of difference that many Americans needed to represent themselves.

Epilogue

IN HER 1927 book *Mother India*, American writer Katherine Mayo asked, "But what does the average American actually know about India?" She answered, "That Mr. Gandhi lives there; also tigers. His further ideas, if such he has, resolve themselves into more or less hazy notions more or less unconsciously absorbed from professional propagandists out of one camp or another; from religious or mystical sources; or from tales and travel-books, novels and verses, having India as their scene."[1] The preceding chapters have accounted for the construction and circulation of these "more or less hazy notions more or less unconsciously absorbed" by nineteenth-century Americans. But more than that, they have argued that these notions played an integral role in American arguments about what counted as religion and what counted as American. Indeed, even Mayo's book, based on her observations traveling around India in 1925, engaged in similar work. She was a member of the Society of Mayflower Descendants "who defined her own mission as a defense of a white, Anglo-Saxon, Protestant establishment at home and of Anglo-U.S. colonialism and imperialism abroad," and her book emphasized the superiority of Protestant Anglo-Saxon society over that of India.[2]

This book has been an attempt to understand where these "hazy notions" came from by choosing a series of sites where Americans deployed a variety of categories and representations of India, the people there, and their religion in a variety of debates about the United States and its religion. The previous chapters have moved back and forth between American religious history, religious studies, and South Asian studies, and have triangulated between Britain, America, and India by paying close attention to the forces, discourses, debates, arguments, and networks that produced constructions of religion in India. Rather than a story of progress or historical development from mistaken images of heathens to accurate representations of Hinduism, these various sites reveal that a variety of representations coexisted, bounced off one another, ignored one another, and even gathered together under the rubric of the World's Parliament of Religions. An extension of this study into the twentieth century would find earlier representations of Hindoos and heathenism continuing right alongside the newly minted world religion of Hinduism.

This genealogical approach provides a much-needed corrective to the history of South Asian religions in the United States. It offers a challenge to the essentialist narratives that assume Hinduism is a unified and timeless religious tradition of India that arrived in the United States through texts and people. It also challenges less blatantly essentialist narratives that narrate a story of greater and greater understanding and accuracy as Americans progressed through the nineteenth century. Such narratives fold every encounter between Americans and religion in India into the category of "Hinduism" without paying close attention to the forces that produced this or that representation of India. Instead, historians must pay attention to how Americans used each of the "more or less hazy notions" of religion in India in their domestic arguments, conflicts, identities, and representations.

Paying close attention to the construction of categories points the way out of what Jason Bivins has called the "lone repertory" of the study of religion in America. The subfield of "American religious history" or, as Bivins has dubbed it, American Religious Studies (ARS), is characterized by a methodology of expanding descriptive narrative.[3] Ethnographic and sociological methods have been a part of the field, especially under the rubric of "lived religion," but even then, the emphasis has been on accurately describing the things so-called religious people do. By forgoing descriptive narrative for interrogating categories, this book offers an example of another approach to religion in the United States that might lead in new fruitful directions.

This book has not followed an arching descriptive narrative but, instead, has paid particular attention to category construction. Thus, it has illuminated the relationship between American representations of religion in India and identity, conflict, and religion in America. For example, representations of heathenism, filth, caste, bloody idolatry, lasciviousness, and sati in missionary reports, popular magazines, and schoolbooks functioned to bolster an American Protestant nationalism. Arguments about true religion between evangelicals and Unitarians and the search for esoteric Wisdom Religion and the Universal Religion took place within a secular state where religion had become a category of choice and a force for uniting across difference. The World's Parliament of Religions was a nationalist argument about the definition of religion and who would be counted within it. Following what

Americans wrote and said about religion in India during the nineteenth century revealed bigger conversations and conflicts about religion and modernity. A number of recent works have hazarded to theorize rather than merely describe, and they have produced important insights into the relationship between religion and secularism, politics, law, capitalism, and popular culture.[4]

Because descriptive narrative has been a mainstay in the study of American religions, the main approach to growing the field and finding new avenues of study has been to expand and include. The study of religion in the United States has grown from its roots in church history to move past Protestant narratives to a broader pluralist narrative. Tracy Fessenden has summed this process up nicely:

> In a nutshell, somewhere between the 1970s and 80s a vanguard among scholars of American religion began at last to leave off writing about white, northeastern, Protestant men and to write instead about everybody: more religions, more relations to religion, more of what counts as religion in the first place.[5]

As recently as 2010, religious studies scholar Thomas Tweed called for scholars to "expand the temporal span and geographical scope of the field and its narratives."[6] The expansionist call turned on itself like a snake eating its tail when historians Kevin Schultz and Paul Harvey noted that we actually needed *more* studies of *Protestantism* in America. "We need more books to explain, for example, the lineage of Presbyterianism, or the divisions within Methodism," they wrote.[7] But outward expansion was not enough. Scholars also began to reach deeper down. Some historians argued that the study of American religion paid too much attention to elite white males and moved toward studying the "lived religion" of everyday people and practices.[8] Whether by reaching outward or downward, Fessenden described this scholarly drive well: "Retell, again retell. No longer, clearly, are we bound by the stodgy confines of Protestant church history. What we study, what we want, is *more*."[9]

As I described in the Preface, when I began writing this book I thought of it as a retelling, a new narrative, *more*. Scholars of American religion were vaguely aware that Emerson and the Theosophists had read some stuff from India. We knew that Vivekananda had come to Chicago. But the story of Hinduism in the United States, especially in the nineteenth century, had not become part of the narrative. It needed to be told—or retold. But as I wrote and rewrote, I realized that my retelling, my addition to the narrative, was actually part of a much larger narrative about the category "religion" in America. Just as Hannah Adams had tried to include every religion she could under her rubric of Christian, Jew, Muslim, and heathen; just as James Freeman Clarke had named ten "great religions;" and just as the World's

Parliament of Religions had named ten "world religions," my attempt at adding "Hinduism" to "American religions" was another step in expanding what counted as "religion" in America. Put another way, both the "old Protestant" and "pluralist" narratives of American religious history were attempts to organize and categorize religion, but neither of them is a self-conscious attempt to analyze how "religion" gets constructed in the first place.

So, rather than pulling "Hinduism" underneath the ever growing big tent of "American religion," this book has traced the contours of how Americans used representations of India in their own constructions and arguments about "religion." To expand what counts as "American religion," a scholar must assume to know what religion is, and then go and find more of it in new places. To write descriptive narratives of religious people is to know what religion is and then go find the people doing it. Rather than landing on a single definition of religion, the previous chapters have analyzed the variety of definitions in the sources themselves. This has revealed how representations of India and religion "over there" were important to American constructions of religion at home. Ironically, this genealogical, rather than expansionist, method has also brought more attention to historical subjects that have been marginal to American religious history. Helena Blavatsky, Lydia Maria Child, Vivekananda, Protap Chunder Mozoomdar, and Rammohun Roy are mentioned in passing but rarely are investigated as they have been in this study.

The further irony is that this genealogy of American representations of India gestures toward the genealogy of the expansionist narrative method. From Cotton Mather's single religion of Christianity to Hanna Adams's four religions to Clarke's and the World Parliament's differing ten religions, the Americans have long desired to enumerate an ever-expanding count of religions. American religious historians have not been the only ones invested in the pluralist drive for more religions. Americans themselves have been, too. Bivins traced this pluralist drive back to "the 1970s-style politics of pluralism and inclusion"[10] but, as the previous chapters show, the expansionist drive goes back even further. Yet, adding more religions can also be a way to control and exclude. Only certain forms of belief and practice were counted as "religion" or "Hinduism," and others, such as sati or hook-swinging, were labeled religion in order to reinforce American superiority and white supremacy. Furthermore, the writings of Hannah Adams and Joseph Priestley reveal that comparative religion was a Protestant American project and so, perhaps, the shift from a Protestant narrative to a pluralist narrative that Fessenden outlines is not the major transition historians have thought it was. Only a further genealogy of "American religion" itself will be able to answer that question.

Religious studies has shown a greater comfort with the analysis of category construction than American religious history. To be sure, many scholars working in

American religious history have been trained and work in religious studies departments. The difference between the two is not a boundary line but a Venn diagram. Nevertheless, whenever scholars of religion get together at conferences or even on social media, it does not take long before disciplinary divisions between "historians" and "religious studies scholars" become apparent. That said, religious studies scholars have taken an eager interest in the invention, construction, and imagining of "religion" and religions.[11] By turning that theoretical and methodological focus on category construction onto American representations of India, the previous chapters gesture toward a different history of the field of religious studies in the United States.

Most histories of the so-called academic study of religion, comparative religion, history of religions, or religious studies have emphasized a nineteenth-century European origin story. German, French, and British thinkers led the way in the study of religion, so the story goes, until something happened in the twentieth century and the United States became the center of the field.[12] In 1905, Henry Louis Jordan noticed that the study of comparative religion in the United States was "a movement which has so recently been launched, that its national type has not yet had time to manifest itself."[13] Yet, throughout the previous pages of this book, Americans engaged in comparative religion over and over again. Hannah Adams, Joseph Priestley, Helena Blavatsky, Samuel Johnson, James Freeman Clarke, Lydia Maria Child, and even geography schoolbook writers engaged in the comparative study of religion. To his credit, Jordan recognized Adams, Johnson, and Clarke in his early history of the field, and Thomas Tweed has argued for the important role that Hannah Adams played in the field of comparative religion. In his 1975 history of the field, Eric Sharpe ignored everyone on the preceding list except Clarke, who received passing mention for his *Ten Great Religions* as an "early milestone" in the field.[14] So, somewhere between 1905 and today, the various comparative approaches to religion analyzed in these chapters have fallen out of the narrative that religious studies tells itself about itself.

It is beyond the scope of this epilogue, or even this book, to figure out how these sites of comparative religion in America fit into the genealogy or history of religious studies as a discipline in the United States. That is a future project for someone to tackle. But the moments of comparative religion revealed in this study do point toward an interesting relationship between comparative religion and American religious history. How does the study of comparative religion fit into American religious history? That is, rather than seeing religious studies as an overlapping field within American religious history or the study of American religions as a subfield of religious studies, how can we see the two as interrelated and co-constitutive discourses? In her study of "world religions discourse," Tomoko Masuzawa noted in passing that "the actual manifestation of the world religions discourse in the form familiar to us today was very much an American phenomenon."[15] Masuzawa never went further than that. Her interests were purely European.[16] But the questions remain: What is *American* about religious studies? What role did the comparative work of the figures in this book play in the genealogy of religious studies? What role does religious studies play in the genealogy of "religion" in America or "American religion" or "American religious history"?

The answers to these questions are each a book in their own right. That said, following the various writers detailed in this book leads to an important transitional figure: William James. James represented a transition point between the Transcendentalists, the Theosophists, and Vivekananda and the academic study of religion that would blossom in the latter half of the twentieth century. James's father was a Swedenborgian and friends with Emerson and Thoreau, and young William grew up in the midst of New England metaphysical religion. Ann Taves noted how much James's thought shared with Theosophy and Spiritualism. [17] Meanwhile, Catherine Albanese described how "the metaphysical version of Asia clearly fascinated" him. Drawing on the metaphysical representation of India as a land of contemplation and mysticism, James described yoga in his chapter on mysticism in his classic *Varieties of Religious Experience*: "In India, training in mystical insight has been known from time immemorial under the name of yoga. Yoga means the experimental union of the individual with the divine."[18] James then quoted extensively from Swami Vivekananda's 1896 *Raja Yoga* and discussed the "Samâdhi" of the "Vedantists." James's representation of India depended on the earlier representations of Theosophists, Transcendentalists, and Vivekananda.

James's representation of mystic India was hardly new, but the larger intellectual project he put it to use within was quite radical. Eric Sharpe recognized James, and the larger psychological study of religion he represented, as the first truly American contribution to the study of comparative religion.[19] James also brought a new emphasis in method and subject for the study of religion in the United States. James Turner described how *Varieties of Religious Experience* "can best be seen, in the longer history of religious studies in the United States, as a strenuous effort at academic intellectual reform."[20] James turned aside from the various taxonomies, dictionaries, encyclopedias, and representations of religious rituals, beliefs, and texts. Instead, he turned attention to "the feelings, acts, and experiences of individual men in their solitude, so far as they apprehend themselves to stand in relation to whatever they may consider the divine."[21] Thus, for James, the mystical experience of the yogi represented religion in India.

With James, the comparisons and representations of religion shift from those in literature, popular books, national magazines, metaphysical treatises, and missionary periodicals discussed in the previous chapters to those of an academic social science. The Transcendentalist Brahmanism, the Theosophical wisdom religion, and Vivekananda's Hinduism are swallowed up by James's "mysticism." The Enlightenment project of cataloging religious belief is replaced by a cataloging of religious experience. Along the way, the missionary and nationalist interests in representing the Hindoo Other dropped away. Yet, the emphasis on interior individual and solitary experience betrays an incipient American Protestantism, the nonspecific Protestantism of American national culture. As the twentieth century opened, the study of religion was finding a place in the academy, and Vedantists and yogis represented India in America.

Pulling back from American religious history and religious studies, representations of heathens, Hindoos, and Hindus provide yet another example of how social actors build their identities. Heathens, Hindoos, and Hindus functioned as representational Others against whom Americans could imagine themselves. Jonathan Z. Smith observed that the most common way to classify religion is "theirs" and "ours."[22] Thus, religion is a classificatory system. Like gender, race, class, nationality, or even college football team, social actors use religion to tell themselves and each other who "we" are and who "they" are. Such classification is a political act. To study religion, then, is to investigate the function of classificatory systems, to historicize their construction, and to analyze their social and political effects.

Notes

PREFACE

1. Parts of this book were published earlier in Michael J. Altman, "Before Hinduism: Missionaries, Unitarians, and Hindoos in Nineteenth-Century America," *Religion and American Culture: A Journal of Interpretation* 26, no. 2 (Summer 2016).

2. Quoted in Thomas Tweed and Stephen Prothero, eds., *Asian Religions in America: A Documentary History* (New York: Oxford University Press, 1999), 110–111.

3. Richard Hughes Seager, ed., *The Dawn of Religious Pluralism: Voices from the World's Parliament of Religions, 1893* (La Salle, IL: Open Court, 1993), 337; John Henry Barrows, *The World's Parliament of Religions: An Illustrated and Popular Story of the World's First Parliament of Religions, Held in Chicago in Connection with the Columbian Exposition of 1893* (Chicago: The Parliament Publishing Company, 1893), 1:101.

4. Marie Louise Burke, *Swami Vivekananda in the West: New Discoveries*, 4th ed., vol. 1 (Kolkata, India: Advaita Ashrama, 1998), 86.

5. Ibid., 1:114.

6. Vasudha Narayanan, "Hinduism in America," in *Cambridge History of Religions in America*, ed. Stephen J. Stein, vol. 3 (New York: Cambridge University Press, 2012), 335.

7. Raymond Brady Williams, *Religions of Immigrants from India and Pakistan: New Threads in the American Tapestry* (Cambridge: Cambridge University Press, 1988), 54.

8. Narayanan, "Hinduism in America"; Lola Williamson, *Transcendent in America: Hindu-Inspired Meditation Movements as New Religion* (New York: New York University Press, 2010); Gurinder Singh Mann, Paul David Numrich, and Raymond Brady Williams, eds., *Buddhists, Hindus, and Sikhs in America: A Short History* (New York: Oxford University Press, 2008);

Prema A. Kurien, *A Place at the Multicultural Table: The Development of an American Hinduism* (New Brunswick, NJ: Rutgers University Press, 2007); Thomas A. Forsthoefel and Cynthia Anne Humes, eds., *Gurus in America* (Albany: State University of New York Press, 2005); Williams, *Religions of Immigrants from India and Pakistan*.

9. For a trenchant critique of such pluralist narratives of expansion in American religions, see Rosemary R. Hicks, "Between Lived and the Law: Power, Empire, and Expansion in Studies of North American Religions," *Religion* 42, no. 3 (July 1, 2012): 409–424.

10. Kurien, *A Place at the Multicultural Table*, 41.

11. Narayanan, "Hinduism in America," 331.

12. Thomas Tweed and Stephen Prothero, eds., *Asian Religions in America: A Documentary History* (New York: Oxford University Press, 1999); Stephen Prothero, "Hinduism," in *Contemporary American Religion*, ed. Wade Clark Roof (New York: Macmillan, 2000), 302–305; Stephen Prothero, "Mother India's Scandalous Swamis," in *Religions of the United States in Practice*, ed. Colleen McDannell, vol. 2 (Princeton, NJ: Princeton University Press, 2001), 418–432; Stephen Prothero, "Hinduphilia and Hinduphobia in American Culture," in *The Stanger's Religion: Fascination and Fear*, ed. Anna Lannstrom (Notre Dame, IN: University of Notre Dame Press, 2004), 13–37.

13. Andrew J. Nicholson, *Unifying Hinduism: Philosophy and Identity in Indian Intellectual History* (New York: Columbia University Press, 2010); Brian Pennington, *Was Hinduism Invented? Britons, Indians, and the Colonial Construction of Religion* (New York: Oxford University Press, 2005); Arvind Sharma, "On Hindu, Hindustān, Hinduism and Hindutva," *Numen* 49, no. 1 (January 1, 2002): 1–36; Gunther-Dietz Sontheimer and Hermann Kulke, eds., *Hinduism Reconsidered* (New Delhi: Manohar, 2001); Richard King, *Orientalism and Religion: Postcolonial Theory, India and "the Mystic East"* (London: Routledge, 1999); David N. Lorenzen, "Who Invented Hinduism?," *Comparative Studies in Society and History* 41, no. 4 (October 1, 1999): 630–659.

14. King, *Orientalism and Religion*, 98.

15. Ibid., 107.

16. Lorenzen, "Who Invented Hinduism?," 631.

17. Nicholson, *Unifying Hinduism*.

18. Jack Miles and Wendy Doniger, eds., *Norton Anthology of World Religions: Hinduism* (New York: W. W. Norton, 2015), 45.

19. Pennington, *Was Hinduism Invented?*, 168–169.

20. King, *Orientalism and Religion*, 138.

21. Will Sweetman, *Mapping Hinduism: "Hinduism" and the Study of Indian Religions, 1600–1776*, Neue Hallesche Berichte 4 (Halle: Verl. der Franckeschen Stiftungen, 2003), 51.

22. Bernard McGrane, *Beyond Anthropology: Society and the Other* (New York: Columbia University Press, 1992), 3.

23. Michel Foucault, "Nietzsche, Genealogy, History," in *The Foucault Reader*, ed. Paul Rabinow (New York: Pantheon Books, 1984), 83–84.

24. Such a method is similar to that sketched out by Mark Jordan. Mark D. Jordan, *The Invention of Sodomy in Christian Theology* (Chicago: University of Chicago Press, 1997), 1–9.

25. Foucault, "Nietzsche, Genealogy, History," 77.

26. Edward Said, *Orientalism* (New York: Vintage Books, 1979), 3.

CHAPTER 1

1. Cotton Mather, *India Christiana: A Discourse, Delivered Unto the Commissioners, for the Propagation of the Gospel Among the American Indians Which Is Accompanied with Several Instruments Relating to the Glorious Design of Propagating Our Holy Religion, in the Eastern as Well as the Western, Indies. An Entertainment Which They That Are Waiting for the Kingdom of God Will Receive as Good News from a Far Country* (Boston: Company for the Propagation of the Gospel in New England and the Parts Adjacent in America, 1721).

2. Ibid., 22; emphasis in the original.

3. Frank E. Manuel, *The Eighteenth Century Confronts the Gods* (Cambridge, MA: Harvard University Press, 1959); David A. Pailin, *Attitudes to Other Religions: Comparative Religion in Seventeenth- and Eighteenth-Century Britain* (Manchester: Manchester University Press, 1984); Peter Harrison, *"Religion" and the Religions in the English Enlightenment* (Cambridge: Cambridge University Press, 1990).

4. Bernard McGrane, *Beyond Anthropology: Society and the Other* (New York: Columbia University Press, 1992), 57.

5. Richard Baxter, *The Reasons of the Christian Religion* (London: R. White for Fran. Titon, 1667), 198.

6. Ibid., 198.

7. Ibid., 199.

8. McGrane, *Beyond Anthropology*, 71.

9. Mather, *India Christiana*, 85–86.

10. Ibid., 28; emphasis in original.

11. Ibid., 29; emphasis in original.

12. Susan S. Bean, *Yankee India: American Commercial and Cultural Encounters with India in the Age of Sail, 1784–1860* (Salem, MA: Peabody Essex Museum, 2001), 69–70.

13. John H. Reinoehl, "Some Remarks on the American Trade: Jacob Crowninshield to James Madison 1806," *The William and Mary Quarterly*, Third Series, 16, no. 1 (January 1, 1959): 110–111.

14. G. Bhagat, *Americans in India, 1784–1860* (New York: New York University Press, 1970), 138.

15. William Bentley, *The Diary of William Bentley, D.D., Pastor of the East Church, Salem, Massachusetts*, ed. Peter Smith, vol. 2 (Gloucester, MA: Essex Institute, 1962), 121.

16. *The East-India Marine Society of Salem* (Salem, MA: W. Palfray Jr., 1821), 50, 64.

17. James Lindgren M., "'That Every Mariner May Possess the History of the World': A Cabinet for the East India Marine Society of Salem," *The New England Quarterly* 68, no. 2 (1995): 200.

18. Bentley, *The Diary of William Bentley*, 2:68.

19. Ibid., 2:361.

20. Caroline Howard King, *When I Lived in Salem, 1822–1866* (Brattleboro, VT: Stephen Daye Press, 1937), 31.

21. Bean, *Yankee India*, 31.

22. *The East-India Marine Society of Salem.*

23. King, *When I Lived in Salem*, 29.

24. This view of the exotic Orient may have had an influence on Salem's own Nathaniel Hawthorne. See Jee Yoon Lee, "'The Rude Contact of Some Actual Circumstance': Hawthorne and Salem's East India Marine Museum," *ELH* 73, no. 4 (2006): 949–73.

25. "To the East India Marine Society," *Salem Gazette*, November 5, 1805.

26. Ibid.

27. Ibid.

28. Will Sweetman has argued that these two figures are foundational to the modern concept of "Hinduism" as a unified religion. He fails, however, to connect these early figures to the later British works. They may have been the first to see some sort of unified "religion" in India, but how that shaped the later formations is left unclear. See Will Sweetman, "Unity and Plurality: Hinduism and the Religions of India in Early European Scholarship," *Religion* 31, no. 3 (July 1, 2001): 209–224, and *Mapping Hinduism: "Hinduism" and the Study of Indian Religions, 1600–1776*, Neue Hallesche Berichte 4 (Halle: Verl. der Franckeschen Stiftungen, 2003), 103–126.

29. Wilhelm Halbfass, *India and Europe: An Essay in Understanding* (Albany: State University of New York Press, 1988), 47.

30. P. J. Marshall, *The British Discovery of Hinduism in the Eighteenth Century* (Cambridge: Cambridge University Press, 1970), 4.

31. Ibid., 5.

32. Ibid., 7.

33. David Kopf, *British Orientalism and the Bengal Renaissance: The Dynamics of Modernization, 1773–1835* (Berkeley: University of California Press, 1969), 17.

34. See Bernard S. Cohn, *Colonialism and Its Forms of Knowledge: The British in India* (Delhi: Oxford University Press, 1997).

35. Ibid.

36. Marshall, *The British Discovery of Hinduism in the Eighteenth Century*, 11.

37. Cohn, *Colonialism and Its Forms of Knowledge*, 21.

38. Ibid., 11.

39. "Advertisement" in Hannah Adams, *An Alphabetical Compendium of the Various Sects Which Have Appeared in the World from the Beginning of the Christian Era to the Present Day* (Boston: B. Edes & Sons, 1784).

40. Jonathan Z. Smith, "Religion, Religions, Religious," in *Critical Terms for Religious Studies*, ed. Mark C. Taylor (Chicago: University of Chicago Press, 1998), 269–284; Brent Nongbri, *Before Religion: A History of a Modern Concept* (New Haven, CT: Yale University Press, 2013), 118–119.

41. Lynn Avery Hunt, Margaret C. Jacob, and W. W. Mijnhardt, *The Book That Changed Europe: Picart and Bernard's Religious Ceremonies of the World* (Cambridge, MA: Belknap Press of Harvard University Press, 2010), 17.

42. See Appendix A in Hunt, Jacob, and Mijnhardt, *The Book That Changed Europe*.

43. Pailin, *Attitudes to Other Religions*, 8.

44. Harrison, *"Religion" and the Religions in the English Enlightenment*, 2.

45. Adams, *An Alphabetical Compendium of the Various Sects Which Have Appeared in the World from the Beginning of the Christian Era to the Present Day*, xliii.

46. Ibid., xliii–xliv.

47. Ibid., xliv.

48. Ibid.

49. Harrison, *"Religion" and the Religions in the English Enlightenment*, 73–98.

50. Marshall, *The British Discovery of Hinduism in the Eighteenth Century*, 27.

51. Ibid.

52. Harrison, *"Religion" and the Religions in the English Enlightenment*, 85–92.

53. Ibid., 85.

54. Hannah Adams, *A View of Religions, in Two Parts*, 2nd ed. (Boston: John West Folsom, 1791), 346.

55. Ibid., 346.

56. Ibid., 346–347.

57. John Zephaniah Holwell, *Interesting Historical Events Relative to the Provinces and the Empire of Indostan*, vol. 2 (London: T. Becket and P. A. De Hondt, 1767), 97.

58. Adams, *A View of Religions* (1791), 349.

59. Ibid., 349.

60. Ibid., 349.

61. Ibid., "Appendix."

62. Gary D. Schmidt, *A Passionate Usefulness: The Life and Literary Labors of Hannah Adams* (Charlottesville: University of Virginia Press, 2004), 116.

63. Hannah Adams, *A View of Religions, in Two Parts*, 3rd ed. (Boston: Manning & Loring, 1801), 504.

64. Harrison, *"Religion" and the Religions in the English Enlightenment*, 99–129.

65. Adams, *A View of Religions* (1801), 406.

66. Ibid., 406.

67. Ibid., 406.

68. Ibid., 407.

69. Ibid., 407.

70. Ibid., 409.

71. Ibid., 409.

72. Ibid., 409–410.

73. Ibid., 412.

74. Thomas Maurice, *Indian Antiquities*, vol. 4 (London: W. Richardson, 1794), Preface.

75. Schmidt, *A Passionate Usefulness*, 290.

76. Hannah Adams, *A Dictionary of All Religions and Religious Denominations: Jewish, Heathen, Mahometan, Christian, Ancient and Modern*, ed. Thomas A. Tweed, 4th ed. (Atlanta, GA: Scholars Press, 1992), xv.

77. Ibid., xv.

78. Ibid., 322.

79. "A Dictionary of All Religions and Religious Denominations," *The North American Review and Miscellaneous Journal* 7, no. 19 (May 1818): 86.

80. James Turner, *Religion Enters the Academy: The Origins of the Scholarly Study of Religion in America* (Athens: University of Georgia Press, 2011), 31.

81. Carl T. Jackson, *The Oriental Religions and American Thought: Nineteenth-Century Explorations* (Westport, CT: Greenwood Press, 1981), 29.

82. Ibid.

83. Joseph Priestley, *A Comparison of the Institutions of Moses with Those of the Hindoos and Other Ancient Nations* (Northumberland, PA: A. Kennedy, 1799), 8.

84. Ibid., 87.

85. Ibid., 84.

86. Ibid., 157.

87. Ibid., 208.

88. Ibid., 223.

89. Ibid., 279.

90. Ibid., 284.

91. For more on Priestley's relationship with Adams and Thomas Jefferson, see Jenny Graham, "Joseph Priestley in America," in *Joseph Priestley, Scientist, Philosopher, and Theologian*, ed. Isabel Rivers and David L. Wykes (Oxford: Oxford University Press, 2008), 203–230.

92. John Adams, *The Adams-Jefferson Letters: The Complete Correspondence Between Thomas Jefferson and Abigail and John Adams*, ed. Lester Jesse Cappon, vol. 2 (Chapel Hill: University of North Carolina Press, 1959), 427.

93. Ibid., 2:428.

94. Ibid., 2:428.

95. Adams's copy of *Comparison* is available in a digital format through the John Adams Library and the Internet Archive at http://www.archive.org/details/comparisonofinstooprie (accessed November 5, 2011). See also Zoltán Harastzi, *John Adams and the Prophets of Progress* (New York: Grosset & Dunlap, 1964).

96. Manuel, *The Eighteenth Century Confronts the Gods*, 271.

97. Adams, *The Adams-Jefferson Letters*, 2:515.

98. Ibid., 2:518–519.

CHAPTER 2

1. Jedidiah Morse and Elijah Parish, *Compendious History of New England Designed for Schools and Private Families* (Charleston, MA: Samuel Ethridge, 1804), iv.

2. For Adams's side of the controversy, see Schmidt, *A Passionate Usefulness*, 154–222; For Morse and his conflicts over Adams and Harvard, see Richard J. Moss, *The Life of Jedidiah Morse: A Station of Peculiar Exposure* (Knoxville: University of Tennessee Press, 1995), 54–80; Joseph W. Phillips, *Jedidiah Morse and New England Congregationalism* (New Brunswick, NJ: Rutgers University Press, 1983), 129–160.

3. Jedidiah Morse, *An Appeal to the Public, on the Controversy Respecting the Revolution in Harvard College, and the Events Which Have Followed It* (Charlestown, MA, 1814), v.

4. Ibid.

5. "Fragment of a Vision," *The Massachusetts Missionary Magazine* 5, no. 6 (November 1807): 225.

6. Ibid.

7. Ibid.

8. Ibid.

9. Ibid.

10. I use the term "evangelical" to indicate Trinitarian Protestants with an actively outward focus. These Christians sought to differentiate themselves from Catholic Christians on one side, and liberal Unitarian Christians on the other. Such Protestants were attracted to revivalism and missionary societies. Also, many missionary societies used the word "evangelical" in the titles of their periodicals. I use the term not as a substantive definition but in order to distinguish one sort of New England Christian from others. This difference is most pronounced in the subtitle of Robert Baird's 1844 book, *Religion in America: Or an Account of the Origin, Relation to the State, and Present Condition of the Evangelical Churches in the United States: With Notices of the Unevangelical Denominations*.

11. Oliver Wendell Elsbree, *The Rise of the Missionary Spirit in America, 1790–1815* (Philadelphia: Porcupine Press, 1980), 104.

12. For Buchanan's role in British evangelical and missionary culture, see Allan K. Davidson, *Evangelicals and Attitudes to India, 1786–1813: Missionary Publicity and Claudius Buchanan*, Evangelicals & Society from 1750, no. 4 (Oxfordshire: Sutton Courtenay Press, 1990); Pennington, *Was Hinduism Invented?*, 85–93; Oddie, *Imagined Hinduism*, 75–83. For the connections between British and American missionary societies, see Emily Conroy-Krutz, *Christian Imperialism: Converting the World in the Early American Republic* (Ithaca, NY: Cornell University Press, 2015).

13. I refer to "Juggernaut" throughout this discussion to highlight the difference between the representation of Juggernaut that moved throughout evangelical print culture and the Jagannath of the Puri temple. One is the construction of British and American evangelical cultures and reflects their concerns, imaginations, and desires. The other is an Indian religious culture with a long history before and after the British East India Company. For more on Jagannath, see Nancy Gardner Cassels, *Religion and Pilgrim Tax under the Company Raj*, South Asian Studies/Heidelberg University, New Delhi Branch, South Asia Institute, no. 17 (New Delhi: Manohar Publications, 1988); Hermann Kulke and Burkhard Schnepel, eds., *Jagannath Revisited: Studying Society, Religion, and the State in Orissa* (New Delhi: Manohar, 2001).

14. Claudius Buchanan, "India," *Panoplist* 3, no. 3 (August 1807): 136–139; Claudius Buchanan, "An Important Letter from the Rev. Claudius Buchanan," *Connecticut Evangelical Magazine and Religious Intelligencery* 2, no. 10 (October 1809): 388–393; Claudius Buchanan, "An Important Letter from the Rev. Claudius Buchanan," *The Adviser; Or, Vermont Evangelical Magazine* 1, no. 11 (November 1809): 286–287.

15. Buchanan, "India," 136.

16. Ibid.

17. Ibid.

18. Ibid.

19. Ibid.

20. Claudius Buchanan, *The Works of the Reverend Claudius Buchanan, LL.D. Comprising His Eras of Light, Light of the World, and Star in the East; to Which Is Added Christian Researches in Asia. With Notices of the Translation of the Scriptures into the Oriental Languages*, 6th American ed. (Boston: Samuel T. Armstrong, 1812), 106.

21. Ibid., 106.

22. Ibid., 105.

23. Ibid., 101.

24. Ibid., 106.

25. Ibid., 104.

26. Ibid., 104.

27. Ibid., 195.

28. Pennington, *Was Hinduism Invented?*, 69.

29. "Work in Press," *The Panoplist, and Missionary Magazine* 4, no. 3 (August 1811): 143.

30. Claudius Buchanan, "Two Discourses Preached before the University of Cambridge, on Commencement Sunday, July 1, 1810; and a Sermon Preached before the Society for Missions to Africa and the East, at Their Tenth Anniversary, July 12, 1810: To Which Are Added Christian Researches in Asia," *The Panoplist, and Missionary Magazine* 4, no. 4 (September

1811): 174–178; Claudius Buchanan, "Dr. Buchanan's Christian Researches in Asia," *The Panoplist, and Missionary Magazine* 4, no. 5 (October 1811): 221–229; "The English Review of Buchanan's Researches," *The Connecticut Evangelical Magazine and Religious Intelligencer* 4, no. 10 (October 1811): 382–393; "The English Review of Buchanan's Researches," *The Connecticut Evangelical Magazine and Religious Intelligencer* 4, no. 11 (November 1811): 429–435; "The English Review of Buchanan's Researches," *The Connecticut Evangelical Magazine and Religious Intelligencer* 4, no. 12 (December 1811): 458–470; "Review of Christian Researches," *The Adviser; Or, Vermont Evangelical Magazine* 4, no. 5 (May 1812): 147–159; "The English Review of Buchanan's Researches," *The Adviser; Or, Vermont Evangelical Magazine* 4, no. 6 (June 1812): 173–183; "The English Review of Buchanan's Researches," *The Adviser; Or, Vermont Evangelical Magazine* 4, no. 7 (July 1812): 200–206.

31. Pennington, *Was Hinduism Invented?*, 59–61.

32. "On the Ruinous Effects of Ardent Spirits," *The Panoplist, and Missionary Magazine* 5, no. 9 (February 1813): 416–417.

33. While at sea on their way to India, the Judsons and Luther Rice had an awakening and became Baptists. Rice returned to the United States to organize a Baptist missionary movement, and the Judsons established a Baptist mission in Burma.

34. Elsbree, *The Rise of the Missionary Spirit in America, 1790–1815*, 110–114; for more on the history of the ABCFM, see Clifton Jackson Phillips, *Protestant America and the Pagan World: The First Half Century of the American Board of Commissioners for Foreign Missions, 1810–1860* (Cambridge, MA: East Asian Research Center, Harvard University, 1969); John A. Andrew, *Rebuilding the Christian Commonwealth: New England Congregationalists & Foreign Missions, 1800–1830* (Lexington: University Press of Kentucky, 1976); Donald Phillip Corr, "'The Field Is the World': Proclaiming, Translating, and Serving by the American Board of Commissioners for Foreign Missions, 1810–40" (Ph.D. diss., Fuller Theological Seminary, 1993); Wilbert R. Shenk, ed., *North American Foreign Missions, 1810–1914: Theology, Theory, and Policy* (Grand Rapids, MI: Eerdmans, 2004); Conroy-Krutz, *Christian Imperialism*. For a larger history of American missionaries in India, see Sushil Madhava Pathak, *American Missionaries and Hinduism* (Delhi: Munshiram Manoharlal, 1967).

35. Harriet Newell, "Letter from Mrs. Newell," *The Panoplist, and Missionary Magazine* 5, no. 11 (April 1813): 515.

36. Ibid.

37. Ibid.

38. Anonymous, "Juggernaut and His Worship," *Monthly Paper of the American Board of Commissioners for Foreign Missions*, no. 11 (May 1833).

39. For the history of hook-swinging and colonial attempts to suppress it, see Geoffrey A. Oddie, *Popular Religion, Elites, and Reform: Hook-Swinging and Its Prohibition in Colonial India, 1800–1894* (New Delhi: Manohar Publishers & Distributors, 1995).

40. Gordon Hall and Samuel Newell, "American Missionaries," *The Panoplist, and Missionary Magazine* 13, no. 7 (July 1817): 323.

41. Gordon Hall, "Journal of the Rev. Gordon Hall, Missionary at Bombay," *The Panoplist, and Missionary Magazine* 12, no. 12 (December 1816): 571.

42. Gordon Hall and Samuel Newell, "Journal of the Mission at Bombay," *The Panoplist, and Missionary Herald* 14, no. 2 (February 1818): 79; italics in the original.

43. Gordon Hall and Samuel Newell, "Journal of the Mission at Bombay," *The Panoplist, and Missionary Herald* 14, no. 1 (January 1818): 31.

44. Ibid., 33.

45. Gordon Hall and Samuel Newell, "Journal of the Bombay Mission," *The Panoplist, and Missionary Magazine* 13, no. 12 (December 1817): 560.

46. Ibid.

47. Hall and Newell, "American Missionaries," 324.

48. Jackson, *The Oriental Religions and American Thought*, 90.

49. Horatio Bardwell, "Mission at Bombay and the Vicinity," *The Panoplist, and Missionary Herald* 16, no. 10 (October 1820): 457.

50. Gordon Hall and Samuel Newell, "Journal of the Bombay Mission," *The Panoplist, and Missionary Magazine* 13, no. 11 (November 1817): 526.

51. Gordon Hall, "American Missionaries," *The Panoplist, and Missionary Magazine* 12, no. 11 (November 1816): 507.

52. Ibid.

53. Gordon Hall, "Journal of the Rev. Gordon Hall," *The Panoplist, and Missionary Magazine* 13, no. 1 (January 1817): 35.

54. Hall, "Journal of the Rev. Gordon Hall, Missionary at Bombay," 571.

55. John Nichols, "Extracts from the Journal of Mr. Nichols at Salsette," *The Panoplist, and Missionary Herald* 16, no. 8 (August 1820): 374.

56. Cyrus Stone, "Extracts from Mr. Stone's Private Journal," *The Missionary Herald* 25, no. 9 (September 1829): 266.

57. William Ramsey, "Journal of Mr. Ramsey: Heathen Worship—Hindoo Indolence," *The Missionary Herald* 28, no. 5 (May 1832): 148.

58. Gordon Hall and Samuel Newell, "Extracts from the Journal of Messrs. Hall and Newell, at Bombay," *The Panoplist, and Missionary Magazine* 13, no. 8 (August 1817): 371.

59. Ibid.

60. American Board of Foreign Missions, "Extracts from a Joint Letter of the Missionaries, Dated January 1829," *The Missionary Herald* 25, no. 11 (November 1829): 340.

61. Gordon Hall, "Extracts from the Journal of Mr. Hall," *The Missionary Herald* 18, no. 7 (July 1822): 220.

62. David Kling, "The New Divinity and the Origins of the American Board of Commissioners for Foreign Missions," in *North American Foreign Missions, 1810–1914: Theology, Theory, and Policy*, ed. Wilbert R. Shenk (Grand Rapids, MI: Wm. B. Eerdmans, 2004), 13.

63. Ibid., 24.

64. Phillips, *Protestant America and the Pagan World*, 273.

65. Pennington, *Was Hinduism Invented?*, 96.

66. Ibid.

67. Bruce Carlisle Robertson, *Raja Rammohan Ray: The Father of Modern India* (Delhi: Oxford University Press, 1995), 12.

68. Ibid., 19.

69. Rammohun Roy, *Translation of an Abridgement of the Vedant, Or, Resolution of All the Veds* (London: T. and J. Hoitt, 1817), iii–iv.

70. Iqbal Singh, *Rammohun Roy: A Biographical Inquiry into the Making of Modern India*, vol. 1 (New York: Asia Publishing House, 1958), 88.

71. Lieutenant-Colonel Fitzclarence, *Journal of a Route across India, Through Egypt, to England, in the Latter End of the Year 1817, and the Beginning of 1818* (London: John Murray, 1819), 106.

72. Sophia Dobson Collet, *The Life and Letters of Raja Rammohun Roy* (Calcutta: A. C. Sarkar, 1913), 1–23; Robertson, *Raja Rammohan Ray*, 10–24; Lynn Zastoupil, *Rammohun Roy and the Making of Victorian Britain* (New York: Palgrave MacMillan, 2010), 25–26.

73. "A Remarkable Hindoo Reformer," *Christian Disciple* 5, no. 4 (April 5, 1817): 123–126; "Account of Rammohun Roy," *Boston Recorder* 2, no. 18 (April 29, 1817): 69.

74. The *Missionary Register* article was itself a reprint of an article from another British magazine, *The Christian Observer*.

75. "A Remarkable Hindoo Reformer," 123; "Account of Rammohun Roy," 69.

76. "Account of Rammohun Roy," 69.

77. "A Remarkable Hindoo Reformer," 124; "Account of Rammohun Roy," 69.

78. "A Remarkable Hindoo Reformer," 124; "Account of Rammohun Roy," 69.

79. "Account of Rammohun Roy," 69.

80. Ibid.

81. "A Remarkable Hindoo Reformer," 126.

82. William Tudor, "Theology of the Hindoos, as Taught by Ram Mohun Roy," *The North American Review and Miscellaneous Journal* 6, no. 18 (March 1818): 386–393; Frank Luther Mott, *A History of American Magazines, 1850–1865*, vol. 2 (Cambridge, MA: Harvard University Press, 1938), 223.

83. Carl T. Jackson identifies Tudor as the author of the anonymously published article. Jackson, *The Oriental Religions and American Thought*, 34.

84. Tudor, "Theology of the Hindoos, as Taught by Ram Mohun Roy," 386.

85. Ibid., 387.

86. Ibid., 393.

87. "Rammohun Roy: The Celebrated Hindoo Reformer," *Boston Recorder* 4, no. 38 (September 18, 1819): 156.

88. Zastoupil, *Rammohun Roy and the Making of Victorian Britain*, 28.

89. Rammohun Roy, *The Precepts of Jesus, the Guide to Peace and Happiness, Extracted from the Books of the New Testament Ascribed to the Four Evangelists. To Which Are Added the First and Second Appeal to the Christian Public, in Reply to the Observations of Dr. Marshman of Serampore* (New York: B. Bates, 1825), xviii.

90. Ibid., xxv.

91. Collet, *The Life and Letters of Raja Rammohun Roy*, 55–77; Singh, *Rammohun Roy: A Biographical Inquiry into the Making of Modern India*, 1:216–243; Jackson, *The Oriental Religions and American Thought*, 33; Dermot Killingley, *Rammohun Roy in Hindu and Christian Tradition: The Teape Lectures 1990* (Newcastle upon Tyne: Grevatt & Grevatt, 1993), 138–143; Robertson, *Raja Rammohan Ray*, 39–42.

92. Southwood Smith, "Rammohun Roy," *Christian Register*, November 23, 1821.

93. H. T., "Rammohun Roy," *Christian Register*, December 7, 1821.

94. Rammohun Roy, "Letter: Clapton, (Eng.) September 3, 1821," *Christian Register* 1, no. 21 (January 4, 1822): 81.

95. "Reply of the Baptist Missionaries at Calcutta, to Rammohun Roy," *Christian Watchman* 4, no. 16 (March 29, 1823): 61.

96. "Rammohun Roy," *Christian Watchman*, November 29, 1823; "Unitarianism in India," *Boston Recorder* 8, no. 49 (December 6, 1823): 193.

97. "Rammohun Roy," *The Missionary Herald*, September 1824; "Rammohun Roy," *Christian Watchman*, September 11, 1824.

98. David Reed, "Rammohun Roy," *Christian Register*, September 10, 1824; David Reed, "Rammohun Roy," *Christian Register*, September 17, 1824.

99. Francis W. P. Greenwood, "Spirit of Orthodoxy," *The Unitarian Miscellany and Christian Monitor* 6, no. 19 (October 1, 1824): 215.

100. Joseph Tuckerman, "Is Rammohun Roy a Christian? Or, in Other Words, Is He a Believer in the Divine Authority of Our Lord?," *Christian Examiner and Theological Review* 3, no. 5 (October 1826): 361.

101. See, for example: *Christian Register* 6, no. 16 (April 21, 1827): 62; *Christian Register* 6, no. 17 (April 28, 1827): 66; "Correspondence with Calcutta Unitarians," *Christian Watchman* 8, no. 56 (December 28, 1827): 222; "Rammohun Roy," *Spirit of the Pilgrims*, May 1829; "Unitarian Mission in India," *Christian Register* 8, no. 21 (May 23, 1829): 82.

102. See, for example: "Burning of Widows," *Christian Register* 1, no. 28 (February 22, 1822): 110; "Poona: Extreme Cruelty Towards a Hindoo Widow," *Christian Register* 3, no. 56 (September 3, 1824): 224; "Burning of Widows and Slaves," *Christian Register* 5, no. 45 (November 11, 1826): 180; "Hindoo Widows," *Christian Register* 8, no. 36 (September 5, 1829): 143.

103. "Hindoo Female Rights," *Christian Register* 2, no. 30 (March 7, 1823): 117; "Abolition of Suttees," *Christian Register* 9, no. 28 (July 10, 1830): 109; "Abolition of Suttees," *Christian Register* 9, no. 29 (July 17, 1830): 113; "Conditions of Females in India," *Christian Register* 11, no. 40 (October 6, 1832): 158.

104. Zastoupil, *Rammohun Roy and the Making of Victorian Britain*, 94.

105. Cited in ibid.

106. Bean, *Yankee India*, 193.

107. Jackson, *The Oriental Religions and American Thought*, 35–36; Spencer Lavan, *Unitarians and India: A Study in Encounter and Response*, 3rd ed. (Chicago: Exploration Press, 1991), 41–72.

108. Adrienne Moore, *Rammohun Roy and America* (Calcutta: Brahmo Mission Press, 1942), vii, 2–3.

109. Jackson, *The Oriental Religions and American Thought*, 36.

110. Bean, *Yankee India*, 193.

111. Jenny Franchot, *Roads to Rome: The Antebellum Protestant Encounter with Catholicism* (Berkeley: University of California Press, 1994), 4–5.

112. Ibid., 5.

CHAPTER 3

1. Lyman Beecher, *A Plea for the West*, 2nd ed. (Cincinnati: Truman & Smith, 1835), 11.

2. Ibid., 12.

3. Alexis de Tocqueville, *Democracy in America*, ed. Harvey Claflin Mansfield and Delba Winthrop (Chicago: University of Chicago Press, 2000), 278.

4. Ibid., 280.

5. Ibid., 281.

6. David Sehat, *The Myth of American Religious Freedom* (New York: Oxford University Press, 2011), 8.

7. Ibid.

8. Tracy Fessenden, *Culture and Redemption : Religion, the Secular, and American Literature* (Princeton, NJ: Princeton University Press, 2007), 55.

9. Samuel Goodrich, *Manners and Customs of the Principal Nations of the Globe* (Boston: Bradbury Soden, 1845), 24.

10. Samuel Mitchell, *Mitchell's Geographical Reader: A System of Modern Geography, Comprising a Description of the World . . .* (Thomas, Cowperthwait, 1840), iii.

11. Ibid.

12. See, for example: Martin Brückner, *The Geographic Revolution in Early America: Maps, Literacy, and National Identity* (Chapel Hill: Published for the Omohundro Institute of Early American History and Culture by University of North Carolina Press, 2006); François Furstenberg, *In the Name of the Father: Washington's Legacy, Slavery, and the Making of a Nation* (New York: Penguin Press, 2006); Carolyn Eastman, *A Nation of Speechifiers: Making an American Public after the Revolution* (Chicago: University of Chicago Press, 2009).

13. Joseph Moreau, *Schoolbook Nation: Conflicts over American History Textbooks from the Civil War to the Present* (Ann Arbor: University of Michigan Press, 2003), 33.

14. Charles Halsey Carpenter, *History of American Schoolbooks* (Philadelphia: University of Pennsylvania Press, 1963), 271.

15. John A. Nietz, *Old Textbooks: Spelling, Grammar, Reading, Arithmetic, Geography, American History, Civil Government, Physiology, Penmanship, Art, Music, as Taught in the Common Schools from Colonial Days to 1900* (Pittsburgh: University of Pittsburgh Press, 1961), 196–200.

16. Roswell Smith, *Geography on the Productive System: For Schools, Academies, and Families*, 2nd ed. (Philadelphia: W. Marshall, 1836), 5.

17. Samuel Mitchell, *A System of Modern Geography, Comprising a Description of the Present State of the World and Its Five Great Divisions: America, Europe, Asia, Africa, and Oceanica: With Their Several Empires* (Philadelphia: Thomas, Cowperthwait, 1844), 42.

18. Smith, *Geography on the Productive System*, 78–80.

19. Mitchell, *A System of Modern Geography*, 43.

20. Ibid., 44–45; Smith, *Geography on the Productive System*, 83–85.

21. Mitchell, *A System of Modern Geography*, 48.

22. Smith, *Geography on the Productive System*, 81.

23. Mitchell, *A System of Modern Geography*, 50.

24. Masuzawa, *The Invention of World Religions*, 61.

25. Nietz, *Old Textbooks*, 229. Nietz has isolated the most popular and widely circulated schoolbooks for each genre before 1900. In the next section of the chapter I rely heavily on books from Samuel Goodrich's Peter Parley series, a series Nietz cites as the most popular series of schoolbooks in the period.

26. Samuel Goodrich, *A System of School Geography*, 6th ed. (New York: F. J. Huntington, 1833); Samuel Goodrich, *Peter Parley's Geography for Beginners* (New York: Huntington and Savage, 1845).

27. Samuel Goodrich, *The Tales of Peter Parley about Asia* (Thomas, Cowperthwait, 1845), 108–109.

28. Salem Town and Nelson M. Holbrook, *The Progressive Third Reader* (Boston: Sanborn, Carter, Bazin, 1857), 176–180.

29. Ibid., 176.

30. Mitchell, *A System of Modern Geography*, 243.

31. Smith, *Geography on the Productive System*, 230.

32. Samuel Goodrich, *The World and Its Inhabitants* (Boston: C. J. Rand, Wm. J. Reynolds, 1856), 258.

33. Goodrich, *The Tales of Peter Parley about Asia*, 122.

34. Goodrich, *Manners and Customs of the Principal Nations of the Globe*, 332.

35. Ibid., 338.

36. Goodrich, *The Tales of Peter Parley about Asia*, 121.

37. Samuel Goodrich, *Lights and Shadows of Asiatic History* (Boston: Bradbury Soden, 1844), 40.

38. Goodrich, *The World and Its Inhabitants*, 258.

39. Goodrich, *Lights and Shadows of Asiatic History*, 48.

40. Goodrich, *The Tales of Peter Parley about Asia*, 119.

41. Goodrich, *Lights and Shadows of Asiatic History*, 38.

42. R. Turner, *The Parlour Letter-Writer* (Philadelphia: Thomas, Cowperthwait, 1845), 236–237.

43. Ibid., 237.

44. Goodrich, *The Tales of Peter Parley about Asia*, 123–124.

45. Frederick Lewis Allen, *Harper's Magazine, 1850–1950: A Centenary Address*, Newcomen Address 1950 (New York: Newcomen Society in North America, 1950), 14.

46. Rather than trying to tease out the various agents, writers, editors, publishers, etc., engaged in the production process of the magazine, I will refer to *Harper's* as a single entity throughout the chapter. Such personification of the magazine's agency "stresses the collaborative nature of periodicals" and coincides with the view "that every periodical has a distinct character" that results from this collaboration. See Jennifer Phegley, *Educating the Proper Woman Reader: Victorian Family Literary Magazines and the Cultural Health of the Nation* (Columbus: Ohio State University Press, 2004), 35.

47. Barbara M. Perkins, "Harper's Monthly Magazine," in *American Literary Magazines: The Eighteenth and Nineteenth Centuries*, ed. Edward E. Chielens, Historical Guides to the World's Periodicals and Newspapers (New York: Greenwood Press, 1986), 167.

48. Phegley, *Educating the Proper Woman Reader*, 33.

49. Ibid., 15.

50. Ibid., 21.

51. Quoted in Frank Luther Mott, *A History of American Magazines, 1850–1865*, vol. 2, (Cambridge, MA: Harvard University Press), 391.

52. "Advertisement," *Harper's New Monthly Magazine* 1, no. 1 (June 1850): i.

53. Lorman Ratner, Paula T. Kaufman, and Dwight L. Teeter, *Paradoxes of Prosperity: Wealth-Seeking versus Christian Values in Civil War America* (Urbana: University of Illinois Press, 2009), 49.

54. Ibid., 53.

55. Ibid., 52.

56. Ibid., 52.

57. Ibid., 53.

58. "Ghosts and Sorceresses of India," *Harper's New Monthly Magazine* 7, no. 42 (November 1853): 830.

59. Ibid., 830.

60. Ibid., 830.

61. Ibid., 831.

62. Victor G. Plarr, *Men and Women of the Time: A Dictionary of Contemporaries*, 14th ed. (London: George Routledge and Sons, 1895), 723.

63. Phil Robinson, "A Priest of Doorga," *Harper's New Monthly Magazine* 71, no. 425 (October 1885): 734–741.

64. "Madras, In Pictures," *Harper's New Monthly Magazine* 16, no. 91 (December 1857): 31–32.

65. William L. Stuart, "Calcutta, the City of Palaces," *Harper's New Monthly Magazine* 34, no. 201 (February 1867): 302.

66. Ibid., 302–303.

67. "Madras, In Pictures," 31.

68. Stuart, "Calcutta, the City of Palaces," 303.

69. A. H. Guernsey, "Juggernaut," *Harper's New Monthly Magazine* 57, no. 338 (July 1878): 222–229.

70. Mott, *A History of American Magazines, 1850–1865*, 2:392–396.

71. Guernsey, "Juggernaut," 226.

72. Ibid., 226.

73. Ibid., 226.

74. Ibid., 227.

75. Ibid., 227–228.

76. Ibid., 227–228.

77. Henry M. Alden, "The Sacred City of the Hindus," *Harper's New Monthly Magazine* 38, no. 228 (May 1869): 754.

78. Ibid., 754.

79. Ibid., 760.

80. Ibid., 756.

81. Ibid., 752.

82. Stuart, "Calcutta, the City of Palaces," 311.

83. Thomas Nast, "The American River Ganges" (Cartoon), *Harper's Weekly* (September 30, 1871): 916.

CHAPTER 4

1. Catherine L. Albanese, *A Republic of Mind and Spirit: A Cultural History of American Metaphysical Religion* (New Haven, CT: Yale University Press, 2007), 1–16. Albanese positions metaphysical religion alongside evangelical and liturgical or state-church religions, which she identifies with the historical work of Nathan Hatch and Jon Butler, respectively.

2. Philip Goldberg, *American Veda: From Emerson and the Beatles to Yoga and Meditation* (New York: Harmony Books, 2010), 26; for another recent example, see Stefanie Syman, *The Subtle Body : The Story of Yoga in America* (New York: Farrar, Straus and Giroux, 2010), 11–19.

3. Albanese, *A Republic of Mind and Spirit*, 347.

4. Arthur Christy, *The Orient in American Transcendentalism: A Study of Emerson, Thoreau, and Alcott* (New York: Columbia University Press, 1932); Frederic I. Carpenter, *Emerson and Asia* (Cambridge, MA: Harvard University Press, 1930).

5. Christy, *The Orient in American Transcendentalism*, 3; emphasis in the original.

6. Carpenter, *Emerson and Asia*; R. K. Gupta, *The Great Encounter: A Study of Indo-American Literary and Cultural Relations* (Riverdale, MD: The Riverdale Company, 1987); Arthur Versluis, *American Transcendentalism and Asian Religions* (New York: Oxford University Press, 1993).

7. Paul Friedrich, *The Gita Within Walden* (Albany: State University of New York Press, 2009); Steven Adisasmito-Smith, "Transcendental Brahmin: Emerson's 'Hindu' Sentiments," in *Emerson for the Twenty-First Century*, ed. Barry Tharaud (Newark: University of Delaware Press, 2010), 131–164.

8. Versluis, *American Transcendentalism and Asian Religions*.

9. Christy, *The Orient in American Transcendentalism*, 14.

10. Versluis, *American Transcendentalism and Asian Religions*, 13.

11. Albanese, *A Republic of Mind and Spirit*, 346.

12. James Elliot Cabot, *A Memoir of Ralph Waldo Emerson*, vol. 1 (Boston: Houghton, Mifflin, 1887), 81.

13. Ibid.

14. Ibid.

15. Carpenter, *Emerson and Asia*, 159–160.

16. Ibid., 27–28, 31–32.

17. Ralph Waldo Emerson, *The Collected Works of Ralph Waldo Emerson*, ed. Wallace E. Williams and Douglas Emory Wilson, vol. 4 (Cambridge, MA: Belknap Press of Harvard University Press, 1987), 28.

18. Ibid., 4:28.

19. Ibid., 4:28.

20. Ibid., 4:29.

21. Ibid., 4:31.

22. Ralph Waldo Emerson, *The Journals and Miscellaneous Notebooks of Ralph Waldo Emerson*, ed. William H. Gilman, vol. 9 (Cambridge, MA: Belknap Press of Harvard University Press, 1960), 321.

23. Ralph Waldo Emerson, "Hamatreya," in *The Collected Works of Ralph Waldo Emerson*, ed. Albert J. Von Frank, vol. 9 (Cambridge, MA: Belknap Press of Harvard University Press, 2011), 68.

24. Ibid., 69.

25. Ibid., 69.

26. Ibid., 70.

27. Ibid., 70.

28. Ibid., 68.

29. Ibid., 70.

30. Ralph Waldo Emerson, "Brahma," in *The Collected Works of Ralph Waldo Emerson*, ed. Albert J. Von Frank, vol. 9 (Cambridge, MA: Belknap Press of Harvard University Press, 2011), 363–366. The version of the poem printed in that text mistakenly starts the final line of the poem with "Fine" instead of "Find." Because every other version of the poem I found uses "Find" and because there is no note in the list of variants of the poem in the text, I can only assume this is a typo and I have corrected it here.

31. Christy, *The Orient in American Transcendentalism*, 167.

32. Carpenter, *Emerson and Asia*, 127.

33. Ibid.

34. "Poems," *The North American Review* 64, no. 135 (April 1847): 410.

35. Ibid., 411.

36. "Emerson Travestie," *New York Times*, November 12, 1857.

37. "Brahma," *New York Times*, November 16, 1857.

38. "A Poetical Explanation," *Boston Herald*, December 3, 1857.

39. "Editor's Easy Talk," *Graham's American Monthly Magazine of Literature, Art, and Fashion* 52, no. 3 (March 1858): 273.

40. "Representative Men," *Christian Watchman and Christian Reflector* 31, no. 4 (January 24, 1850): 14.

41. Henry David Thoreau, *A Week on the Concord and Merrimack Rivers*, ed. J. Lyndon Shanley (Princeton, NJ: Princeton University Press, 2004), 126.

42. Ibid., 126.

43. Ibid., 136.

44. Ibid., 136.

45. Ibid., 136–137.

46. Ibid., 137.

47. Ibid., 140.

48. Ibid., 138–140.

49. Ibid., 141.

50. Ibid., 141.

51. Ibid., 76.

52. Ibid., 77.

53. Ibid., 78.

54. Henry David Thoreau, *Walden*, ed. J. Lyndon Shanley, 150th anniversary ed. (Princeton, NJ: Princeton University Press, 2004), 19–20.

55. Ibid., 90–91.

56. Christy, *The Orient in American Transcendentalism*, 199; emphasis in the original.

57. Ibid., 201.

58. Shreena Niketa Divyakant Gandhi, "Translating, Practicing, and Commodifying Yoga in the U.S." (Ph.D. diss., University of Florida, 2009), 54.

59. Alan D Hodder, *Thoreau's Ecstatic Witness* (New Haven, CT: Yale University Press, 2001), 184.

60. Ibid., 184–190.

61. Thoreau, *Walden*, 219.

62. Ibid., 218.

63. Ibid., 221.

64. Ibid., 221.

65. Ibid., 222.

66. Ibid., 287.

67. Ibid., 297–298.

68. George Ripley, "H. D. Thoreau's Book," *New-York Tribune* (June 13, 1849) and *New-York Weekly* (June 16, 1849), reprinted in Samuel Arthur Jones, ed., *Pertaining to Thoreau: A Gathering of Ten Significant Nineteenth-Century Opinions* (Hartford, CT: Transcendental Books, 1970), 9.

69. Ibid., 11.

70. James Russell Lowell, "A Week on the Concord and Merrimack Rivers," *Massachusetts Quarterly Review* 3 (December 1849): 40–51, reprinted in Jones, ed., *Pertaining to Thoreau*, 15.

71. Ibid., 16.

72. Edwin Morton, "Thoreau and His Books," *Harvard Magazine* 1 (January 1855): 87–99, reprinted in Jones, ed., *Pertaining to Thoreau*, 26.

73. Ibid.

74. Ibid.

75. "Veeshnoo Sarma," *The Dial* 3, no. 1 (July 1842): 82.

76. Ibid.

77. Ibid.

78. Versluis, *American Transcendentalism and Asian Religions*, 188.

79. Ibid.

80. "Veeshnoo Sarma," 82.

81. Ibid., 83.

82. "The Laws of Menu," *The Dial* 3, no. 3 (January 1843): 331.

83. Versluis, *American Transcendentalism and Asian Religions*, 189.

84. "The Laws of Menu," 332.

85. Ibid., 337.

86. Lydia Maria Child, *The Progress of Religious Ideas Through Successive Ages* (New York: C. S. Francis, 1855), 1:x.

87. Ibid., 3:450.

88. "New Publications," *New-York Observer*, November 15, 1885, 366.

89. Carolyn L. Karcher, *The First Woman in the Republic: A Cultural Biography of Lydia Maria Child* (Durham, NC: Duke University Press, 1994), 383.

90. The religions Clarke covered were Chinese (or Confucianism), Brahmanism, Buddhism, Zoroastrianism, Egyptian, Grecian, Roman, Scandinavian, Judaism, Islam, and Christianity. Christianity, being a universal religion, was left out of his count of the ten "great" religions.

91. James Freeman Clarke, *Ten Great Religions: An Essay in Comparative Theology* (Boston: James R. Osgood, 1872), 21.

92. Ibid., 9.

93. Eric J. Sharpe, *Comparative Religion: A History* (New York: Charles Scribner's Sons, 1975), 137n.

94. Samuel Johnson, *Lectures, Essays, and Sermons* (Boston: Houghton, Mifflin, 1883), 2.

95. Samuel Johnson, *Oriental Religions and Their Relation to Universal Religion: India* (Boston: James R. Osgood, 1873), 6.

96. Johnson, *Lectures, Essays, and Sermons*, 96.

97. Child, *Progress of Religious Ideas*, 3; Clarke, *Ten Great Religions: An Essay in Comparative Theology*, 83.

98. Johnson, *Oriental Religions and Their Relation to Universal Religion: India*, 58.

99. Clarke, *Ten Great Religions: An Essay in Comparative Theology*, 86.

100. Child, *Progress of Religious Ideas*, 1:11.

101. Johnson, *Oriental Religions and Their Relation to Universal Religion: India*, 343.

102. Clarke, *Ten Great Religions: An Essay in Comparative Theology*, 136.

103. Child, *Progress of Religious Ideas*, 1:116–117.

104. Ibid., 1:117.

105. Ibid., 1:117.

106. Johnson, *Oriental Religions and Their Relation to Universal Religion: India*, 252–255, 299.

107. Ibid., 574.

108. Ibid., 574.

109. Albanese, *A Republic of Mind and Spirit*, 170, 168.

110. Ibid., 169.

111. Ibid., 167.

112. Ibid., 171.

CHAPTER 5

1. Henry Steel Olcott, *People from the Other World* (Hartford, CT: American Publishing Company, 1875), 293.

2. Henry Steel Olcott, *Old Diary Leaves: The True Story of the Theosophical Society* (New York: G. P. Putnam's Sons, 1895), 8.

3. Olcott, *People from the Other World*, 359.

4. Ibid., 360.

5. Olcott, *Old Diary Leaves: The True Story of the Theosophical Society*, 118.

6. Ibid., 120.

7. Henry Steel Olcott, *Inaugural Address of the President-Founder of the Theosophical Society*, Adyar Pamphlet Series 5 (Madras: The "Theosophist" Office, Adyar, n.d.), 10.

8. Ibid., 6.

9. Ibid., 6.

10. Ibid., 11.

11. Ibid., 12.

12. H. P. Blavatsky, *Isis Unveiled* (Wheaton, IL: The Theosophical Publishing House, 1972), 1:ix.

13. Ibid., 1:vii.

14. Ibid., 1:vii.

15. Ibid., 1:xiv.

16. Ibid., 1:5.

17. Ibid., 1:5. The term "phenomenon" became an important one for Theosophy. It referred to any manifestation of occult power, such as a mysteriously appearing letter, a spirit in the style of spiritualism, or finding lost objects.

18. Ibid., 1:9.

19. Ibid., 1:38.

20. Ibid., 2:2.

21. Ibid., 2:53.

22. Ibid., 2:54.

23. Ibid., 2:79–80.

24. Ibid., 2:80.

25. Ibid., 2:99.

26. Ibid., 2:99.

27. Ibid., 2:99.

28. Ibid., 1:585.

29. Ibid., 2:589.

30. Ibid., 1:576.

31. Ibid., 1:576.

32. Ibid., 1:576.

33. Ibid., 1:578.

34. Ibid., 2:170.

35. Ibid., 2:531.

36. Ibid., 2:531.

37. Ibid., 2:531.

38. Ibid., 1:xxii.

39. Ibid., 1:xxvii.

40. Ibid., 1:xl.

41. Ibid., 1:xl.

42. Ibid., 1:xxxviii.

43. Ibid., 2:636.

44. Ibid., 2:639.

45. Ibid., 2:639.

46. Ibid., 1:139.

47. Ibid., 1:383; 2:103–107, 383.

48. Blavatsky, *Isis Unveiled*, 1:139; 2:106–107.

49. Blavatsky, *Isis Unveiled*, 1:141; emphasis in the original.

50. Ibid., 2:98.

51. Ibid., 2:106.

52. Ibid., 2:369.

53. Olcott, *Old Diary Leaves: The True Story of the Theosophical Society*, 395.

54. Ibid., 396.

55. Ibid., 396.

56. Henry Steel Olcott, "Swami Dayanand's Charges," *Theosophist* 3, no. 10 (July 1882): S5.

57. Olcott, *Old Diary Leaves: The True Story of the Theosophical Society*, 403.

58. Olcott, "Swami Dayanand's Charges," S5.

59. Henry Steel Olcott, *Old Diary Leaves: The Only Authentic History of the Theosophical Society, Second Series, 1878–83* (London: The Theosophical Publishing Society, 1900), 224.

60. Har Bilas Sarda, *The Life of Dayanand Saraswati World Teacher* (Ajmer: Vedic Yantralaya, 1946), 556–559.

61. Ibid., 556.

62. Ibid., 557.

63. Ibid., 559.

64. Olcott, *Old Diary Leaves: The True Story of the Theosophical Society*, 398.

65. Stephen Prothero, *The White Buddhist: The Asian Odyssey of Henry Steel Olcott* (Bloomington: Indiana University Press, 1996), 107.

66. Ibid., 69.

67. Olcott, *People from the Other World*, 454.

68. Ibid., 454–459, 464.

69. Ibid., 480.

70. Ibid., 453.

71. Olcott, *Old Diary Leaves: The True Story of the Theosophical Society*, 11–12.

72. "Important Note" in ibid., 14.

73. Ibid., 15.

74. Prothero, *The White Buddhist*, 59–60; Bruce F. Campbell, *Ancient Wisdom Revised: A History of the Theosophical Movement* (Berkeley: University of California Press, 1980), 24; Olcott, *Old Diary Leaves: The True Story of the Theosophical Society*, 75–76.

75. Olcott, *Old Diary Leaves: The True Story of the Theosophical Society*, 379.

76. Ibid., 380.

77. Ibid., 380.

78. Henry Steel Olcott, "Theosophy, the Scientific Basis of Religion," in *A Collection of Lectures on Theosophy and Archaic Religions* (Madras: A. Theyaga Rajier, 1883), 164.

79. Campbell, *Ancient Wisdom Revised*, 56–57, 80–81.

80. A. P. Sinnett, *The Occult World*, 9th ed. (London: The Theosophical Publishing House, 1969), 8–9.

81. Ibid., 4.

82. Ibid., 180.

83. Ibid., 83–84.

84. Kirin Narayan, "Refractions from the Field at Home: American Representations of Hindu Holy Men in the 19th and 20th Centuries," *Cultural Anthropology* 8 (1993): 491.

85. Jane Naomi Iwamura, *Virtual Orientalism: Asian Religions and American Popular Culture* (New York: Oxford University Press, 2011), 6.

86. Ibid., 20; emphasis in original.

87. H. P. Blavatsky, *The Secret Doctrine* (Los Angeles: The Theosophy Company, 1947), xxii–xxiii.

88. Ibid., 157.

89. H. P. Blavatsky, *The Key to Theosophy* (Los Angeles: The Theosophy Company, 1962), 10.

90. Blavatsky, *The Secret Doctrine*, 95.

91. William Q. Judge, *The Yoga Aphorisms of Patanjali* (Los Angeles: United Lodge of Theosophists, 1920), vi.

92. Ibid., ix.

93. Ibid., 1.

94. Ibid., 2.

95. William Q. Judge, *Echoes of the Orient: The Writings of William Quan Judge*, ed. Dara Eklund (Pasadena, CA: Theosophical University Press, 2011), 3:259.

96. Judge, *The Yoga Aphorisms of Patanjali*, ix.

97. Judge, *Echoes of the Orient*, 3:308.

98. Ibid., 2:416–417.

99. Ibid., 3:327.

100. Ibid., 3:327.

101. For a more on the history of yoga in American culture from this period into the early twentieth century, see Andrea R. Jain, *Selling Yoga: From Counterculture to Pop Culture* (New York: Oxford University press, 2015), 20–41.

102. Elizabeth De Michelis, *A History of Modern Yoga* (London: Continuum, 2005), 179.

103. Mark Singleton, *Yoga Body: The Origins of Modern Posture Practice* (New York: Oxford University Press, 2010), 80.

104. King, *Orientalism and Religion : Postcolonial Theory, India and "the Mystic East,"* 33.

105. Hugh B. Urban, "Magia Sexualis: Sex, Secrecy, and Liberation in Modern Western Esotericism," *Journal of the American Academy of Religion* 72, no. 3 (September 1, 2004): 695–731; Hugh B. Urban, "The Omnipotent Oom: Tantra and Its Impact on Modern Western Esotericism," *Esoterica: The Journal of Esoteric Studies* 3 (2001): 218–259; Leigh Schmidt, *Heaven's Bride: The Unprintable Life of Ida C. Craddock, American Mystic, Scholar, Sexologist, Martyr, and Madwoman* (New York: Basic Books, 2010), 89–135.

106. King, *Orientalism and Religion : Postcolonial Theory, India and "the Mystic East,"* 33.

CHAPTER 6

1. Walter Houghton, ed., *Neely's History of the Parliament of Religions and Religious Congresses at the World's Columbian Exposition*, 4th ed. (Chicago: F. Tennyson Neely, 1894), 34–35.

2. Charles Carroll Bonney, "The Genesis of the World's Religious Congresses of 1893," *New Church Review* 1 (January 1894), quoted in Richard Hughes Seager, ed., *The Dawn of Religious Pluralism: Voices from the World's Parliament of Religions, 1893* (La Salle, IL: Open Court, 1993), 5.

3. Kathryn Lofton, "Religious History as Religious Studies," *Religion* 42, no. 3 (July 2012): 390.

4. Jonathan Z. Smith, "Religion, Religions, Religious," in *Critical Terms for Religious Studies*, ed. Mark C. Taylor (Chicago: University of Chicago Press, 1998), 281.

5. Richard Hughes Seager, *The World's Parliament of Religions: The East/West Encounter, Chicago, 1893* (Bloomington: Indiana University Press, 1995), 51.

6. Martin E. Marty, "A Cosmopolitan Habit in Theology," in *A Museum of Faiths: Histories and Legacies of the 1893 World's Parliament of Religions*, ed. Eric Jozef Ziolkowski (Atlanta: Scholars Press, 1993), 165.

7. Ibid., 165.

8. Ibid., 168.

9. Houghton, *Neely's History of the Parliament of Religions and Religious Congresses at the World's Columbian Exposition*, 15.

10. Ibid., 15.

11. Ibid., 15.

12. Ibid., 15–19.

13. John Henry Barrows, *The World's Parliament of Religions: An Illustrated and Popular Story of the World's First Parliament of Religions, Held in Chicago in Connection with the Columbian Exposition of 1893* (Chicago: The Parliament Publishing Company, 1893), 1:74.

14. Houghton, *Neely's History of the Parliament of Religions and Religious Congresses at the World's Columbian Exposition*, 22–23.

15. Barrows, *The World's Parliament of Religions*, 1:10. Note the ambiguity of the address. While inviting all religions, Barrows used biblical verses for his rationale drawing on Acts 14:17, "God has not left himself without a witness" and Acts 10:34–35, "God is no respecter of persons . . . righteousness is accepted of him." Thanks to Arun Jones for the insight into these scriptural invocations.

16. Ibid., 1:10.

17. Ibid., 1:61.

18. Ibid., 1:61.

19. Seager uses a similar inclusivist/exclusivist rubric in his analysis of the Parliament's Christian speakers. Seager, *The World's Parliament of Religions*, 54–55.

20. Houghton, *Neely's History of the Parliament of Religions and Religious Congresses at the World's Columbian Exposition*, 218.

21. Barrows, *The World's Parliament of Religions*, 1:538.

22. Ibid., 1:542.

23. Ibid., 1:538.

24. Ibid., 1:541.

25. Ibid., 1:494.

26. Ibid., 1:495.

27. Ibid., 1:500.

28. Ibid., 1:500.

29. Ibid., 2:1247.

30. Ibid., 2:1249.

31. Ibid., 2:1249.

32. Houghton, *Neely's History of the Parliament of Religions and Religious Congresses at the World's Columbian Exposition*, 765.

33. Ibid., 766.

34. Ibid., 766.

35. Ibid., 766.

36. Leigh Eric Schmidt, *Restless Souls: The Making of American Spirituality*, 1st ed. (San Francisco: Harper San Francisco, 2005), 111–114.

37. Barrows, *The World's Parliament of Religions*, 1:781.

38. Ibid., 1:784.

39. Ibid., 2:1186.

40. Ibid., 2:1186.

41. Ibid., 2:1186.

42. Ibid., 2:1186.

43. Ibid., 2:1270.

44. Ibid., 2:1269.

45. Ibid., 2:1272.

46. Ibid., 2:1272.

47. Ibid., 2:1172.

48. Ibid., 2:1173.

49. Ibid., 2:1174.

50. Ibid., 1:345.

51. Ibid., 1:345.

52. Ibid., 1:346.

53. Ibid., 1:351.

54. Daily Inter-Ocean, September 14, 1893, quoted in Seager, *The Dawn of Religious Pluralism*, 450.

55. Barrows, *The World's Parliament of Religions*, 1:143.

56. Ibid., 1:145.

57. Ibid., 1:145.

58. Daily Inter-Ocean, September 20, 1893, quoted in Seager, *The Dawn of Religious Pluralism*, 338.

59. For a brief biography of Vivekananda, see Amiya P. Sen, *Swami Vivekananda* (New Delhi: Oxford University Press, 2000); for more on Ramakrishna and his Tantra, see Jeffrey J. Kripal, *Kālī's Child: The Mystical and the Erotic in the Life and Teachings of Ramakrishna* (Chicago: University of Chicago Press, 1995).

60. Barrows, *The World's Parliament of Religions*, 1:129.

61. Ibid., 1:129.

62. "Hindoo Criticises Christianity," *Chicago Daily Tribune*, September 20, 1893.

63. Daily Inter-Ocean, September 20, 1893, quoted in Seager, *The World's Parliament of Religions*, 337–338.

64. Barrows, *The World's Parliament of Religions*, 2:976.

65. Ibid., 2:975.

66. Ibid., 2:968–969.

67. Ibid., 2:977.

68. Ibid., 2:977.

69. Ibid., 2:978.

EPILOGUE

1. Katherine Mayo, *Mother India* (New York: Harcourt, Brace, 1927), 11.

2. Mrinalini Sinha, *Specters of Mother India: The Global Restructuring of an Empire* (Durham, NC: Duke University Press, 2006), 69.

3. Jason C. Bivins, "'Only One Repertory': American Religious Studies," *Religion* 42, no. 3 (July 1, 2012): 395–407.

4. Notable examples include: Tisa Wenger, *We Have a Religion: The 1920s Pueblo Indian Dance Controversy and American Religious Freedom* (Chapel Hill: University of North Carolina Press, 2009); Kathryn Lofton, *Oprah: The Gospel of an Icon* (Berkeley: University of California Press, 2011); John Lardas Modern, *Secularism in Antebellum America: With Reference to Ghosts, Protestant Subcultures, Machines, and Their Metaphors: Featuring Discussions of Mass Media, Moby-Dick, Spirituality, Phrenology, Anthropology, Sing Sing State Penitentiary, and Sex with the New Motive Power* (Chicago: University of Chicago Press, 2011); Amanda Porterfield, *Conceived in Doubt: Religion and Politics in the New American Nation* (Chicago: University of Chicago Press, 2012).

5. Tracy Fessenden, "The Objects of American Religious Studies," *Religion* 42, no. 3 (July 2012): 374.

6. Thomas A. Tweed, "Expanding the Study of U.S. Religion: Reflections on the State of a Subfield," *Religion* 40, no. 4 (October 1, 2010): 255.

7. Kevin M. Schultz and Paul Harvey, "Everywhere and Nowhere: Recent Trends in American Religious History and Historiography," *Journal of the American Academy of Religion* 78, no. 1 (March 1, 2010): 152.

8. Tweed has produced a broad survey, history, and appraisal of this work that he calls "the Quotidian Turn." Thomas A. Tweed, "After the Quotidian Turn: Interpretive Categories and Scholarly Trajectories in the Study of Religion since the 1960s," *The Journal of Religion* 95, no. 3 (2015): 361–385.

9. Fessenden, "The Objects of American Religious Studies," 374.

10. Bivins, "'Only One Repertory': American Religious Studies," 399.

11. Jonathan Z. Smith, *Imagining Religion: From Babylon to Jonestown* (Chicago: University of Chicago Press, 1982); Ronald B. Inden, *Imagining India* (Oxford: Basil Blackwell, 1990); J. Samuel Preus, *Explaining Religion: Criticism and Theory from Bodin to Freud* (Atlanta, GA: Scholars Press, 1996); Sharada Sugirtharajah, *Imagining Hinduism: A Postcolonial Perspective* (London: Routledge, 2003); Tomoko Masuzawa, *The Invention of World Religions* (Chicago: University of Chicago Press, 2005); Brian Pennington, *Was Hinduism Invented?: Britons, Indians, and the Colonial Construction of Religion* (New York: Oxford University Press, 2005); Geoffrey A. Oddie, *Imagined Hinduism: British Protestant Missionary Constructions of Hinduism, 1793–1900* (New Delhi: Sage Publications, 2006); Jason Ānanda Josephson, *The Invention of Religion in Japan* (Chicago: University of Chicago Press, 2012); Brent Nongbri, *Before Religion: A History of a Modern Concept* (New Haven, CT: Yale University Press, 2013).

12. Louis Henry Jordan, *Comparative Religion, Its Genesis and Growth* (Edinburgh: T. & T. Clark, 1905); Eric J. Sharpe, *Comparative Religion: A History* (New York: Charles Scribner's Sons, 1975); Ivan Strenski, *Thinking about Religion: An Historical Introduction to Theories of Religion* (Malden, MA: Blackwell, 2006).

13. Jordan, *Comparative Religion, Its Genesis and Growth*, 208.

14. Sharpe, *Comparative Religion: A History*, 137.

15. Masuzawa, *The Invention of World Religions*, 32.

16. Fessenden, "The Objects of American Religious Studies," 377.

17. Ann Taves, *Fits, Trances, and Visions: Experiencing Religion and Explaining Experience from Wesley to James* (Princeton, NJ: Princeton University Press, 1999), 279.

18. William James, *The Varieties of Religious Experience: A Study in Human Nature*, 2nd ed. (New York: Longmans, Green, 1902), 400.

19. Sharpe, *Comparative Religion: A History*, 97.

20. James Turner, *Religion Enters the Academy: The Origins of the Scholarly Study of Religion in America* (Athens: University of Georgia Press, 2011), 79.

21. James, *The Varieties of Religious Experience*, 31.

22. Jonathan Z. Smith, "Religion, Religions, Religious," in *Critical Terms for Religious Studies*, ed. Mark C. Taylor (Chicago: University of Chicago Press, 1998), 276.

Index